W9-ABM-045

WITHDRAWN

Post-Cold War America, 1992-present

Post–Cold War America: 1992–Present

VOLUME 9

Other titles in the
American History by Era series:

AMERICAN HISTORY BY ERA

Post–Cold War America: 1992–Present

VOLUME 9

James Haley, *Book Editor*

Daniel Leone, *President*
Bonnie Szumski, *Publisher*
Scott Barbour, *Managing Editor*

GREENHAVEN
PRESS ®

THOMSON

™

GALE

San Diego • Detroit • New York • San Francisco • Cleveland
New Haven, Conn. • Waterville, Maine • London • Munich

© 2003 by Greenhaven Press. Greenhaven Press is an imprint of The Gale Group, Inc., a division of Thomson Learning, Inc.

Greenhaven® and Thomson Learning™ are trademarks used herein under license.

For more information, contact
Greenhaven Press
27500 Drake Rd.
Farmington Hills, MI 48331-3535
Or you can visit our Internet site at http://www.gale.com

Cover inset photo credits (from left): Planet Art; Corel; Digital Stock; Corel; Library of Congress; Library of Congress; Digital Stock; Painet/Garry Rissman

Main cover photo credit: © Reuters NewMedia Inc./CORBIS

John F. Kennedy Library, 149
Library of Congress, 134, 156
PhotoDisk, 207
UNHER/22021/05.1992/A. Hollmann, 90

LIBRARY OF CONGRESS CATALOGING-IN-PUBLICATION DATA

Post–Cold War America, 1992–present / James Haley, book editor.
   p. cm. — (American history by era; v. 9)
  Includes bibliographical references and index.
  ISBN 0-7377-1148-5 (lib. : alk. paper) — ISBN 0-7377-1147-7 (pbk. : alk. paper)
   1. United States—History—1969– . 2. Nineteen nineties. I. Haley, James, 1968– .
II. Series.
E839 .P67 2003
973.92—dc21   2002024293

Printed in the United States of America

CONTENTS

Chapter 1: 1992–1995: Unrest at Home and Abroad

1. The Rodney King Verdict and the Los Angeles Riots

On April 29, 1992, rioting broke out on the streets of Los Angeles in reaction to a jury's acquittal of white police officers accused of beating black motorist Rodney King. For four days and four nights, mobs attacked motorists, set fires, and looted stores.

2. Gangsta Rap Captivates the Mainstream

The early 1990s saw the rise of "gangsta" rap, an offshoot of rap music chronicling the violence and mayhem of the black ghetto. The genre's commercial success quickly overshadowed rap styles conveying more positive political and cultural messages.

3. The World Trade Center Bombing: The Growing Threat of Islamic Terrorism

Islamic fundamentalists bombed the World Trade Center on February 26, 1993, killing six people. The bombing exposed the hatred many Muslims around the world feel toward the United States and the willingness of some Muslims to commit terrorism in the name of Islam.

Chapter 2: 1995–1998: Technology and Scandal

and business leaders with mail bombs, killing
three people and injuring more than two dozen.
He was identified and captured in 1996 after insist-
ing that two major newspapers publish his treatise, "Industrial Society and Its Future."

2. Television Comedy Embraces Irony

Television comedies in the mid-1990s, following
the success of hit shows like *Seinfeld* and *The Simpsons*, abandoned political correctness in favor of ir-
reverent satire. The popularity of the new programs reflected America's changing sense of
humor and social mores.

3. Tiger Woods Makes Golf History

A twenty-year-old Tiger Woods took the golf
world by storm when he joined the professional
golf tour in the summer of 1996. Not only did
Woods prove to be an outstanding golfer, his
mixed-race ethnicity drew many new fans to a
sport once seen as unfriendly to minorities.

4. Cloning: A Scientific Breakthrough Challenges Medical Ethics

In 1997, scientists announced that they had successfully cloned an adult mammal for the first
time. The announcement generated concern that
the technology might eventually be used to clone
humans, raising numerous ethical questions.

5. The Bombing of U.S. Embassies in Africa

On August 7, 1998, terrorist bombs exploded at the
U.S. embassy buildings in Nairobi, Kenya, and Dar
Es Salaam, Tanzania. A total of 213 American
diplomats, embassy employees, and civilians were
killed. The bombings raised concerns that the Clinton administration had not taken sufficient action
against international terrorists.

Chapter 3: 1999–2001: Youth Violence, an Election Dispute, and Fleeting Dot-Coms

Chapter 4: 2001 and Beyond: A Tragic Introduction to a New Era

the Pentagon. In addition, any nation providing a safe haven for terrorists would be considered hostile to the United States.

3. Responding to Terror: Waging War in Afghanistan
In early October 2001, the United States embarked on a military campaign against the Taliban government in Afghanistan after it refused to turn over Osama bin Laden and other terrorists linked to the September 11, 2001, attack on America.

4. Civil Liberties and the War Against Terrorism
In response to the continuing threat of terrorism, Congress passed the USA Patriot Act of 2001, which broadened the surveillance powers of law enforcement agencies in investigations related to terrorism.

5. The Rise of Anti-Americanism in the Post–Cold War Era
America's rise as the sole superpower since the end of the Cold War has created resentment abroad. The unsympathetic reaction to the September 11 attacks in some corners of the world shocked many Americans.

During the sixteenth century, events occurred in North America that would change the course of American history. In 1512, Spanish explorer Juan Ponce de León led the first European expedition to Florida. French navigator Jean Ribault established the first French colony in America at Fort Caroline in 1564. Over a decade later, in 1579, English pirate Francis Drake landed near San Francisco and claimed the country for England.

These three seemingly random events happened in different decades, occurred in various regions of America, and involved three different European nations. However, each discrete occurrence was part of a larger movement for European dominance over the New World. During the sixteenth century, Spain, France, and England vied for control of what was later to become the United States. Each nation was to leave behind a legacy that would shape the political structure, language, culture, and customs of the American people.

Examining such seemingly disparate events in tandem can help to emphasize the connections between them and generate an appreciation for the larger global forces of which they were a part. Greenhaven Press's American History by Era series provides students with a unique tool for examining American history in a way that allows them to see such connections. This series divides American history—from the time that the first people arrived in the New World from Asia to the September 11 terrorist attacks—into nine discrete periods. Each volume then presents a collection of both primary and secondary documents that describe the major events of the period in chronological order. This structure provides students with a snapshot of events occurring simultaneously in all parts of America. The reader can then gain an appreciation for the political, social, and cultural movements and trends that shaped the nation. Students reading about the adventures of individual European explorers, for instance, are invited to consider how such expeditions compared in purpose and consequence to earlier and later expeditions. Rather than simply learning that Ponce de León was the first Spaniard to try to colonize Florida, for example, students can begin to understand his expedition in a larger context. Indeed, Ponce's voyage was an extension of Spain's desire to conquer the Caribbean and Mexico, and his expedition was to inspire other Spanish explorers to head north from Hispaniola and New Spain in search of rich empires to conquer.

Another benefit of studying eras is that students can view a "snapshot" of America at any given moment of time and see the various social, cultural, and political events that occurred simultaneously. For example, during the period between 1920 and 1945, Charles Lindbergh became the first to make a solo transatlantic flight, Babe Ruth broke the record for the most home runs in one season, and the United States dropped the atomic bomb on Hiroshima. Random events occurring in post–Cold War America included the torching of the Branch Davidian compound in Waco, Texas, the emergence of the World Wide Web, and the 2000 presidential election debacle in which ballot miscounts in Florida held up election results for weeks.

Each volume in this series offers features to enhance students' understanding of the era of American history under discussion. An introductory essay provides an overview of the period, supplying essential context for the readings that follow. An annotated table of contents highlights the main point of each selection. A more in-depth introduction precedes each document, placing it in its particular historical context and offering biographical information about the author. A thorough chronology and index allow students to quickly reference specific events and dates. Finally, a bibliography opens up additional avenues of research. These features help to make the American History by Era series an extremely valuable tool for students researching the political upheavals, wars, cultural movements, scientific and technological advancements, and other events that mark the unfolding of American history.

On September 11, 2001, nineteen Islamic extremists, armed only with pocket knives and box cutters, hijacked four commercial jetliners shortly after takeoff from three East Coast airports. Two of the planes were crashed into the twin towers of the World Trade Center in New York City, and a third was flown into the side of the Pentagon outside Washington, D.C. A fourth plane, thought to have been headed for the White House, crashed in rural Pennsylvania after passengers attempted to thwart the hijackers. In New York City, more than two thousand people were killed when the twin towers collapsed from the explosive impact of the planes. At the Pentagon, the heart of the nation's military defense operations, close to two hundred people lost their lives. These horrific acts of mass murder exposed a gaping vulnerability in the domestic security of the nation. U.S. officials now warn that repeat attacks may be inevitable and that terrorists may escalate the scale of their assaults through the use of nuclear and biological weapons.

The attacks of September 11 were not only enormously tragic; they seemed to mark the end of an era of a largely isolationist foreign policy that had begun with the end of the Cold War ten years earlier. In the early years of the post–Cold War era, the United States sought to define its role as the world's only remaining "superpower." President George H. Bush envisioned a "new world order" in which the United States led the international community in the protection of democracy and the provision of humanitarian aid. This vision seemed to be confirmed by America's success in the Gulf War of 1990.

After this initial victory, however, subsequent American interventions proved less fruitful and lost the support of the American people, causing the United States to refocus its energies on domestic concerns. Throughout the remainder of the 1990s, the United States, for the most part, intervened directly in international affairs only when vital U.S. interests were at stake. Although this policy resulted in an era of peace and prosperity for the nation, America would eventually pay for its lack of attention to developments in foreign lands. By neglecting the fate of impoverished countries like Somalia, Sudan, Ethiopia, and Afghanistan, which were no longer regarded as strategically important, the United States failed to prevent the further destabilization of countries already on the brink of disaster and the rise of anarchic, rogue nations in which terrorists, criminals, and warlords flourished. In Afghanistan and Somalia, especially, warlords and extremist groups took over, providing a fertile breeding ground for the terrorists who would carry out the attacks of September 11.

SOMALIA: A PEACEKEEPING MISSION TURNS VIOLENT

In late 1992, Somalia had devolved into utter chaos, a country full of disease and extreme famine. Armed gangs roamed the streets of Mogadishu, Somalia's largest city, exacting street justice in their quest for territory and control of the food supply. In December 1992, President George Bush, in his last days in office, ordered thousands of U.S. troops into Somalia on a peacekeeping mission. Public outcry over disturbing television pictures of starving Somalis and pressure from the United Nations (UN) may have been a factor in Bush's decision to intervene. The mission was primarily humanitarian in nature: The troops were to distribute food, open roads, and engage in the limited disarmament of local gangs. The mission went smoothly for several months. In May 1993, Congress, working with President Bill Clinton's administration, passed a resolution expanding the U.S. role in Somalia to include nation-building tasks such as establishing regional councils and elections. This expanded role was offset by the fact that U.S. forces were being reduced from twenty-eight thousand to forty-five hundred.

By the early summer of 1993, the U.S. distribution of food, in cooperation with UN peacekeepers, had antagonized local warlords. The warlords' control of the food supply was a key factor in their struggle to gain control of the country, and their power was undermined by the fact that food was reaching more of the Somali people. Somali warlord Mohammed Farah Aidid also felt that his militia had been singled out by the UN for disarmament. In retaliation, he ordered his forces to ambush Pakistani UN peacekeepers on June 5, killing twenty-four. According to George J. Church, a reporter for *Time* magazine, the assault led to the passage of a UN Security Council resolution authorizing the "arrest and detention for prosecution, trial and punishment" of those responsible and marked the moment when "the humanitarian mission began to turn into a mini-war against Aidid."[1]

As a result, U.S. forces in Somalia found themselves engaged in a manhunt for Aidid and his followers. On October 3, 1993, intelligence reports indicated that Aidid's top lieutenants were meeting at the Olympic Hotel in Mogadishu. Approximately one hundred American army rangers repelled onto the hotel from Blackhawk helicopters and captured nineteen of Aidid's cohorts. In a 1993 article Louise Lief reported on the events that followed: "Unable to climb back up to their helicopters with their prisoners, the soldiers waited for another Ranger detachment to make its way to the hotel through Mogadishu's shattered streets in trucks and humvees. Then disaster struck. One Blackhawk was hit by 23-mm cannon fire from the hotel and crashed. Minutes later a second helicopter was hit and went down about 1¼ miles from where the first Blackhawk had crashed."[2] The rangers were attacked by Aidid's forces on all sides. After a nine-hour gun battle, fifteen rangers were dead, scores were wounded, and four were missing in action. Chief Warrant Officer Michael Durant, a pilot of one of the downed helicopters, was held hostage by Aidid's men and released after eleven days. The final death toll would be eighteen Americans killed and 197 wounded.

Most disturbing, however, were the images of Somalis dragging the mutilated corpses of U.S. soldiers through the streets of Mogadishu, which were broadcast on television newscasts. The shocking pictures outraged many Americans, who began to question what American troops were trying to accomplish in Somalia, a mission whose purpose had never been clearly articulated by either the Bush or Clinton administration. To many observers, the vague mission had gotten out of control and had become a terrifying example of what can go wrong when the United States chooses to intervene in the affairs of distant, distressed nations where no clearly defined U.S. interests are at stake. In response to public and political pressure, the Clinton administration announced that it would withdraw American troops by March 31, 1994. But this did little to quell the firestorm of controversy surrounding the debacle.

In November 1993, Eliot A. Cohen, a professor of strategic studies at the Paul A. Nitze School of Advanced International Studies, maintained that the Bush and Clinton administrations had failed to understand that the famine in Somalia was caused by the anarchy of men, not nature, a fact that would inevitably necessitate military conflict. Said Cohen, "The American intervention came to remedy the chaos bred by years of civil war. To end the famine, the occupying forces had to restore order. . . . Unwilling to buy off the bandits, we chose to coerce them. They fought back. We have pursued the most wily of these bandit chieftains with the results we have seen."[3] In Cohen's opinion, once troops were committed to Somalia, the United States should have been prepared for the kind of large-scale military action that would have achieved the goal of restoring order. Instead, the message to warlords was "kill a dozen Americans and desecrate their corpses, and the Yanks will cave in."[4] A U.S. soldier in Mogadishu leveled more succinct criticism at the assumption that U.S. troops could be deployed for strictly humanitarian purposes. He wondered, "What good does it do just to distribute food and supplies? As soon as we leave Aidid's people will take everything back and extend their reign of misery even further."[5] Other observers were critical of the mission's escalation from humanitarian to military action. An editorial in the liberal political magazine the *Nation* that appeared soon after the disastrous raid on the Olympic Hotel asserted that "the mistake is in thinking that complex political situations—in Somalia or anywhere—can be resolved by sending in the troops and trying to 'take out' some troublesome leader. From Panama to Iraq we have witnessed the unwisdom of such a strategy; there is no reason to think that escalating the urban-guerilla war in Mogadishu will somehow defy this wretched history."[6]

The Somalia mission, widely regarded as an American foreign policy failure, coincided with another largely unsuccessful intervention against the military-led regime in Haiti. By the close of 1993, public support for peacekeeping and nation building in countries where no U.S. interests were at stake was clearly diminished. As a result, the Clinton administration retreated somewhat from the interventionist course it had charted for the United States. Other impoverished trouble spots that had surfaced at the end of the Cold War, such as the African nation of Rwanda, were neglected in favor of the containment of

Iraq and U.S. bombing campaigns in Bosnia and Serbia, newly independent and deeply troubled states of the former Yugoslavia. One area of neglect that would prove particularly disastrous was the nation of Afghanistan.

AFGHANISTAN: HISTORICAL BACKGROUND

Afghanistan, deeply scarred by events of the Cold War, was one country that received little beyond limited humanitarian assistance from the United States throughout most of the 1990s. In the early 1990s, however, Afghanistan bore a striking resemblance to Somalia. Warlords in charge of ethnic factions had carved up the country and proclaimed themselves provincial rulers, blocking the establishment of a unified national government. Anarchy, hunger, and civil war prevailed.

Afghanistan has a long history of ethnic strife between its four main ethnic groups, the Pashtuns, Tajiks, Uzbeks, and Hazaras. According to Zalmay Khalilzad, an Afghan-born scholar of the Middle East and a National Security Council official under President George W. Bush, "A variety of political movements were formed in and across these ethnic groups. These movements included ethnic nationalists; centrists or Afghan nationalists; Islamists; and Communists. . . . However, a major change took place in 1978. Two factions of the Communist Party—Kalq and Percham—seized power in a military coup." Khalilzad contends that the Soviet Union may have encouraged the coup and "provided military, political, and economic support to the regime, including the sending of several thousand military advisors."[7] The new Communist government, which was installed in Afghanistan's capital, Kabul, drew opposition from religious and nationalist forces, who "resented the centralized control coming out of Kabul,"[8] according to Khalilzad. These groups that supported Afghan nationalism and traditional values weakened the authority of the Communist regime. Sensing the Communists' imminent collapse, the Soviet Union invaded Afghanistan in 1979 and installed Babrak Karmal as president with the support of 100,000 troops.

The United States considered Afghanistan to be of strategic value as a buffer against Soviet expansion into the Middle East, a region containing most of the world's oil reserves. The U.S. government under President Jimmy Carter took immediate steps to destabilize the Soviet "puppet" government by supplying the anti-Communist rebels with weapons through neighboring Pakistan. The plan was to bog the Soviet Union down in a protracted guerrilla war, much like the United States had experienced in Vietnam. The Afghan resistance groups, known as the mujahedin, were strongly united by their Islamic faith. They believed that they were fighting a jihad, or holy war, against godless Communist oppressors. The mujahedin were joined by freedom fighters from all over the Muslim world who were eager to participate in the jihad. One such participant was Osama bin Laden, the son of a wealthy Saudi real estate magnate, who had shunned his privileged background in favor of Islamic fundamentalism. Reportedly worth $20 to $30 million, bin Laden offered financial and strategic assistance to the mujahedin and is thought to have participated in key battles against the Soviets. His ties to Afghanistan would later have dire consequences for the United States.

By 1985, the mujahedin were clearly losing ground against the superior Soviet air forces, but their commitment to the battle was unflagging. According to the Pentagon, Soviet forces had begun to concentrate their attacks on the Pakistan border in an effort to shut down the flow of weapons to the mujahedin. In March 1985, U.S. military assistance underwent a major escalation after President Ronald Reagan signed classified National Security Decision Directive 166, which authorized assistance to the mujahedin "by all means available" and changed the purpose of U.S. aid to Afghanistan from enabling the "harassment" of the Soviets to compelling their withdrawal. In 1986, the United States decided to arm the mujahedin with Stinger antiaircraft missiles, which greatly increased their defenses against Soviet air forces. According to Alan J. Kuperman, a visiting scholar at the Center for International Studies of the University of Southern California, the Stinger missiles were the first American-made weapons used against Soviet troops. This escalation of U.S. support (in 1986, the United States contributed nearly $500 million in aid to Afghanistan) is cited as a factor in the Soviet Union's decision to begin the withdrawal of its troops in the late 1980s. Kuperman maintains that the Soviet Union was interested in renewing economic cooperation with the West in order to restore its ailing economy; the occupation of Afghanistan was regarded by Soviet leader Mikhail Gorbachev as a hindrance to that effort. In February 1989, after nearly ten years of war, the Soviet Union pulled the last of its 115,000 troops out of Afghanistan.

The Soviet occupation was not yet entirely defeated; the Soviet-backed regime in Kabul, now led by Mohammed Najibullah, remained in control. In 1992, Najibullah was finally toppled, but a peaceful transition toward new leadership eluded Afghanistan. Khalilzad maintains that "without the glue of a common enemy, the mujahedin turned their guns on each other in a brutal civil war."[9] Conditions in Afghanistan, already devastated by ten years of war and an estimated 1 million casualties, deteriorated into anarchy as the nation once again fractured into competing ethnic groups. But this discord was no longer of much concern to the United States. Its main objective of driving the Soviets out of Afghanistan had been achieved, and the Soviet Union's sudden collapse in 1991 shifted the attentions of American foreign policy elsewhere.

THE RISE OF THE TALIBAN

Unlike with Somalia, the chaos in Afghanistan received scant media coverage. According to Khalilzad, the U.S. role in Afghanistan was reduced to humanitarian aid and support for the UN to negotiate an end to the civil war. Fears that Afghanistan might become a haven for drug smugglers and international terrorists were expressed, but the United States lacked the political will to get further involved in the affairs of a nation gripped by a violent civil war, particularly following its experience in Somalia. After the events of September 11, however, many observers would come to regret this hands-off approach to Afghanistan in the immediate post–Cold War years. Zbigniew Brzezinski, who served as national security adviser under President Jimmy Carter, has concluded that "America's most significant mistake was to abandon [Afghanistan] to its unhappy fate following the Soviet withdrawal."[10]

What transpired in Afghanistan during the early 1990s proved to be unfavorable to both the United States and the Afghan people. By 1994, an Islamic fundamentalist movement known as the Taliban, meaning "students of religion," had attracted, according to Khalilzad, many "disgruntled former mujahedin and students of religious studies from the madressas or 'religious schools' located in Pakistan along the Afghan border."[11] Emerging from the surrounding anarchy, the Taliban managed to attract other mujahedin parties and by 1996 had control of over two-thirds of Afghanistan, including Kabul. Under the leadership of Mullah Omar, the Taliban enforced a strict interpretation of Islamic law on the areas under its control. Women could no longer work outside the home and were required to wear a *burqa*, a veiled dress that covered them from head to toe, in public. Young girls were not permitted to attend school, and radios and television sets were banned. The extremism of the Taliban attracted Muslim fundamentalists from Africa and other Middle Eastern countries who relished the prospect of living in a true Islamic state. Some of these arrivals were connected with the anti-Western terrorist group al-Qaeda, which operated terrorist "cells" in countries throughout the Muslim world, including Pakistan, Sudan, and Somalia. With funding from the Taliban government, al-Qaeda operated several terrorist training camps in Afghanistan.

THE START OF A TERRORIST CAMPAIGN

Following the Soviet defeat in Afghanistan, bin Laden had left Afghanistan for the African nation of Sudan, where his financial largesse was welcomed for a time by Sudan's Islamic fundamentalist government. It was from Sudan in 1992 that bin Laden is thought to have led al-Qaeda terrorists in their first attack on the United States as U.S. troops were preparing to enter Somalia on their peacekeeping mission. In protest of the Somalia mission, al-Qaeda terrorists under the leadership and financial backing of bin Laden bombed a hotel in Yemen where U.S. troops were staying en route to Somalia. The bombing was not a success, but one person, an Australian tourist, was killed. In addition to this attack, according to journalist Deborah Scroggins of the *Atlanta Journal-Constitution*, "Bin Laden provided military training and assistance to Somali opponents of the U.S. presence and later claimed the U.S. pullout from Somalia as the first of his followers' victories over what he called the U.S. 'paper tiger.'"[12]

From 1992 on, bin Laden escalated his terrorist activity. As reported by Douglas Waller in *Time* magazine, U.S. intelligence officials from the FBI and the CIA made a disturbing discovery as they brought Rami Yousef, the mastermind of a 1993 attack on the World Trade Center, into custody in 1995. (Yousef had fled to Pakistan after the attack.) According to Waller, Yousef boasted to authorities that "next time, if I have more money . . . I'll knock it down."[13] The boast was not taken lightly by authorities because they had discovered that Yousef now had a benefactor, most likely Osama bin Laden. As Waller describes it, this connection caused intelligence officials to discover that "by 1993 bin Laden had begun hunting for nuclear weapons. First on his shopping list was a Russian nuclear warhead he hoped to buy on the black market. He abandoned that effort when no warhead could be found. Instead, his agents began scouring former Soviet republics for enriched uranium and weapons components that could be used to set off the fuel."[14]

America's worst nightmare for the post–Cold War era seemed to be coming true: A wealthy madman with terrorist connections around the world was searching for weapons of mass destruction. The Taliban government in Afghanistan only intensified the threat to U.S. security interests. Aware of bin Laden's terrorist activity, the Sudanese government pressured him to leave after a five-year stay. Since few countries were willing to accept a known terrorist, bin Laden headed back to Afghanistan in 1996, just as the Taliban was coming to power. From there, he was free to lead al-Qaeda terrorists in more attacks against the United States, unconstrained by the laws of the civilized world.

On August 7, 1998, the U.S. embassies in Nairobi, Kenya, and Dar es Salaam, Tanzania, were bombed by terrorists, killing 223 people, and bin Laden was linked to the attacks. Thirteen days later, on August 20, the United States retaliated with missile attacks aimed at al-Qaeda training camps in the Kowst region of Afghanistan. The Shifa pharmaceutical plant in North Khartoum, Sudan, was also targeted with missiles. U.S. intelligence officials maintained that the factory was producing nerve-gas weapons materials, although Sudan's health minister, Ihsan el Ghabsawi, denied these assertions. He protested that the plant was producing drugs to fight tuberculosis and other medicines for humans and animals. In May 1999, the United States unfroze the assets of the owner of the plant, Salih Idris, implying that a mistake had been made in targeting the factory and that funds from bin Laden had not been funneled into the plant.

RESPONDING TO TERROR: TROUBLING QUESTIONS ABOUND

For the first time, President Bill Clinton had mustered the political will to take direct action against bin Laden and al-Qaeda. However, the Monica Lewinsky sex scandal and the impending impeachment proceeding that had engulfed the president's administration clouded the U.S. retaliation with troubling questions. Particularly in the Middle East, some observers felt that Clinton had ordered the attacks to distract the attentions of the American people from the scandal. Beirut's *Al Kifah Al Arabi* newspaper featured a front-page editorial that asserted, "Lewinsky's dress is no longer the preoccupation of the world after Clinton has discovered Osama bin Laden's (Arab robe)."[15] Others questioned whether there was enough evidence to target the pharmaceutical plant in Sudan and doubted the effectiveness of a piecemeal assault on terrorist camps in Afghanistan. Michael Collins Dunn, the editor and publisher of the *Estimate*, a newsletter of intelligence analysis on the Islamic world, raised these concerns soon after the U.S. attacks: "Even if the factory had done everything it is accused of doing, its connection with bin Laden seems somewhat tenuous at best, and therefore its selection as a target may be questionable. . . . The attack on the training camps . . . has come in for less criticism, since there is little doubt that the camps were in fact used for training fighters . . . loosely allied with bin Laden. . . . Though camps were destroyed, such camps are easy enough to rebuild, and Bin Laden can afford to rebuild them."[16] On the whole, the ensuing controversy over Clinton's motives rendered the retaliation ineffective, and bin Laden and the terrorist activity in Afghanistan lost the attention of most Americans.

Undeterred, bin Laden and his terrorist agents struck again just over two years later. The USS *Cole*, a navy destroyer, was attacked by suicide bombers as it refueled in Aden, Yemen, on October 4, 2000, killing seventeen sailors. It was later determined that one of the terrorists, Hassan Said Awadh Khemeri, had been arrested and released seventeen months earlier by authorities in Yemen for conspiring to kidnap Americans working there. Khemeri had also trained at one of bin Laden's terrorist camps in Afghanistan. The bin Laden connection did not surprise U.S. intelligence officials, but revelations that Yemeni officials may have had prior knowledge of the bombing plot were not encouraging. Without the full cooperation of Middle East governments, the United States was bound to lose its struggle against terrorism, short of invading Afghanistan. Meanwhile, Americans were preparing to cast their votes for presidential candidates Al Gore and George W. Bush. Domestic issues topped voter concerns, and neither candidate was pressed to offer his solutions to the rise of rogue nations harboring well-funded terrorist groups.

Terrorists Target the United States

The grave security threats confronting America in the post–Cold War era were brought home with terrifying clarity on September 11, 2001. More than three thousand people were mass murdered in acts of terrorism unprecedented in scale and evilness. Bin Laden and his terror network finally achieved their goal of toppling the twin towers of the World Trade Center, delivering a powerful punch to the nation's financial services sector in downtown New York City. Just over two hundred miles to the south, shock waves of fear reverberated through the nation's capital after terrorists took aim at the Pentagon, the stronghold of America's military might. The attacks left no doubt in the minds of many Americans that the heady prosperity of the 1990s, precipitated by the end of the Cold War, had lulled the country into a sense of invincibility. The 1993 World Trade Center bombing and its connections to Islamic terrorist groups had faded all too quickly from memory. After all, the Oklahoma City bombing, the worst act of domestic terrorism prior to September 11, was committed by Timothy McVeigh, a former U.S. Army ranger. Although bin Laden had taken American lives before, most of the attacks had been carried out in distant nations and engendered the impression that, for the most part, Islamic terrorism happened in the Middle East and Africa. In addition, many Americans trusted that the intelligence-gathering efforts of the FBI and the CIA would unravel plots against the country from terrorists operating in the rogue nations before they came to pass. After September 11, Americans would never feel the same sense of security when boarding a domestic flight, visiting prominent national landmarks, or working in high-rise office buildings.

The Threat of Weapons of Mass Destruction

Perhaps the greatest fear expressed by both U.S. leaders and the American public in the wake of September 11 is that terrorists or rogue nations will seek to acquire nuclear and biological weapons on a burgeoning black market. The end of the Cold War raised serious questions about the fate of the former Soviet Union's nuclear arsenal and the proliferation of weapons of mass destruction. The initial euphoria over the end of the arms race and the reduced chances for a nuclear holocaust quickly evaporated. The grim reality was that nuclear weapons were left without adequate controls in some of the newly independent states of the Soviet Union. Explains Thomas E. McNamara, who served as the assistant secretary for political-military affairs in President Clinton's administration, "Russia and the other New Independent States—NIS—face new economic incentives to export WMD [weapons of mass destruction]–related technologies, material, and equipment at a time of grave economic crisis. . . . The collapse of totalitarian controls opened up the risk that individuals with access to dangerous materials or with sensitive knowledge could be persuaded to smuggle it to rogue states of terrorists."[17] U.S. officials also feared that scientists with weapons expertise, desperate for work in the collapsed economies of the former Soviet Union, would be lured away in a "brain drain" to countries like Iraq and North Korea. To reduce the incentive of Soviet scientists to sell their knowledge abroad, the U.S. government provided funding in 1994 for several government agencies administered by the International Science and Technology Center (ISTC) in Moscow. According to journalist Nicholas Kralev, participating scientists are employed in peaceful scientific projects and are "banned from working with countries that have [nuclear and biological weapons] proliferation programs or sponsor terrorists."[18] The program seems to have precluded a large-scale defection of scientists, but it offers no guarantee against the trafficking of weapons technology. In addition, treaties such as the Nonproliferation Treaty, the Missile Technology Control Regime, and the Biological Weapons Convention have all played a role in controlling deadly weapons.

Unfortunately, however, the demand for nuclear and biological weapons technology abroad has increased with the collapse of the Soviet Union. During the Cold War, Iraq and North Korea, aligned with the Soviet regime, had come to rely on formidable Soviet military strength as a powerful deterrent to would-be aggressors. With that sense of protection gone, Iraq and North Korea, along with other countries, sought to acquire weapons of mass destruction. Thomas E. McNamara maintains that "the breakup of the FSU [former Soviet Union] has increased the level of insecurity of the FSU's former clients and their motivation to acquire weapons of mass destruction. Iraq and the Democratic People's Republic of Korea—D.P.R.K.—are cases in point. . . . Unknown to any of us, coalition forces in the [1991] Gulf faced a series of Iraqi biological and chemical weapons. . . . Worse, we now know that [Iraqi ruler] Saddam Hussein had plans that would have allowed him to target most of the capitals of Europe and the Middle East with missiles tipped with nuclear, chemical, and biological weapons. . . . North Korea's use of . . . technology to create a nuclear weapons program also put us on the edge of a major crisis."[19] The threat of these nations, unconstrained by the diplomatic checks and balances imposed by the Cold War and demonstrating a willingness to acquire and use weapons of mass destruction, cannot be underestimated and presents a complex challenge to the United States. In addition, countries like Iraq may actively provide terrorists with the funding and materials needed to carry out a nuclear or biological attack against the United States.

AMERICA RESPONDS TO TERRORISM AND THE "AXIS OF EVIL"

In response to the events of September 11, American foreign policy has abruptly shifted its focus to routing out terrorists who operate with impunity in rogue nations. On September 20, 2001, President George W. Bush, in a speech to Congress and the American people, announced his plans for a "war on terrorism," which will involve a series of steps to make life uncomfortable for terrorists abroad. Counterintelligence, diplomacy, freezing the financial assets of terror networks, and direct military action against states that harbor terrorists are all part of the president's plan. The Taliban government was the first casualty in the war on terrorism. In early October 2001, after Taliban leader Mullah Omar refused to hand over bin Laden and members of al-Qaeda, U.S. forces began a bombing campaign that led to the collapse of the Taliban regime just two months later. Many al-Qaeda terrorists were brought into custody, but bin Laden eluded capture. The president also laid down the gauntlet in his January 2002 State of the Union address against three countries—Iran, Iraq, and North Korea—which he described as representing an "axis of evil" because of their support of terrorist activities and their development of weapons of mass destruction. Cuba, Libya, and Syria were also named as rogue states.

The looming security threats of the post–Cold War years have proven to be a disheartening replacement for the era when the two superpowers (the Soviet Union and the United States) engaged in a tense competition for global influence. The world somehow seems to have become a free-for-all in which diplomacy has been superseded by chaos, fear, and a new willingness to target large civilian populations in the name of radical religious movements or political agendas. Americans must now come to accept the threat of terrorism as a fact of life, adjusting their routines and sacrificing certain freedoms that were once taken for granted. The United States may have won the Cold War, emerging as the world's sole superpower, but its role in this new world order has yet to be clearly defined. Only time will tell if the United States must play the role of the world's policeman indefinitely to protect its homeland security interests. Nearly ten years after the American mission in Somalia, the United States is still searching for a footing in the post–Cold War world.

NOTES

1. George J. Church, "Anatomy of a Disaster," *Time*, October 18, 1993, p. 44.

2. Louise Lief, Bruce B. Auster, and Sam Kiley, "What Went Wrong in Somalia?" *U.S. News & World Report*, October 18, 1993, p. 33.

3. Eliot A. Cohen, "A Nasty Little War," *National Review*, November 1, 1993, p. 50.

4. Cohen, "A Nasty Little War," p. 51.

5. Ian Alexander, "There Oughta Be a Law," *National Review*, February 7, 1994, p. 33.

6. *Nation*, "Include Us Out," October 25, 1993, p. 448.

7. Zalmay Khalilzad, "Anarchy in Afghanistan," *Journal of International Affairs*, Summer 1997, p. 38.

8. Khalilzad, "Anarchy in Afghanistan," p. 39.

9. Khalilzad, "Anarchy in Afghanistan," p. 37.

10. Quoted in Eric Alterman, "Blowback, the Prequel," *Nation*, November 12, 2001, p. 12.

11. Khalilzad, "Anarchy in Afghanistan," p. 42.

12. Deborah Scroggins, "Somalia: Old Hot Spot May Be Next in War Against Terrorism," *Atlantic Journal-Constitution*, January 3, 2002, p. A8.

13. Douglas Waller, "Inside the Hunt for Osama," *Time*, December 21, 1998, p. 33.

14. Waller, "Inside the Hunt for Osama," p. 33.

15. Quoted in *Nando Times*, "Arabs Suggest Clinton-Lewinsky Scandal Behind Attacks," August 21, 1998. http://archive.nandotimes.com.

16. Michael Collins Dunn, "Usama Bin Laden: The Nature of the Challenge," *Middle East Policy*, October 1998, p. 23.

17. Thomas E. McNamara, "Rethinking Proliferation in the Post–Cold War Era: The Challenge of Technology," *US Department of State Dispatch*, December 1995, p. 928.

18. Nicholas Kralev, "Cold War in the Hot Zone," *Insight on the News*, December 10, 2001, p. 27.

19. McNamara, "Rethinking Proliferation in the Post–Cold War Era," p. 929.

AMERICAN HISTORY BY ERA

1992–1995: Unrest at Home and Abroad

CHAPTER 1

THE RODNEY KING VERDICT AND THE LOS ANGELES RIOTS

JUAN GONZALEZ

On April 29, 1992, a jury concluded its deliberations in the trial of four white Los Angeles police officers accused of using excessive force against black motorist Rodney King following a high-speed chase. The trial had garnered national attention stemming from a videotape an onlooker had recorded of King being repeatedly clubbed and kicked by several police officers. The videotape had aired on national television and was regarded by many in the black community as evidence of the brutality routinely committed by police against minorities. Due to the widespread media coverage and concerns over a prejudiced jury pool, the trial had been moved from Los Angeles to Simi Valley, a mostly white suburb north of the city. The jury was comprised of ten whites, one Filipina woman, and one Hispanic woman and was equally divided between the sexes. To the bewilderment of many of those who had seen the videotape, the jury found one officer guilty of one count of excessive force against King and acquitted the remaining three officers of all charges.

As news of the verdict spread through the black community later that afternoon, rioting broke out at the intersection of Florence and Normandie in South Central Los Angeles. Mobs pulled unsuspecting white, Hispanic, and Asian motorists out of their vehicles and attacked them, beating truck driver Reginald Denny nearly to death. The rioting quickly spread to other sections of the city as hundreds of stores were burned and looted. For four days and four nights, anarchy reigned on the streets of Los Angeles. When the fires and angry mobs finally began to subside on May 3, fifty-two people were dead, over 2,500 injured, and close to 1,100 stores and businesses destroyed. In the following diary of the riots, Juan Gonzalez, then a journalist at New York City's *Daily News*, captures the devastation and anger he encountered reporting from South Central beginning on May 1, the second day of the riots. Gonzalez is the author of *Roll Down Your Window: Stories of a Forgotten America*, from which this excerpt was taken.

Yesterday afternoon, National Guard troops drove down Figueroa Street and occupied this country's second-largest city. The military marched in to secure the scorched hell of South Central Los Angeles in the aftermath of the Rodney King decision, arguably the most racist verdict in memory.

MAY 1–8, 1992: VIEWING THE DESTRUCTION

A liquor store at 56th and Broadway had gone up in a flash around 1 P.M., as had its neighbor, A.J. Sedberry's Tailor Shop. "I been here twenty-five years and these motherfuckers took fifteen minutes to destroy it all," Sedberry said of the looters who had pillaged and set fire to his shop.

Sedberry supervised one young worker who was training a faint spray from a garden hose on the smoldering wall between the two stores and another who was tossing big embers from the building's roof. Inside, the shop was ruined. The interior walls were charred and most of the side wall had collapsed. Big spools of thread were strewn on the wet black soot behind the counter. Tramping through the rubble in his gray rubber boots, Sedberry appeared distressed and defeated. His shirt was misbuttoned. A blue baseball cap, emblazoned with the word Cadillac, sat askew on his salt-and-pepper hair.

"They weren't satisfied just taking the liquor," Sedberry said. "They started stealing liquor cases last night. But this afternoon I heard a big boom. I rushed out and the fire was all over the place. Koreans owned it. These kids are going after all the Korean places.

"This Rodney King thing on top of that teenage black girl killed couple of months back, that's all the excuse they needed.

You know, the Korean woman who shot that girl got off with probation. Now that ain't right."

Like many of the older people in the neighborhood, Sedberry had survived the Watts riot of 1965. "I had a place over on the West Side," he recalled. "They didn't touch it. But this time . . . I may as well retire."

Just up Broadway, at 47th Street, a young black couple, Marcus and Carolyn Selestein, stood guard with their Latino kitchen staff outside their restaurant, Jacob's Cafe. Two doors away the gate to the video store came crashing down and scores of young blacks and Latinos charged in, only to emerge minutes later with armfuls of video tapes and VCRs. Parents double-parked, leaving the kids in the back seat, while they rushed in for the week's supply of movies. Five black men started shaking the gates of a shuttered variety store with a handwritten sign in the window: Black Owned Store. The Selesteins rushed over. "Now, you know your mothers and sisters need that store to shop. Don't go destroying it," Carolyn barked at the men. Like kids caught with their hands in the cookie jar, all five turned and sheepishly walked away.

"People around here figure, 'We don't own or lease any of these stores, so why worry what happens to them,'" Marcus said. "This is all just mindless kids. They don't know how long it will take to rebuild the community." He had watched last night as a crowd looted the big Broadway Food Market across the street from his restaurant. "The owner was Korean," Marcus reported. "Someone shot him in the back of the head and then people just stepped over the body as they took things out. After the cops arrived and removed the body, the people came back and burned the store."

Ronnie Harrison stood at 58th and Figueroa as a small complex of stores was engulfed in huge flames. "I was here for Watts," she said. "This is much worse. Then it was all in one area. Now, there's fires everywhere. They hit first one place, then another."

As I drove up Vermont, black smoke from more than a dozen fires spiraled into the smog. At Vermont and Martin Luther King, the smoke was so thick you couldn't see twenty feet in front of you.

"They started in Atlanta," Harrison had explained. "And I spoke to someone in Boston who said black people there are angry, too." Here in Los Angeles, though, the conflict was not solely about race. Latinos rioted, as did a few whites. More was clearly at stake than skin color. . . .

AWAKENING FROM A NIGHTMARE

Around six o'clock on the morning of May 1st, Edward James Olmos and two friends pulled up in front of the First AME Zion Cathedral, one of the city's oldest black churches, in a garbage truck. Armed with push brooms and trash bags, they went to work in the deserted streets.

Los Angeles was just waking up from two nights of the worst looting and arson in American history. There were 38 dead, 1,300 injured and 2,000 torched buildings. The country, too, was awakening from a nightmare. In a haunting return to the 1960s, civil unrest had spread to a dozen other cities and the president had alerted troops in most major urban areas. In 1968, the assassination of Dr Martin Luther King Jr ignited rebellions in 125 cities. Now another King emerged, a man named Rodney, whose ruthless beating by crazed cops was captured on video for all the world to see. From King to King, the years of neglect, denial and economic inequality visited upon black and Latino America by the justice system and our so-called free market have resulted in a rage unleashed to frightening result.

Yesterday, a few people dared to ask, Where do we go from here? Olmos is a successful actor who grew up on the hard streets of East Los Angeles and has never lost his ties to his old neighborhood. For two days he watched his city burn to the ground at the hands of vengeful residents. "I saw whole families looting in their cars and thought of the damage this was doing to these kids," Olmos said. "I decided we had to do something. We have to get parents and their kids to rebuild this."

So Olmos got on television Thursday night and challenged the people of Los Angeles to meet him the next morning with brooms. And the people came.

He started in front of the First AME, equipped with work gloves and a push broom, and then headed south along Western Avenue through the heart of the riot area. Each block he traveled the rubble disappeared, and the cleanup crew grew. They came from the suburbs, colleges and local neighborhoods: black, white, Hispanic and Asian, young and old. All were frustrated and pained by what had happened to their city. Elias Boca Negra, fifty-one years old, brought his two sons; Tina Robinson came with her children and several neighbors' kids.

"The same way it got burned down, we can get our community built up. It's called teamwork," said a young woman named Slim in a UCLA sweatshirt. "We live here. Why should we have to wake up each morning and see all this destruction?"

By noon, the group had grown to more than five hundred. They attacked the blocks of rubble energetically, filling the garbage truck with bags of charred debris. At the intersection of Slauson and Western, a parking lot overflowing with discards from the looting was cleared of trash within minutes. Clearly pleased with his group's efforts, a very grimy, sweaty Olmos offered his opinion on what should happen next: "The whole world is watching Los Angeles. We've got a generation of youth who have lost all sense of value. Maybe this will force us to do something about it." In the meantime, he added, "The politicians need to stop talking and pick up some brooms."

A few blocks away, more than a thousand people were in line at the post office. With no mail delivery, they had come for their monthly checks. The Reverend Jesse Jackson arrived and began shaking hands, kissing babies and urging people to stay calm. A young woman, Charlotte McKay, tried to talk to Jackson but broke down crying instead. "We already got the Crips and Bloods killing each other and now we got this," she wailed. "We just don't have to riot and steal and vandalize. We got to do something." Visibly shaken by her outburst, Jackson threw his arms around McKay and tried to comfort her. "He ain't even from Los Angeles but he cared enough to come here," remarked a woman in the crowd. "Where are all the other leaders, the ones from right here?"

At Western and Jefferson, about twenty-five jittery National Guardsmen, not a black face among them, were posted at a burnt-out shopping center. Across the street, Charles Jones waited for a bus and watched the guardsmen. "This is all over now. All these troops—ain't nobody going to be doing nothing. But what about the buses?" he asked anxiously. "They say most of them are running. I been waiting here two hours. I got to get downtown to get my check. There's no stores open. People ain't got food."

There are those who say the looting and vandalism have nothing to do with the verdict. These people simply don't understand. The mad violence of a group of sadistic, out-of-control cops went unpunished. This miscarriage of justice provoked even more senseless violence, this time from youths across the

country who watched Rodney King being pummeled merci-
lessly and saw themselves on the ground. What do you expect
from undereducated, alienated and unorganized youth? A rational argument? A disciplined protest? A letter to the editor? . . .

BURNT-OUT STORES AND HOMELESS FIRE VICTIMS

Four vicious-looking dogs snarled at me from behind the iron
grates of what was once a string of shops on Vermont Avenue
near 51st Street. A tall, spry, white-haired black man could be
seen between the twisted pillars and steel. Protected by the
dogs, 81-year-old Albert Sampson filled small buckets with water from a garden hose and tried to douse the burning embers.

Sampson, who lived in a small house behind the row of
shops and kept guard over them, was overpowered last Thursday afternoon when ten carloads of looters descended on the
property. "They started on the corner with the TV shop," he recalled. "Shows you how stupid they were—that was a repair
shop. How did they know if the TVs they carried out were even
working?" According to Sampson, the looters were of all races.
A few hours later, a small group returned and set fire to the corner store.

Like many in the community, Sampson believes that the fires
were too numerous and systematic to be purely spontaneous
and that many were set by some of the most notorious of the
city's street gangs. As if to buttress his suspicions, just a few
blocks away someone had spray-painted the words "Crips,
Bloods and Mexicans Together—Tonite 4/30" and "Fuck LAPD"
on the wall of a burnt-out store. "I used to think that, at this age
of civilization, people would know better than to do this,"
Sampson said, shaking his head. "I guess I was wrong."

Just then, Frank Lem, the owner of the TV shop, drove up to
have a word with Sampson.

"How you doin', Al?"

"Okay, Frank. Not much left of your store."

"I know. I drove by yesterday, but my wife didn't want to
stop. Thursday morning, everything was fine. Now this. At
least your house is all right, isn't it?" Lem asked.

"No. All that's left is the bedroom. The fire got everything
else. I got a bed, but no place to sleep in," Sampson replied.

Lem came to Los Angeles from China fifty years ago. He settled in the neighborhood, ran his corner shop for thirty-five

years, raised his children here, and sent them all to the University of Southern California down the road.

"You gonna rebuild, Frank?"

"Me? How could I afford the insurance after this? No. I'm past retirement anyway. This is it for me."

At 49th and Western, Samuel and Magdalena Duarte, immigrants from Guatemala, were sitting on the stoop of a house adjacent to a giant Tru-Value Hardware Store that had been burned to a crisp. The Duartes and four other families had lived in apartments over the store until looters torched it on Thursday night. The trouble had started on Wednesday. "They broke into the store in the afternoon from the back, and all day people went in and out stealing," Duarte said. "There were police and fire trucks up and down the street all day, but they never went into the alley. That's where the stealing was."

Duarte and his neighbors stayed awake on Wednesday night, handguns by their sides for protection. "The owner is Chinese. I called him and told him to do something. He said if the police weren't doing anything, he wasn't coming down." On Thursday, the Duartes packed their suitcases and waited, still praying that no one would set a fire. Then at 10 P.M., as the couple watched coverage of the riot on TV, Samuel heard an explosion. The floor of the apartment shook. "In no time the floor was so hot our feet were burning," he recalled. "We just had enough time to grab a suitcase, warn the neighbors, and run out." Once outside, Magdalena saw the two arsonists dash to a waiting pick-up truck and speed off. "They were Latinos. Our own people did this to us."

A few miles north, at Pico Boulevard and Hoover Avenue, the Korean owner of a photo supply store and his wife were digging through the rubble of their business. A dozen stores in the same commercial strip had burned down Thursday afternoon. "The police and firemen just stood around all day and did nothing," said the owner, J. Cho. "I couldn't believe. A hundred people robbing. They spend all day. They went from one store to another. Firemen fight big fire across street but not touch my store. Why? Why no help?"

As I drove down the streets of South Central, I fought back feelings of despair. Everywhere there were burnt-out stores, each representing the hard-fought dream of an American family; everywhere, homeless fire victims rummaging to retrieve items under a brilliant Los Angeles sun. . . .

A PRESIDENTIAL VISIT

The black letters on the six white trucks outside Mt Zion Missionary Baptist Church spelled "Feed the Children." The shiny 40-foot rigs were parked methodically at intervals around the block, across from the green church, engines running, like settler wagons circled against the Indians.

Inside the church, President Bush was rubbing elbows at an ecumenical service with a select group of the city's elite and members of the Reverend E.V. Hill's congregation. The president's staff and the Secret Service, fearing protests by angry residents, had turned the trucks loaded with food donated for the victims of last week's riot into temporary shields, blocking sight lines for the ordinary people who had come to get a glimpse of their president. Call it food for defense.

Like everything else about Bush's short trip, originally planned as a fund-raising swing, the scene in front of the church showed just how isolated this Yale preppie is from the people he governs. "We've seen the tip of his hair," said Luis Limon. "He didn't even as much as wave." Limon, in his early twenties, was standing on a corner outside the church with his cousin Robert Ruvalcaba and about fifty neighborhood residents. "He ain't never come around here. Whenever he visits LA he goes to Century City with all his rich friends."

The first they heard of Bush's visit was when police cars began surrounding the church around dawn. The security was so tight that the Secret Service had asked television networks not to transmit live broadcasts so the local community wouldn't find out where the president was. Reporters were not given Bush's schedule of visits in advance.

Pressing the food trucks into double duty as barricades, though, testified to a new level of Republican ingenuity. The food had been brought by the Reverend Larry Jones, a Southern Baptist minister from Oklahoma City who heads a charity group called International Ministries Inc. Jones's group has been supplying food for local churches and agencies to distribute for years, and he is a personal friend of Mt Zion pastor Hill.

"When I called and told the Bush people I was bringing the trucks, the Secret Service said, 'Fine, you've solved one of our problems,'" Jones said proudly. "As you can see, the trucks have been placed strategically by them to protect the president. Why, I even have one around back blocking access to the parking lot." Of course, with a couple of hundred reporters and cameras stationed outside the church, Jones got priceless exposure for his charity.

LINGERING ANGER AND FRUSTRATION

Inside, Bush tried his best to be relevant. "We've seen the hatred. We've got to heal and see the love," said the man who captured the White House only four short years ago by milking racist images like that of Willie Horton. But even this appeal for healing was hollow and rife with political partisanship. The neighborhood's top black official, Democratic Senator Diane Watson, for instance, wasn't even invited to the service or to Bush's meeting with black leaders afterward—although she crashed it anyway. "He has a group of leaders in there, mostly Republicans from Sacramento who do not know this area and its people" was her reaction. Neither was Gloria Molina, a Democrat and the first Hispanic to be elected to the Board of Supervisors, invited to the church service or to Bush's meeting with Hispanic leaders later in the day. Edward James Olmos, who did receive an invitation to the service because of his cleanup efforts, emerged from the church furious that Molina and other key Latino leaders had been neglected and that the riots continue to be characterized as a "black problem."

Olmos has good reason to be angry. As information about the racial and ethnic composition of those arrested for rioting is made available, the depiction of the disorders as a predominantly black uprising is being shattered. Of the first 5,438 people arrested, only 37 percent were black, while 51 percent were Hispanic and the rest were either white or of other races.

As people started filing out of Mt Zion, the Los Angeles air, which for days had been filled with the acrid smell of smoke, was suddenly filled with the suffocating aroma of heavy perfume and cologne. Politicians and ministers waited eagerly to be interviewed by reporters desperate for reactions. After a half-hour meeting with black leaders, Bush emerged from a side door. He stood on the sidewalk for several moments, talking with aides, then waved once to the crowd and disappeared into his limousine.

"It'll take more than a wave to get you reelected," yelled a white man in the crowd. His name is Robert Conrardy and he's a postal worker from Orange County. Conrardy had taken the day off with some friends to bring some food to some of South Central's homeless. "We don't need a ghost," he said. "We need someone who's going to change things for this town. I brought Bush some Carefree gum. He could use it right now."

The evidence is in. There is so much anger and frustration among the forgotten have-nots of this country and it has been building for so long that when it erupts, as it now has in Los Angeles, it becomes a sight more ghastly than any we have yet imagined. This was, after all, the riot America has always feared—the one that spilled out of the ghetto and into every corner of town.

GANGSTA RAP CAPTIVATES THE MAINSTREAM

IAN STEAMAN

Beginning in the late 1980s, politicians and the parents of young children expressed concern over the increasingly violent lyrical content of rap music and its most controversial offshoot, "gangsta" rap. Popular rap musicians like Ice Cube, Dr. Dre, and Ice-T had begun to incorporate graphic stories of gang life into their rhymes, rapping about brutal murders, dealing crack cocaine, and killing police officers. Critics found the casual violence of the music disturbing and questioned whether it was an accurate portrayal of life in the ghetto, as gangsta rappers maintained, or merely a glorification of senseless violence and immoral behavior. In the following analysis, written in the fall of 1992, Ian Steaman describes the development and commercial success of gangsta rap. The author contends that the enormous popularity of gangsta rap detracts attention from more positive styles of rap music. Ian Steaman is an arts and repertoire executive with Tommy Boy records.

W hen hip-hop began its development some 15 years ago in New York, it was dismissed as a passing fad by critics. Simple chanting over beats wasn't music, they said; rap was merely the crude utterances of ghetto hoodlums who didn't have the musical training and sophistication to create "real" music like the sung disco enjoyed by the more up-

From "Gangsta Rap Runs Risk of Becoming Passe," by Ian Steaman, *Billboard*, September 19, 1992. Copyright © 1992 by Billboard Magazine. Reprinted with permission.

scale, middle-class blacks in downtown Manhattan discos. Set to the rhythms of some of these same disco and R&B tracks, hip-hop was tagged as mere party music.

That attitude persisted, with few exceptions, until the release of Public Enemy's ground-breaking 1988 album, "It Takes a Nation of Millions to Hold Us Back." Suddenly, rap was no longer just party music. It was a method of conveying political statements and promoting a world view that wasn't reflected in the mainstream media. It was also a perfect medium for teaching a young, impressionable audience about their culture and for motivating them to question the society they lived in.

THE RISE OF GANGSTA RAP

While the music media fell over themselves discussing the new political rap and its influences, from the Nation of Islam to the Afrocentricity movement, another genre of socially infused hip-hop was evolving. Gangsta rap had its first major success with L.A. group N.W.A, whose second album, "Straight Outta Compton," went platinum in the United States. It did so with no airplay, little video play, and precious little (at first) commercial support from the traditional hip-hop strongholds in New York and other Northeastern cities. The music emphasized the rough street sensibilities from which it sprang, and listeners loved it.

What began as a cousin to its more serious Afrocentric and political rap relatives has since become the new patriarch in the hip-hop musical family. Gangsta rap now reigns supreme in terms of commercial success. Myriad groups following in the footsteps of N.W.A, the Geto Boys, and Ice Cube are all trying to attract their share of a seemingly inexhaustible pie. Even venerable institutions of New York hip-hop are jumping on the bandwagon. Def Jam Records, for example, recently announced plans to start a California-based label called DJ West to sign West Coast (read gangsta) hip-hop artists.

There is a troubling side, however, to this trend: While gangsta rap has captured the ear of the hip-hop nation and many of those outside it, other socio-political rappers, Afrocentric culturalists, and those who simply want to develop hip-hop music as an art form have been left behind in terms of sales and interest from record companies. Many wonder whether those artists can ever catch up and whether they'd ever made an impact in the first place.

Has gangsta rap taken over for good? Is it the inevitable out-come of an evolution in a music that is the one medium through which young black rage can be channeled? Or is it a temporary blip in hip-hop's overall development?

PEDDLING VIOLENCE FOR PROFIT?

Critics of gangsta rap argue that it's not constructive criticism or commentary on the social problems being described. Gangsta rappers, they say, are merely feeding off these problems for profit by creating violent heroes for young record buyers to look up to and emulate. But how valid an argument is that, really? After all, gang turf battles and drug dealing were problems in black neighborhoods long before hip-hoppers began telling mainstream America and the rest of the world about it.

Take the case of N.W.A's "Straight Outta Compton," released in 1989. The album's release left many gasping, the FBI harass-ing the group, and police around the country threatening to cancel their shows because of the incendiary, anti-police bru-tality track, "F— Tha Police." People were shocked by the amount of violence described in the track; the level of lyrical profanity reached a new high; and some questioned the social relevance and truth of the group's rhymes.

Three years later, though, the group's detractors were forced to swallow those words when an 81-second home video of Rod-ney King being brutally beaten by L.A. police surfaced. After the L.A. riots protesting the acquittal of the four police officers involved, N.W.A's defense of "F— Tha Police" as a "revenge fantasy" seemed less like a copout and more like a prescient view of how people felt in neighborhoods like Compton.

"Straight Outta Compton," despite its profanity, violence, and misogyny, contains undeniable truths. On the other hand, how many kids are buying albums by groups like N.W.A and the Geto Boys because they aren't satisfied with the mainstream media's performance and realize these groups are dropping the real 411 on black America?

Some of these groups' fans live the lifestyle these songs de-scribe and don't need to be informed about it. As for the signif-icant number of white fans, it has been argued that gangsta rhymes reveal the allure of the "mysterious" black ghettos; lis-tening to the albums gives the white listeners a feeling of hip-ness, of being down and living the ghetto life, if only vicari-ously. And the music's graphic violence and language carry the same kind of appeal as [an Arnold] Schwarzenegger flick or an Andrew Dice Clay [comedy] album.

The social relevance of these rhymes isn't diminished by these arguments, but it does explain the incredible number of new gangsta groups using the N.W.A line about being "street reporters," just telling it like they see it on their streets. Some are good and some aren't, just as in any kind of music. For every Ice Cube, there's a Nu Niggaz On Tha Block that bites ideas already used by other artists.

Ice Cube established himself as an innovative artist with his 1990 solo debut, the hip-hop masterpiece "Amerikkka's Most Wanted." His lyrics covered many of the same subjects that he rhymed about with N.W.A, but from new perspectives. For example, instead of "Gangsta, Gangsta," gang-bangers were now the "Endangered Species." The swagger of his earlier work was there, but Cube was viewing the world from a wider perspective than just being one of the boyz in the 'hood.

The members of N.W.A, on the other hand, have transformed their socially aware style into a pure entertainment commodity. On "Efil4zaggin," they rhymed about how hard and ruthless they were in a fictional world that seemed closer to Hollywood movies than to the reality of inadequate health care and funerals for slain friends described by Ice Cube.

Unfortunately, many of the groups releasing albums in this genre are following N.W.A's example. Groups like Gangsta N-I-P and Too Much Trouble shock and disgust with the negativity of the unprecedented violent and sexual content in their songs without having a social agenda to justify it. N-I-P says in his bio that he grew up watching horror movies and that, as sick as that stuff is, "it happens every day." It is claimed that "his cold, horrific rhymes reveal a perspective that can only be grasped from living under the ruthless grasp of the ghetto." But, clearly, artists like N-I-P realize that the horrific sells and that cloaking it under the guise of street reality legitimizes it.

Gangsta rap still has a function, but whether it can continue to contribute anything positive to hip-hop's musical development and its social agenda depends on whether artists are sincere in making this kind of music. The hip-hop nation has made it clear it wants the gangsta stuff, and groups who want to survive will have to at least acknowledge, if not accommodate, that economic reality.

THE WORLD TRADE CENTER BOMBING: THE GROWING THREAT OF ISLAMIC TERRORISM

MARTIN KRAMER

In September of 1992, several men began to meet in an apartment in Jersey City, New Jersey, to plot the bombing of the World Trade Center. Most were recent immigrants from Middle Eastern countries and adherents of the Islamic faith. One of the conspirators, Palestinian Mohammad Salameh, had ties to El Sayid Nosair, an Islamic fundamentalist who had murdered Meir Kahane, a right-wing Jewish American, in New York City in 1990. Others in the group were congregants at a Jersey City mosque whose cleric, Sheikh Omar Abdel-Rahman, delivered speeches advocating violence against Americans. It did not take long for the conspirators to hatch their plot to topple the Twin Towers of the World Trade Center: They would detonate 1,500 pounds of explosives in a van parked in the center's basement garage.

On February 26, 1993, their plot proceeded as planned. The blast killed six people, injured over a thousand, and caused nearly half a billion dollars' worth of damage. But their plan was carelessly executed. A vehicle identification number discovered on a piece of wreckage was matched to a rental van that had been reported stolen in New Jersey on February 25. As

From "Islam & the West (including Manhattan)," by Martin Kramer, *Commentary*, October 1993. Copyright © 1993 by Martin Kramer. Reprinted with permission.

investigators interviewed the manager of the Ryder rental agency in Jersey City, conspirator Mohammad Salameh called, attempting to get his $400 deposit back for the van he had rented and reported as stolen. A meeting was set up to lure Salameh back to Ryder for his deposit, and he was arrested on March 4. This major break in the case led investigators to a house in Jersey City where traces of explosives were discovered, and the identity of the perpetrators was quickly revealed.

Five weeks after the World Trade Center bombing, four of the perpetrators were in custody. Undeterred, a group of Muslim radicals led by Sheikh Omar Abdel-Rahman continued with their plans to blow up the United Nations and bridges and tunnels around New York City. Luckily, authorities foiled the plot and arrested the conspirators in June 1993. Abdel-Rahman was later found to have participated in the conspiracy to bomb the World Trade Center. In 1994, four of those responsible for the bombing were convicted and sentenced to life in prison. In January 1996, Sheik Omar Abdel-Rahman was sentenced to life in prison, and each of his nine followers received severe sentences. Ramzi Yousef, the plot's mastermind, was apprehended in 1995 and sentenced to life in prison in January 1998.

In the following viewpoint, written in the fall of 1993, Martin Kramer describes how these disturbing events expressed the hatred of Islamic fundamentalists for the United States and the willingness of some Muslims to perpetrate terrorism in support of their beliefs. He asserts that evading the "hard truths" about the connection between Islamic fundamentalism and terrorism will only lead to more bombings. Kramer is the editor of the *Middle East Quarterly* and the author of *Ivory Towers in the Sand: The Failure of Middle Eastern Studies in America*.

O n a weekend in New York this past June [1993], the Middle East Institute at Columbia University convened a conference with the title "Under Siege: Islam and Democracy." Invitations to the conference spoke of a "gathering atmosphere of crisis" which had "stimulated in this country a sense of confrontation between Islam and democracy," and which the organizers hoped their conference would help to "dispel." That ominous atmosphere of crisis, the invitation asserted, had "most recently been fueled by reactions to the bombing of the World Trade Center" in February.

EVADING THE ISLAMIC CONNECTION

Thus, while downtown New York limped from a blast that had killed six, injured 1,000, and done half-a-billion-dollars' worth of damage, uptown New York anguished over the "reactions" to the blast—as if they, and not the terrorist act itself, were what had inflamed the "crisis." To the assembled academics, the worrisome "reactions" included, no doubt, any number of newspaper headlines in the style of "Muslim Arrested."

But in point of fact, Muslims had been arrested—men whose commitment to their understanding of Islam provided motive for their acts. Within days of the bombing, evidence collected by the FBI had produced a strong prima-facie case against a number of recent immigrants from Arab countries, who were duly arrested and charged. Prior to their arrest, the suspects had frequented the Jersey City mosque of Sheikh Omar Abdel-Rahman, confidant of the assassins of Egyptian President Anwar al-Sadat, who had been using his American pulpit to lambaste the West and preach Islamic revolution in Egypt. The press, the public, and agencies of public order thus had every reason to ask whether the bombing had been intended, by some stretch of logic, to serve the interests of Islam.

Fortunately, even as the participants at Columbia's conference busily deconstructed the media's putative bias against Islam, the authorities understood that the most dangerous possible effect of the World Trade Center bombing was not offensive headlines or attacks by bigots against innocent Arab-Americans. It was more bombings. Their hunch resulted in the arrest of eight more of the Sheikh's acolytes and translators, allegedly caught in the act of mixing fertilizer and diesel fuel, with which they intended to deconstruct the United Nations (UN) and FBI headquarters, as well as the Lincoln and Holland tunnels. The Columbia conferees had hoped to "contribute to a modus vivendi between Islam and the West." A week later, the FBI's round of arrests made a more thorough contribution to just that end.

Through all this, it was hard to discern any serious effort to place the bombing and arrests in a credible context. Following the capture of the alleged conspirators in the UN bomb plot, New York Mayor David Dinkins adopted what by then had become the characteristic tone of evasion. In warning New Yorkers against projecting "outrage onto the whole community from which these individuals came," the mayor did his civic duty. But he leaped headlong into surmise when he determined that "these are individuals acting on their own, or in concert among other criminal collaborators." In fact, there was every likelihood that the bombing plot was political as well as criminal, and that its political context extended far beyond New York.

Dinkins could be excused—he was out of his depth—but many of America's academic interpreters of Islam, at the Columbia conference and elsewhere, in effect seconded such evasions. Some simply averred that the bombing and the foiled conspiracy, even if hatched by Muslims, had nothing to do with any extant reading of Islam. Some offered that the bombing was the work of "extremists," and that the only way to undermine them was by supporting "moderates." (On further elaboration, these "moderates" often turned out to be other Islamic fundamentalists, who may have drawn the line at blowing up skyscrapers and traffic tunnels but otherwise subscribed to the same principles as the "extremists.") One instant expert, writing in the pages of *Foreign Affairs*, confidently categorized the bombing as an "isolated event" which only "frustrated cold warriors," sold on an "Islamic conspiracy theory," could possibly tie to other events like terrorist attacks in Egypt.

In short, conventional wisdom decreed that the bombing occurred in a vacuum: it was pathological, not political. This abdication on the part of the professional interpreters of Islam left it to the investigative press to draw an outline of the suspects' murky world. Intensified reportage from New York, Khartoum, and Cairo began to untangle an informal but far-flung network of Islamic activism—a network which most academic experts had denied even existed. Many of the threads led by twists and turns back to Afghanistan, where Arab Muslim money and volunteers had contributed to the successful jihad [holy war] against Soviet forces in the 1980's.

This reportage also raised an issue that has yet to be addressed: the extent to which the U.S., which also backed the Afghan jihad, coddled its Arab veterans with visas and other protection after the war ended. Sheikh Abdel-Rahman himself had been a fund-raiser and meddler in Afghanistan. The State Department's lame explanation for his (repeated) entries into the U.S.—a computer error—suggested a preference for evasion in government as well.

In any case, were it not for the press, whose coverage of Islam is routinely maligned for its supposed bias, none of these fascinating lines of inquiry would have been opened up. A public hungry for analysis would have had to subsist only on the thin gruel of banalities served up by the scholars.

OUTRIGHT DENIAL FROM THE ARAB WORLD

That which American academics and officials evaded, many Arab interpreters openly denied. They professed astonishment that anyone could attribute the planning or execution of such an attack to any Arab or Muslim. Rather than admit even the remote possibility, they did what they have long done: they blamed the Mossad, Israel's secret service, or they simply blamed the Jews.

This view was not confined to the fundamentalist fringe press (where it flourished). It also surfaced in some of the leading newspapers in the Arab world. The columnists of the Cairo daily *al-Ahram*, which purports to be the most respected of Arab newspapers, led the charge. One writer announced with certainty that "the Islamic groups could not have carried out such an action," because it "would have such serious repercussions for them. Many of them could find no better place than the West, and particularly the United States, to take refuge in." Nor could any Palestinian have done it, for the same reasons. But Israel, the writer went on, had long sought to tarnish the image of the Arabs, and to undermine Arab and Muslim communities in Europe and America through its agents. The conclusion: "Look for Israel's and the Mossad's hand in this dirty operation."

Another columnist in *al-Ahram* called the plotters behind the bombing both "devilish and clever," since they had found in Muhammad Salameh, the principal suspect, someone combining the perfect features of a fall guy: he was a Palestinian, at one time he carried an Egyptian passport, and he belonged to a group of Muslim extremists. "Some widespread international planning must have gone into finding this needle in the haystack," the writer insinuated, and then supplied the clue:

> The only way to put the puzzle together is to resort to the Israeli Mossad. It alone is capable of deciphering the act, pinpointing the real culprits, and revealing the real objectives behind this terrorist action, which ultimately serves only one party—which is, coincidentally or not, Israel itself.

If the responsible Arab press fingered the Mossad, others in the Arab world glared accusingly at the inhabitants of New

York, who deserved divine retribution. Hezbollah's radio in Lebanon offered this commentary: "We have the right to ask about the crazy and shameless residents of New York, its gangsters, nightclubs, and brothels. The answer emerges very clearly that the explosion that rocked New York merely expressed its identity." This apocalyptic vision gained respectability in a column in the Beirut daily *al-Safir*, the newspaper that is supposed to represent the views of the serious, progressive Left:

> New York is the city of crime, the Mafia, and organized gangsters who are stronger than armies. It is the jungle where one cannot move without fearing for one's life. New York is the capital of the Jews with all their perversions, including politics, sex, media, forgery, cinema, drugs, and money laundering. It is the greatest arena for crime, most terrible fortress of discrimination, and ugliest example of class and race oppression.

New Yorkers, the columnist concluded, were thus in no position to claim that terror came to their city only when the "dark-skinned and red-eyed Arabs appeared."

The press of Cairo and Beirut will continue to debate whether the bombing of the World Trade Center was a Mossad plot or a blast of hellfire. But for the people most at risk, the question is whether the bombing was indeed the disembodied work of individual criminals, cut loose from any known reading of Islam. Those who take this view may imagine that they are promoting interfaith understanding, but it is an approach that misses the bombing's import entirely—and perhaps helps to invite its repetition.

ISLAMIC RESENTMENT

There is a wider context. The Magjid al-Salaam mosque in Jersey City stands at the far edge of a vast pool of resentment in Islam, fed by a steady stream of fundamentalist complaint against the West in general and the United States in particular. The collapse of the Soviet Union, the survival of the United States as the sole great power, the slogan of a "new world order"—these developments have brought that pool of resentment to overflowing. The bombing should be read as a warning: that a part of Islam dissents from the new ascendancy of the United States. Evasion and denial will not make this animus disappear.

The first context to be grasped is the world inhabited by the defendants in the bombing and conspiracy. As fundamentalists and immigrants, they personify the discontent that afflicts much of Islam today. For fundamentalism and migration have been the two major avenues of escape from the desperate crisis that now besets Muslim countries. They are also the two major sources of friction between Islam and the West. It is at the points of overlap between them, in storefront mosques from Brooklyn, New York, to Bradford, England, that angry preaching wins an especially attentive hearing.

For growing numbers of the young, the poor, and the credulous in the lands of Islam, fundamentalism has provided both escape and hope in circumstances that grow more dire with each passing year. These movements express a widespread frustration at the inability of regimes to deliver on the promise of a quantum leap to power and prosperity, whether by imitation of the Soviet model or by mimicry of capitalism. In appealing to that frustration, fundamentalists propose to abandon all the political and social models of the West. Instead, raising the slogan "Islam is the solution," they offer the vague but alluring ideas of Islamic government and Islamic economics. Most importantly, they hold the West responsible for the present malaise of Islam—a malaise that is understood to be the result of a deliberate Western effort to destroy Islam.

So far, this brand of fundamentalism has seized power only in Islamic lands more distant from the West—Iran in the heart of Asia, Sudan in the heart of Africa. But recently Islamic fundamentalism has made impressive gains on the Muslim shores of the Mediterranean, especially in Algeria, Tunisia, Egypt, Lebanon, and Turkey. These are the Muslim societies closest to the West in geography and culture, and the spread of fundamentalism there is compelling evidence for the depth of the crisis in Islam. The zealots have yet to acquire power in a Mediterranean country, but they have come close in Algeria, and they may yet make a serious bid in Egypt.

MUSLIM IMMIGRANTS: RENOUNCING ACCULTURATION

Muslim immigration to the West has been an equally telling sign of crisis. This immigration, especially to Western Europe and North America, is a result of the vast asymmetry of opportunity between the economies of the West and Islam. Since decolonization, the movement of millions of Muslims has rapidly transformed Islam into the second religion in much of the West. The influx continues unabated, as the fast-growing populations of Muslim countries far outstrip productive capacity.

In recent years, this immigration has taken on a new character, drawing upon more traditional classes in Muslim societies. For the newer immigrants, seeking a livelihood in the lands of unbelief is not without social stigma. Many of them have justified their choice by renouncing acculturation—this, at a time when economic recession in the West has diminished the willingness of host societies to assimilate foreigners anyway. The result has been a backlash of bigotry, epitomized by the repeated and sometimes deadly attacks on Muslim foreigners in Germany.

The prevalence of fundamentalism among more recent Muslim immigrants has tempted fundamentalist states and movements to open a second front in their struggle for political and cultural domination at home. The Paris bomb attacks of 1985 and 1986, the agitation against [author] Salman Rushdie in Britain, and the bombing of the World Trade Center have uncovered remote outposts of Muslim resentment in the West which are highly susceptible to suggestion by fundamentalists abroad.

To be sure, the vast majority of Muslim immigrants to the West, including fundamentalists, have come in search of opportunity, and would never imagine committing acts of political violence. But there are those who simply await a word of encouragement or inspiration offered by a visiting cleric or foreign diplomat. This is an unpleasant truth, but one which must no longer be ignored by immigration services, law-enforcement agencies, and organized Muslim communities themselves.

CHALLENGING THE "NEW WORLD ORDER"

The second, broader context of the bombing has to do with what might be called the fundamentalists' narrative of history. According to this narrative, the grand objective, first of Christendom and then of the West, has been the subordination, if not the destruction, of Islam. The medieval Crusades represented the first attempt; but Islam contained and repelled that aggression, which ultimately left no trace. Modern European imperialism, a far more dynamic force, constituted the next attempt; this proved far more successful, bringing nearly all of Islam under European rule. But while Europe promptly stole the wealth and independence of Muslims, it did not succeed in destroying their identity. The tenacious preservation of their identity has given them the power to rise up in wars of resistance, to reclaim their formal independence and control of their resources.

But now—the narrative continues—Islam faces the most dangerous and insidious challenge yet: America, as heir to Europe and hence to the role of leader of unbelief against Islam, has produced a model of culture, society, and politics which pretends to universal validity. This model exercises so seductive an appeal that it threatens to bring about what one fundamentalist thinker has called "the extinction of the distinctive identity of the Islamic community." This final assault on Islam is now concealed beneath the American slogan of a "new world order."

Rashid al-Ghannushi, exiled leader of the Tunisian Islamic movement, puts the case most succinctly. The "new world order," he says,

> is even more oppressive and severe than the old world order, which tried to banish Islam and ruin it. For the first time, the United Nations has become a real international government with a president—none other than the President of the United States. It has a legal branch to endorse American decisions—the Security Council—and an executive branch, in the form of the U.S. military. It has a financial apparatus—the World Bank and other giant financial institutions—and it has a massive media machine. Government by the United Nations is really government by the United States, which is the main characteristic of the "new world order." This "new world order," from the point of view of its intellectual content, its ideology, and its religion, isn't new. It is simply American hegemony over the world, clothed in the ideology of human rights.

This kind of logic no doubt lay behind the choice of the United Nations as the target of the second bomb plot. Ghannushi, it should be added, is presented by his Western apologists as the most moderate and least anti-American fundamentalist leader.

In the fundamentalist narrative, Muslims are not without their defenses against the "new world order." The hope has been most effectively articulated by Sayyid Muhammad Husayn Fadlallah, mentor and oracle of Lebanon's Hezbollah. His purpose has been to persuade Muslims that "reports about the multifaceted and unrivaled strength of the United States are greatly exaggerated." While America looms large, "its shadow is greater than its substance. It possesses great military power, but that power is not supported by commensurate political or economic strength." Even its much-touted democracy is deeply flawed. And so the collapse of the Soviet Union, far from confirming American power, only presages its fall. Within a generation or two, America will lose its power, and Islam will begin to realize its own massive potential.

"Power is not the eternal destiny of the powerful," Fadlallah reminds the faithful. "Weakness is not the eternal destiny of the weak. We may not have the actual power the U.S. has, but we had the power previously and we have now the foundations to develop that power in the future." Islam might even end by bringing America and Europe into its fold; already, the spread of Islam into these areas

> represents a great problem for the arrogant powers that seek to preserve the status quo and their own character. We should remember that Hulegu [the Mongol conqueror of Baghdad in 1258] overwhelmed the lands of Islam, but Islam overwhelmed the minds of his descendants, who became Muslims. Their power became Islamic power. I believe it is possible that Islam will storm many of the bastions that are now a danger to Islam, turning them to the benefit of Islam.

America's assault on Islamic identity, its bloated power cloaked as a "new world order," its hidden vulnerabilities, Islam's ultimate triumph, the final conversion of America—millions have been irradiated by this narrative, which might well have served as the underlying motif for the bombing of the World Trade Center. When the FBI arrested Muslims for the bombing, Fadlallah himself was quick to blame Israel and "Jewish circles in the United States." Yet he, and many other fundamentalist theoreticians, had been assuring Muslims repeatedly that if they looked, they would find "chinks in the armor of the United States, and we can penetrate these chinks and enlarge them." It could have come as no surprise to him that some Muslims living in the United States overheard these admonitions and acted upon them.

An Iranian commentator put the bombing precisely in the

context of the fundamentalist narrative. Asadollah Badamchian, the deputy head of the Iranian judiciary for political affairs, and a well-known hardliner, wrote an analysis that was published the day before the arrest of Mohammad Salameh, when no one could yet make the damaging association between the bombing and Islam:

> If the United States cannot safeguard even one floor of the most important building in the heart of New York, how can [it] ever put into practice the foolish policy of Bush—the establishment of a new world order or a new chapter of U.S. domination? And Badamchian concluded: Even though initially tyranny inflicts anguish on the oppressed, ultimately divine wrath gives the devout persons the upper hand and they annihilate the tyrant.

That the seemingly omnipotent U.S. was vulnerable at its heart, and that the "new world order" could be stopped—this was the message the fundamentalists were reading into the bombing before the evidence began to point precisely in their direction.

APPROACHING ISLAMIC FUNDAMENTALISM WITH CAUTION

Paradoxically, of course, and thanks to the arrests, the bombing had the opposite of its intended effect. Fundamentalists who would have been only too glad to hammer home Badamchian's point about American vulnerability instead had to denounce the bombing, blame it on Israel, and declare the United States off-limits to their struggle. Even Sheikh Abdel-Rahman, who was later indicted for, among other things, ordering the bombing, pronounced it incompatible with Islam. In the end, a chorus of fundamentalist voices affirmed the immunity of American soil.

The American response to the bombing also belied the fundamentalist portrayal of the United States as arch foe of the Muslims. The Egyptian fundamentalist newspaper *al-Nur* ran a commentary acknowledging that there was no popular wave of retribution against American Muslims, no random arrests, no mass interrogations, no storming of mosques in search of terrorists—the opposite, in fact, of what usually occurs in Egypt. Even the suspects "were treated in a civilized manner, and their lawyers were allowed to be present with them as soon as they were arrested." The simple workings of due process conveyed an image of immense power. So did the endless footage on Arab and Muslim television of the skyline of New York, unaltered by the bombing. In the end, ironically, one lasting effect of the bombing and trial may be to fill Arabian nights with many more dreams of Manhattan.

But Manhattan's own nightmare could recur. The fundamentalist struggle continues back in the capitals of Islam. It has lasted for nearly two decades, and its outcome is still far from decided. The Shah of Iran, one nemesis of the fundamentalists, is gone, but other secular kings and presidents rule on. Women are returning to the veil in Egypt, but a woman has become prime minister of Turkey. Islam, in short, remains divided against itself, and seems to be moving toward a civil war between two antagonistic blocs—social blocs within countries, and strategic blocs among states. The dividing issue is whether or not Islam should exist as a closed system, in constant tension with the world. The United States has obvious preferences in this struggle, and it is always possible that it may be threatened for holding them. It would therefore be foolish to rely on fundamentalist denunciations of this latest bombing. They were made under extreme duress.

Two bits of truth lie beneath the bomb rubble and should be embedded in the wall of Western defense. First, no one has the clairvoyance to sort the "moderates" from the "extremists." Those Arabs who waged jihad in Afghanistan, including some of the defendants now on trial, were supposed to be America's domesticated fundamentalists. They were often cited as prime evidence that not all Muslim fundamentalists are anti-American, that they are a "politically 'tamable'" force, in the words of one former CIA analyst. But as the World Trade Center bombing suggests, the conduct even of those fundamentalists who were once American allies and clients cannot be predicted, even in the short term. In dealing with Islamic fundamentalism, the United States now has an obligation to its own citizenry to err on the side of caution.

Second, the systematic preaching of hatred eventually will produce violence. Even if others strike the detonator, the kind of vitriol against America so widely retailed by the likes of Sheikh Abdel-Rahman is the fuel. And even if, in the trial of the alleged plotters in the New York bombing, the court should rule that the defendants acted alone, they are not lone men. They belong to a society with its own code, which they call true Islam, and whose interpreters have condemned America as the seat of evil.

As the bombing trials unfold, those who have made blithe assurances about "Islamism" would do well to reexamine the content and appeal of this code. The more they continue to evade hard truths, the more their credibility is bound to be questioned by the press and public alike. As for government, the case of the Sheikh should be a reminder that the preaching of hatred is still protected speech in America—which is why it is vital to keep such preachers at a safe distance from America's shores, even when they claim to bear the divine message of Islam.

DISASTER AT WACO: A CULT UNDER FIRE

JANET RENO

In the early spring of 1993, the Branch Davidians, a doomsday religious cult, had segregated themselves from the world of non-believers and were living in a self-contained complex of buildings on the outskirts of Waco, Texas. The cult consisted of 130 men, women, and children who had come strongly under the influence of their leader, David Koresh. They believed that Koresh could predict the end of the world and guarantee their immortality in the coming battle of Armageddon.

The Branch Davidians had attracted the attention of agents from the Bureau of Alcohol, Tobacco, and Firearms (ATF), who alleged that the cult was stockpiling illegal firearms. While attempting to serve an arrest warrant for David Koresh on February 28, 1993, a deadly gun battle erupted; four ATF agents were killed and sixteen wounded. An undetermined number of Branch Davidians inside the compound were also killed and injured, but Koresh and his followers refused to surrender. On April 19, 1993, after a fifty-one-day standoff, U.S. attorney general Janet Reno ordered a tear-gas assault on the compound using tanks and other assault vehicles. After several hours and six deliveries of tear gas, the compound was engulfed in a catastrophic fire, believed to have been set by the Davidians. Nine individuals survived the fire, while the remains of fifty adults and twenty-five children were recovered in the compound's ruins.

The government received heavy criticism for its handling of the Waco situation, with many observers arguing that the standoff could have been resolved peacefully. Subsequent investigations revealed that government agents had used pyrotechnic

Excerpted from Janet Reno's statement before the Committee on the Judiciary, House of Representatives, April 28, 1993.

devices to inject three rounds of tear gas near the compound on the final day of the standoff. The FBI initially denied the use of pyrotechnic devices, but in 1999 it admitted that such devices had in fact been used. A final independent investigation conducted by former senator John Danforth in 2000 concluded that the firing of these rounds was inconsequential: The three pyrotechnic rounds were fired four hours before the fire at the compound broke out and in a direction away from the building itself. Danforth's report also stated that Janet Reno and former FBI director William Sessions had no knowledge that pyrotechnic devices were used on April 19. Groups on the far right-wing, however, remain convinced that Reno and the FBI participated in a cover-up. In the following statement made at a congressional hearing just nine days after the disaster, Janet Reno defends her decision to order the assault on the Branch Davidian compound, having determined that a peaceful resolution was not attainable. Janet Reno served as U.S. attorney general from 1993 to 2000.

I truly appreciate this opportunity to appear before you to discuss the tragic events at the compound in Waco, Texas, this past week.

I want to be as open as possible with you and with all the American people about what we knew before; what we knew on that day; and what we know now and as our investigation proceeds. I want to be responsible and accountable to the Congress and to the American people in every way I possibly can.

This is one of the hardest decisions that anybody could ever be asked to make. We deliberated long and carefully before reaching a decision. Nothing we do now can change the suffering felt by the families of the Bureau of Alcohol, Tobacco and Firearms [ATF] agents or the families of those who perished in the compound; but as you have pointed out so eloquently, we must do everything we can to learn from these events about what we can do in the future to prevent people like David Koresh, or people motivated by other thoughts from causing such a senseless, horrible loss of human life.

A Deadly Shootout

On February 28, 1993, 4 agents of the Bureau of Alcohol, Tobacco and Firearms were killed and 16 were injured in a shootout that occurred when they attempted to execute an arrest warrant for Vernon Howell, also known as David Koresh, and a search warrant at the Branch Davidian compound near Waco, Texas. The agents were met by a barrage of gunfire from numerous firing points in the compound that lasted 45 minutes, involved thousands of rounds of ammunition, and left the agents dead and injured.

Weapons used by the Branch Davidians included .50-caliber rifles having an effective range of 3,000 yards, a distance from the Capitol to the White House. All of those killed or wounded were shot or injured by homemade hand grenades. While several members of the commune were killed and injured, there was apparently no serious injury to any of the children.

After the shootout, the remaining ATF agents established a protective perimeter around the compound. A few hours later, three Branch Davidians attempted to enter the compound, resulting in a second shootout with ATF agents in which one Davidian was killed. Attempts were made to further secure the perimeter. ATF officials then requested that the FBI dispatch its Hostage Rescue Team, which we refer to as HRT.

On February 28, 1993, agents of the Federal Bureau of Investigation, including the HRT, arrived on the scene. The FBI found an armed fortress compound consisting of approximately 70 acres located on Route 7 near Waco.

NEGOTIATION TACTICS

I took office on March 12, 1993. After my FBI clearance, I had been briefed previously by the Acting Attorney General and was thereafter briefed specifically on the situation at Waco.

I was advised that the primary goal of the FBI's Hostage Rescue Team was to negotiate with Koresh to secure the release of the children and the surrender and prosecution of all those who participated in the murder and assault of the Federal agents without further violence or injury to anyone concerned. I concurred that we must try to negotiate to avoid further bloodshed to the extent that we could.

As this situation evolved, the FBI had consistently rejected a direct assault on the compound because of the danger of heavy casualties to the agents and to the children and because of the layout which prevented a surprise assault. I was told, as I was briefed, that the FBI had a trained negotiator on the scene and that they had, and during the course of these deliberations, continued to consult with behavioral experts and others who had knowledge of the cult to determine how best to proceed to negotiate with Koresh.

From the start, the negotiation tactics focused on restricting the activities of those inside the compound and of depriving them of a comfortable environment so as to bring the matter to a conclusion without further violence.

Those inside the compound were advised of the FBI's rules of engagement. Under those rules, the agents conveyed the information that they would not use deadly force against any person except when necessary in self-defense or defense of another, or when they had reason to believe that they or another were in danger of death or grievous bodily harm.

The FBI installed lights to illuminate the compound at night and loudspeakers to ensure they could communicate with all members of the compound at once rather than to rely solely on a single telephone line available to speak to Koresh and those he permitted to talk on the phone. They also used loudspeakers to disrupt their sleep. They cut off their electricity and they sought to restrict communications of those within the compound just to the hostage negotiators.

Additionally, they sent in letters from family members and made other good-faith efforts designed to encourage surrender by those who wished to leave the compound. In particular— and I asked about this during the course of our deliberations— they made repeated efforts to secure the release of the children.

In further efforts to encourage the negotiating process, attorneys representing Koresh and Steve Schneider were allowed to enter the compound or communicate by telephone with them on several occasions. Throughout this 51-day process, Koresh continued to assert that he and others inside would at some point surrender. However, the FBI advised that at no point did he keep his word on any of his promises.

Despite all efforts, the negotiators concluded that negotiations were at a standstill and that they had not been able to negotiate a single item with Koresh. Although 21 children and 14 adults had been allowed to leave the compound between February 28 and March 23, 1993, those persons who left the compound did so because Koresh affirmatively wanted them out as they were not fully committed to his cause; they were a drain on his efforts in internal discipline and resources; or he viewed them as potential spokespersons to the media.

CONSIDERING TEAR GAS

During the week of April 5, the FBI advised me that they were developing a plan for the possible use of tear gas in an effort to increase the pressure on those in the compound to surrender. Thereafter, I had a series of meetings with the FBI to discuss the emerging proposal.

The threshold question I asked was whether the gas would cause permanent injury to the children. I did not even want to consider the matter further if we could not be certain about this factor. The FBI assured me that the gas would not cause permanent injury.

I asked them to research further, and subsequently, they arranged for me to meet with Dr. Harry Salem, a top expert in toxicology, who is chief of the Life Sciences Department at the Edgewood Arsenal. He reviewed with me case studies which confirmed that it would not cause permanent injury.

Then the primary question I asked again and again during the ensuing discussion was: "Why now? Why not wait?" I asked about their food and water supply and was told that it could last at least a year or more. I asked that the information about the water supply be checked and doublechecked by observing the level in the water tanks. We explored but could not develop a feasible method for cutting off their water supply.

I asked my staff to have direct personal discussions by phone with the chief negotiator on the scene to satisfy ourselves that we had, indeed, reached an impasse in discussions and in negotiations. After a 2½-hour conversation, that seemed clear. I became convinced that short of allowing David Koresh to go free, he was not coming out voluntarily.

Given that unacceptable result, in light of the fact that he was such a dangerous criminal, allowing the status quo to remain was not going to lead to an ultimate peaceful resolution and eliminate any risk to the safety of the innocent children in the compound, the public at large or the Government agents at the scene. On the contrary, the passage of time only increased the likelihood of incidents and possible injuries and attendant injuries and harm.

But we continued to deliberate; and in the course of our deliberations, we met with General Peter Schoomacher and Colonel Jerry Boynkin, former and present commanders of Delta Force, respectively, the Army's equivalent to the FBI's HRT, to review the plan. Their comments were instructive.

While indicating that the plan appeared to be sound, one suggestion was that rather than an incremental approach for the use of the gas as proposed by the FBI, gas should be inserted into all portions of the compound simultaneously. I preferred the FBI approach which called for a gradual increase in pressure over time. It seemed to me that that would be best to ensure the safety of those inside.

I directed that if at any point Koresh or his followers threatened to harm the children, the FBI should cease the action immediately. Likewise, if it appeared that as a result of the initial use of tear gas, Koresh was prepared to negotiate in good faith for his ultimate surrender, the FBI was to cease operation.

On the other hand, if Koresh and his followers endangered the agents by firing upon them, they were authorized to return the fire. To the great credit of the FBI, they received substantial fire from within the compound, both at the vehicles and at sniper positions surrounding the compound, without returning any fire. In fact, throughout the 51-day siege, the FBI never fired a single shot. Instead, when fired upon, the FBI responded by beginning to insert gas throughout the compound, consistent with what the Delta Force commanders had suggested.

The commanders also expressed concern about the length of time the HRT had been on the scene and in the state of constant readiness, and all expressed the view that the team would have to be pulled back for retraining very quickly if they were going to come back to the scene. All advised that there was not a substitute civil force that could secure the extensive area around the compound that had the expertise of the Hostage Rescue Team.

We continued deliberations. I wanted, and received, assurances that the gas and its means of use were not pyrotechnic. I was concerned about intentional or accidental explosions and ordered that additional resources be provided to ensure that there was an adequate emergency response if we should go forward.

THREATS OF SUICIDE AND CHILDREN AT RISK

I also considered that Koresh had talked about suicide, and that might occur at any time under conditions that the FBI might be less likely to control. Experts, however, advised the Bureau that the chances of suicide were not likely; but I again emphasized that it was something that was considered, something that was considered that might happen at any point along the way regardless of what the FBI did.

In considering the FBI proposal, I weighed the many concerns of the Government with respect to the state of affairs inside the compound. They included: First, the well-being of the children in the compound, given the deteriorating sanitary conditions, the apparent lack of adequate medical care inside and reports of sexual and other abuse in the past.

Second, the vulnerability of the outer perimeter, which created a threat to public safety and the Federal agents at the perimeter. The outer perimeter was vulnerable because there were inside the compound .50-caliber weapons having an effective killing range of 3,000 yards, a distance that would reach from the U.S. Capitol to the White House.

Third, our inability to maintain the presence of the HRT onsite indefinitely, and the advice I received that there was a lack of a suitable substitute force that could replace them at the compound and ensure the security of all involved.

Fourth, the increasing risk, as the standoff continued, of injury to Federal agents whether by accident or by the risk of shooting from the inside.

Since being sworn in as Attorney General, I have had numerous conversations with people both inside and outside the Department of Justice concerning the Waco situation. In addition, I directed my staff to keep the White House apprised of ongoing developments. My discussions with representatives of the White House were predicated on the premise that as chief law enforcement officer, the decision on how to proceed was mine.

I advised the President on the Sunday before the operation of my decision to authorize the FBI's use of tear gas at the compound, and he said he would support my decision.

I believed that we were dealing with a situation that would not resolve itself by mere acquiescence to the standoff. Negotiations had proven to be fruitless; and despite our best efforts, we could not secure the release of the children.

It was a situation that suggested to me that time would only increase the risk to public safety, to the safety of Government agents and to those within the compound, without any realistic expectation that the matter would be resolved peacefully if we did nothing. It was my call, and I made it the best way I know how.

Let me urge that we focus on the future to try to determine how we can best avoid a recurrence of this tragedy. In this regard, at the President's request, we and the Department of Treasury are looking at a process whereby the events at Waco will be examined by experts both within and outside the Government to consider the following questions: One, in the execution of the arrest and search warrants by ATF, were established procedures followed and, if so, were they adequate?

Two, is Federal law enforcement adequately prepared to negotiate in dangerous situations in terms of training, staffing, and available techniques?

Three, is training for the execution of warrants involving barricaded suspects who may be holding innocent third parties adequate for all law enforcement agencies?

Four, are improvements needed in coordinating the activities of the various investigative agencies.

Five, how should Federal law enforcement agencies marshal resources in various disciplines, including psychology and psychiatry, in situations involving cults and other groups using barricades and holding innocent people?

Six, what systems and understandings about command and control should guide the relationships among leaders of the departments and career officials in operating the units when field operations impose a substantial risk of danger to law enforcement officials and others?

The incident at Waco ended tragically for all involved. I have thought every day since April 19 about what I might have done differently. I only hope that we can work together to make sure that I never have to make such a decision again.

THE SIMPSON TRIAL: FAME, RACE, AND MURDER

JEWELLE TAYLOR GIBBS

In the early 1990s, O.J. Simpson, an African American from humble beginnings, was enjoying the lingering wealth and status he had earned as an award-winning professional football player in the 1970s. On June 13, 1994, however, the bloodied bodies of Simpson's ex-wife Nicole Brown Simpson and her acquaintance Ronald Goldman were found lying in front of Nicole's townhouse in the wealthy Los Angeles enclave of Brentwood. Days later, Simpson had become a suspect in the murders. Refusing to surrender to police, Simpson fled, heading south of Los Angeles with his best friend Al Cowlings in a white Ford Bronco. The slow-moving police chase was televised live to 95 million Americans and lasted over two hours, ending with the Bronco's return to Simpson's Brentwood estate, where he surrendered.

The trial of O.J. Simpson, which lasted from September 26, 1994 to October 3, 1995, received unprecedented media coverage and was televised live in its entirety. Much of the nation was captivated by the lurid spectacle of a celebrity accused of brutally stabbing his ex-wife and her presumed lover to death. As the trial progressed, however, public opinion regarding Simpson's guilt increasingly split along racial lines. His "Dream Team" of elite criminal attorneys argued that he had been framed by racist police detectives. This led some blacks to grow more supportive of Simpson's innocence, while many whites saw him as shamelessly exploiting his race.

In the following chronology, Jewelle Taylor Gibbs recounts the public's reaction to the *not guilty* verdict delivered to millions of anxious television viewers on October 3, 1995. In a poll conducted immediately after the verdict, 85 percent of blacks agreed with the *not guilty* verdict compared to only 32 percent of whites. The case had become a flashpoint for unspoken tensions between white and black Americans. Gibbs describes how many blacks publicly celebrated the verdict, rejoicing that for once the justice system had worked for a black man. Many whites, on the other hand, believed that a mostly black jury had ignored key evidence and allowed a murderer to go free. Gibbs is the author of *Race and Justice: Rodney King and O.J. Simpson in a House Divided*.

On September 29, 1995, the last Friday of the month, the jurors in the Simpson case hoped that this would be their final weekend sequestered in a hotel; the prosecution and defense lawyers looked forward to two days of unwinding from their intense contest of wills; the mass media went into overdrive predicting the jury's verdict; and the public began to cope with withdrawal symptoms from the daily diet of Simpson mania. The whole nation was poised for the final act of this national tragedy.

THE CONCLUSION OF THE CASE

On Monday, October 2, a subdued and exhausted Judge Lance Ito referred the case to the jury, sternly admonishing the jurors of their solemn duty to follow his instructions in their deliberations and to take their responsibilities seriously. After the jury retired to discuss the case, people in the courtroom seemed suspended, at loose ends and unsure of what to do with themselves while the jury was out. Feelings on both sides were intense, particularly since the Goldman family had objected so strenuously to parts of [defense attorney] Johnnie Cochran's closing arguments comparing [police detective] Mark Fuhrman to Adolf Hitler. Both sides had spent the weekend spinning their cases with the media and positioning themselves to win or lose gracefully.

The polls reflected growing polarization between blacks and whites, not only on the question of O.J.'s guilt or innocence but also on the tactics used by both sides to bolster their case. The racial split was further exacerbated by the ethnic tensions between blacks and Jews, fanned by Cochran's provocative use of security guards from the Nation of Islam and his gratuitous comments about racial genocide.

After one year of intense discussion and debate, it was clear that there was a deep fault line in the society over this case and that there would be an inevitable upheaval in the community no matter what verdict was rendered.

Reporters were beginning to close down their portable computers and lawyers were making their lunch plans as Judge Ito abruptly reconvened court to respond to the jury's request to read the testimony of Alan Park, the limousine driver who picked up O.J. Simpson on the night of June 12. This request caused considerable anxiety in and around the courthouse as both teams of lawyers and all the reporters tried to second-guess the jury's intent. The consensus seemed to be that this was favorable for the prosecution, particularly since the defense looked visibly distressed.

Shortly after 3:00 P.M. Pacific Daylight Time (PDT) and before the reporters could complete their stories on this development, Judge Ito made an even more surprising announcement. The jury had notified the judge that they had reached a verdict—after less than four hours of deliberation! Pandemonium broke out in the courthouse as Judge Ito, noting that several of the principal lawyers were out of town, decided to postpone the reading of the verdict until the next day. He also wanted to give the Los Angeles Police Department ample time to place officers on a contingency plan to avert any potential replay of the 1992 civil disturbances after three of the four officers were acquitted in the Rodney King case.

Again the media rose to the challenge and filled the evening news, talk shows, and morning newspapers with predictions of O.J.'s verdict. Expert defense lawyers and prosecutors pronounced diametrically opposing opinions: that it would be a "guilty" verdict because the jury reached a decision so quickly (prosecutors) or that it would be a "not guilty" verdict for the same reason (defense lawyers). Previous experience with brief deliberations actually seemed to favor the defense viewpoint, but logic was overcome by emotion for those who strongly felt that O.J. deserved to be convicted of these two heinous murders. More polls were taken in anticipation of the verdict, and blacks and whites were again on opposite sides of the issue. Predictably, the verdict was like a Rorschach test—prosecutors, conservatives, and most whites believed that the jury would find O.J. guilty; defense lawyers, liberals, and most blacks believed that he would be acquitted.

One indisputable fact emerged in all of the polls—the American public had faithfully followed this trial, had heard even more evidence than the jury, and had reached a decision about O.J. Simpson's guilt or innocence. Though dramatically divided, the public had judged O.J. Simpson and was simply waiting to hear that judgment confirmed by the jury.

THE VERDICT

At 10:00 A.M. PDT on Tuesday, October 3, the country came to a virtual standstill as 150 million people watched television sets at homes and department stores or tuned in to portable radios in offices and on construction sites, all anxiously awaiting the verdict. In San Francisco, friends and former neighbors of the Simpson family gathered at the Potrero Hill Neighborhood Community Center to hear the verdict. In Los Angeles, Rev. Cecil Murray of the First African Methodist Episcopal Church (FAME) had again invited his parishioners and community leaders to gather at his church to await the verdict, as they had done after the trial of the police officers in the King beating. Members and friends of the Brown and Goldman families had gathered in the prosecutor's office on the eighteenth floor of the Criminal Courts Building, where they did not have to face the inquisitive and invasive probes of the press.

AT&T reported that the volume of phone calls between 10:00 and 10:10 A.M. plummeted by 58 percent as the business and social calls of the nation were put on hold. On Wall Street, the brokers had placed personal bets on the outcome with a payoff of $18 for a verdict of guilty in the first degree and $10 for a verdict of guilty in the second degree; Wall Street was betting on a conviction, and the price was still rising at noon on the East Coast (9:00 A.M. PDT), an hour before the verdict would be announced in Los Angeles. Airplane flights at the Hartsfield International Airport in Atlanta were delayed as passengers boarded late so they could watch the verdict. Even President Clinton left the Oval Office to join his aides, who were gathered around a television set in a nearby office. The climax of the long-running Simpson serial drama was imminent; the suspense was palpable as people waited for the final curtain to come down on this infamous case.

As the jurors filed into the jury box, their faces impassive, they studiously avoided eye contact with the defendant. A nervous Judge Ito asked O.J. Simpson and his lawyers to stand while the court clerk read the verdict, and he cautioned the courtroom to remain calm and to refrain from any disruptions during the reading. Observers and participants alike seemed to hold their collective breath as the suspense became nearly unbearable. Deirdre Robertson, the court clerk, also nervous, stumbled over Simpson's full name, then solemnly read the verdict: "We, the jury, in the above entitled action, find the defendant, Orenthal James Simpson, not guilty of the crime of murder . . . upon Nicole Brown Simpson." Before she could read the second count, the courtroom erupted in a dramatic display of pent-up emotions. O.J. Simpson, the celebrity defendant, at first looked stunned, then let out a deep sigh of relief and smiled broadly when he grasped the full impact of the verdict. Johnny Cochran, his celebrity lawyer, hugged him and punched a victorious fist in the air. Behind the defense table, O.J.'s mother, sisters, and two older children alternately cried, smiled, and lifted their hands in thankful prayer.

But on the prosecutor's side of the courtroom, the camera showed the stunned expressions of Marcia Clark and Chris Darden, looking dazed and disbelieving that the jury had failed to convict this defendant in spite of all the incriminating evidence against him. Sitting behind the prosecution table, the members of the Goldman family were also shocked by these "not guilty" verdicts. Ron Goldman's father tried to comfort his sister Kim, sobbing uncontrollably, and was heard to mutter "murderer, murderer" as O.J. Simpson looked over in their direction. Nicole's parents sat there in stoic silence, seemingly resigned to this outcome, but Nicole's sisters looked angry as they turned to comfort each other.

THE PUBLIC RESPONSE: BLACKS VERSUS WHITES

Outside the courtroom, pandemonium reigned. Blacks, dressed in African liberation colors and brandishing banners professing Simpson's innocence, were shouting for joy, raising their fists in victory, and dancing in the streets. Whites, standing symbolically on the other side of the barricades, seemed shocked and bewildered at first, then frustrated and angry, women crying and hugging each other to seek solace from their pain at this miscarriage of justice. With the instant access of cameras and satellite feeds, television screens showed the reaction of people in Los Angeles, San Francisco, New York, Washington, Atlanta, and Buffalo.

This time, the congregants at Rev. Murray's church were celebrating the verdict, clapping their hands and singing "Hallelujah!" On Potrero Hill, O.J.'s old friends and neighbors were jumping up and down, yelling that their homeboy had been vindicated. Black law students at Howard University in Washington, D.C., were overjoyed, loudly proclaiming that the system had finally worked for a black man.

This sentiment was repeated over and over by blacks shown greeting the verdict with jubilation or resignation in bars, beauty shops, department stores, and subway stations. They were celebrating the verdict of a jury that could not find Simpson guilty "beyond a reasonable doubt." Despite their obvious excitement and enthusiasm, many blacks quite seriously and emphatically made it clear to reporters that they were not celebrating the brutal murders of two innocent people but rather the release of a black celebrity whose guilt had not been proved in a court of law.

Whites all over the nation initially responded to the verdicts with shock, anger, and outrage. Scenes of whites in corporate offices, suburban shopping malls, and upscale restaurants showed expressions of dismay, disgust, and even despair. White women, like their counterparts in front of the Los Angeles Criminal Courts building, seemed particularly upset about the verdict, protesting that O.J. had gotten away with spouse abuse and murder, sending a chilling message to battered women everywhere.

At the coffee bars and boutiques in Brentwood, casual acquaintances of Nicole and Ron were visibly distressed, denouncing the verdict, the defendant, and Simpson's defense team for this "travesty of justice." In New York's Times Square, where people watched the verdict as it flashed on the huge Sony television screen looming among the skyscrapers, the large, frenetic crowd of shoppers, tourists, and bike messengers suddenly turned into two opposing camps, people of color and whites—one group enjoying the ecstacy of victory, the other feeling the agony of defeat. It appeared that blacks and Latinos were hugging each other and exuberantly exchanging high fives, while whites were momentarily stunned and immobilized by the news. In corporate law offices in Chicago and Atlanta, young white lawyers seemed surprised at the verdicts, injudiciously criticizing the jurors for their hasty deliberations and the judge for his conduct of the case. . . .

THE SPECTRUM OF REACTIONS

The African-American community in cities and suburbs, in schools and offices, in barber shops and pool halls had felt a great sense of relief and satisfaction—for the first time in memory, black Americans had witnessed something unusual, something that had restored their faith in American justice. No matter what their personal beliefs or doubts about O.J.'s culpability for these crimes, he had been tried and found not guilty by a jury of his peers and the system had set him free.

In Brentwood, O.J.'s neighbors kept a low profile but made it clear that they were not pleased with the outcome and that he was no longer welcome in their neighborhood. Likewise, members of his exclusive country club, where he had been a frequent golfer with some of the Southern California gentry, sent word that he would be asked to resign his membership. His neighbors and golfing buddies were unimpressed with the jury's verdict; they were convinced of his guilt and wanted to exclude him as quickly as possible from their privileged enclaves.

While reporters on the ground were searching for significant sound bites, reporters following Simpson from the courthouse to the jail produced the most riveting photos of the day. After his release from custody, a news helicopter showed the white Ford police van driving up Freeway 10, then turning onto Freeway 405 to return O.J. to his Rockingham Avenue estate. It was an eerie scene, so reminiscent of the white Bronco chase that had captured the nation's imagination as Al Cowlings led a procession of police cars waiting to arrest his friend just over fifteen months earlier.

This time, the Los Angeles Police Department was escorting O.J. home as a free man after 473 days of incarceration at the Los Angeles County Central Men's Jail. It was only fitting that Al Cowlings, his lifelong friend and protector, would be there to meet him when the van arrived in the driveway. Al embraced O.J. with a bear hug and, with tears in his eyes, led him into his Brentwood home. The nightmare was over. The Dream Team had restored O.J.'s dream.

THE AFTERMATH

In many circles, the superficial congeniality between blacks and whites, gained at considerable expense since the Rodney King beating, was shattered by this verdict in the Simpson murder trial. The races divided almost seamlessly into two camps: whites who believed that the verdict was a travesty of justice and blacks who believed that the verdict was a triumph for the criminal justice system. Voices of reason and moderation in both groups could not be heard above the shouting, the name-calling, and the vituperation. Blacks who believed that Simpson was guilty and whites who agreed that there was reasonable doubt were drowned out by the angry debate between the true believers on each side of the racial divide.

Polls taken immediately after the verdict confirmed that the racial divisions were not simply manufactured by the media. The poll results reflected quite disparate views of the prosecution's case, of the defense team's strategy, and of the outcome. White women emphatically declared their outrage that Simpson, an admitted wife beater caught in a web of convincing circumstantial evidence, was exonerated. Black women indignantly responded, echoing the words of juror Brenda Moran, that Simpson was not on trial for spousal abuse; he was on trial for murder.

As days grew into weeks without any surcease from the charges and countercharges, the smoldering tensions between blacks and whites bubbled closer and closer to the surface. As magazine and newspaper feature articles solemnly reported, neighbors stopped speaking to each other, colleagues stopped having lunch together, store clerks and customers stopped exchanging pleasantries, and even college students on well-integrated campuses exchanged hostile glances. The verdict in the O.J. Simpson murder case, much like the verdict in the Rodney King assault case, had again exposed the fault line in American society—the deep and dangerous division between blacks and whites. And again this society had to confront the reality that we inhabited one country geographically but were divided into two nations racially, culturally, economically, and politically. There was no consensus and no common ground.

TERROR IN THE HEARTLAND: THE OKLAHOMA CITY BOMBING

MARK S. HAMM

On the morning of April 19, 1995, a bomb exploded in a rental truck parked outside the Alfred P. Murrah federal building in Oklahoma City, Oklahoma, killing 168 people. A little over an hour after the bombing, Oklahoma state police arrested Timothy McVeigh for speeding and driving a car without a license plate. McVeigh remained in the Noble County jail for two nights as he awaited arraignment. In the meantime, FBI investigators had traced a vehicle identification number taken from a fragment of the truck used in the bombing to a rental agency in Junction City, Kansas. Based on physical descriptions of the two men who had rented the truck, provided by the rental agency's employees, a motel clerk in the vicinity determined that one of the men had stayed at his motel. A check of the motel guest book turned up the name Tim McVeigh. The FBI ran the name through the national police computer and discovered that McVeigh was already in custody.

The deadly attack occurred two years to the day after a standoff between federal agents and members of the Branch Davidian religious group had ended in a deadly fire outside Waco, Texas.

Timothy McVeigh, a former U.S. Army sergeant and a veteran of the Persian Gulf War, had traveled to Waco during the standoff to express his support for the Davidians. The federal

Excerpted from *Apocalypse in Oklahoma: Waco and Ruby Ridge Revenged,* by Mark S. Hamm (Boston, MA: Northeastern University Press, 1997). Copyright © 1997 by Mark S. Hamm. Reprinted with permission.

government's actions at Waco infuriated McVeigh, and he blamed the government for the deaths of the seventy-five Davidians killed in the fire.

Determined to avenge the civilian deaths at Waco, McVeigh began to plot the bombing of the Alfred P. Murrah federal building with the help of Terry Nichols, an Army buddy also enraged at the government. McVeigh chose the building mostly due to its light security and easy accessibility. He also believed that it housed some of the federal agents who had participated in the Waco siege. In addition to killing 168 people, 19 of whom were children, the bombing injured 500 people and caused over $600 million worth of damage. McVeigh was subsequently tried and found guilty of the attack, and on June 11, 2000, the thirty-three-year-old was executed by lethal injection. Terry Nichols received a life sentence for his role in the bombing. In the following report, Mark S. Hamm describes the events of April 19, 1995, and the devastation wrought by the bombing. Hamm is the author of *Apocalypse in Oklahoma: Waco and Ruby Ridge Revenged.*

O klahoma City has always been a place where people take care of themselves. Unusual events rarely occur in "the buckle" on the Bible Belt, where the violent crime rate is far below the national average and a sign on the outskirts of town proudly reads, "Oklahoma City, Home of Vince Gill." So safe was the Alfred P. Murrah Federal Building presumed to be that in April 1995 it had only one security guard for the entire complex.

A BATTERED MERCURY AND AN OVERLOADED TRUCK

Daylight broke on a crisp, blue-sky Oklahoma morning. The azaleas and dogwoods were blooming along Robinson and Harvey, and April 19 was shaping up to be a beautiful spring day. By 7:30, downtown was in the full throes of morning rush-hour traffic. Cars were pulling into the Murrah Building garage and the curbside area in front of the building where parents dropped off their children for day care.

By 8:30, most of the Murrah Building employees had arrived. Coffee machines were put to percolating, fax machines and computers began purring, phones started ringing, and people began exchanging early-day chit chat. In America's Kids [the building's day-care center], the teachers were cleaning up a mess of breakfast muffins and spilled milk. It was especially hectic because one of the [four] teachers had called in sick. On balance, it was an unremarkable morning in an unremarkable building set in the middle of an unremarkable city in the heart of America.

But there was something unusual about the big yellow 1977 Mercury Marquis that pulled into the Journal Record [a daily business newspaper] parking lot [250 feet directly north of the Murrah Building] at about 8:45 and came to a stop beside the adjacent two-story Athenian Building. While most drivers on 5th were behind the wheel of clean, well-maintained late-model cars, the Mercury was old, dirty, and battered. Its yellow paint had faded from neglect. The car's Arizona license plate was dangling by one bolt.

At 8:59, a bright yellow, twenty-four-foot Ryder rental truck moved slowly across Harvey and pulled into the curbside parking area in front of the Murrah Building, slightly east of the building's midpoint. Most drivers who approached the curb let someone out and took off. Rarely did they come in bright yellow rental trucks. This was, obviously, an unusual event—one that might have been detected by an alert security guard, had one been assigned to the front of the building.

Perhaps the most pertinent thing a guard could have noticed was the vehicle's overloaded midsection. There was good reason: The truck carried twenty fifty-five-gallon white plastic barrels with blue tops, which were placed in five rows against the front of its cargo compartment. Each barrel was half filled with a mixture of ammonium nitrate fertilizer and diesel fuel. Attached to the barrels was an already burning ten-foot fuse running through a hole connecting the cab to the cargo bay, and attached to the barrels was a detonating cord (an explosive device designed to make a powerful spark), seven high-pressure acetylene gas cylinders made of metal, a string of blasting caps, and several sticks of TNT. These were intended to boost the explosive capability of the ammonium nitrate and diesel fuel. The bomb weighed two and a half tons.

VIOLENCE ERUPTS

At 9:01—when most of the Murrah Building employees were at their desks, when most of the children in America's Kids were singing the Barney song "I Love You, You Love Me," and just as the infants were being placed in their cribs for a morning nap—the driver jumped from the truck and ran to the Athenian. He took the wheel of the battered Mercury and raced down the alley beside the Journal Record building. Just before swinging right onto Robinson, the Mercury struck a cement parking lot marker, leaving its license plate dangling by a thread.

Inside the Ryder truck, the silence was punctuated only by the fuse burning toward its cargo. A few seconds past 9:02, the detonation system kicked in.

Words cannot adequately describe the violence that followed.

With a deafening roar, a red-orange fireball lit the sky as the payload tore upward at more than 7,000 miles per hour, ripping a huge crater from the ground to the roof. The blast hurled people through the air, crushing them under falling walls and ceilings as the gouged north face came down in a gigantic cascade of concrete, steel, and shattered glass.

The explosion simultaneously pushed the first two floors upward and destroyed three of the four columns supporting the second-floor beam. The steel beam toppled, sending the building into progressive collapse as ceilings crashed into floors. Desks, chairs, filing cabinets, refrigerators, and business machines cascaded down with a tangle of live electrical wires, exploding hot water pipes, and whiplashing cables.

The bomb blew the roof off of the Journal Record building, shattering its windows inward. The front of the Athenian Building was blown off, crushing a young woman to death. The bomb blasted the windows of the Water Resources Building inward, showering workers with a blizzard of glass and killing two people. Hundreds of windows at the YMCA [across the street] were blown inward. Its steel-framed doors were twisted and torn from their hinges as the explosion blew a playground fence through its day-care center, spraying children with splintered glass, sheetrock, and raw insulation. The explosion blew out the post office windows, cracked the support columns and shattered the windows of the federal courthouse, and blew out the stained glass windows of the Methodist church and St. Joseph's Cathedral, crumbling their century-old lobbies. Parking meters were ripped from the ground. Cars overturned and ignited, causing a second blast as gas tanks and tires erupted in flames, filling the sky with thick black smoke. Lethal shards of glass, steel, and concrete rocketed over a four-block area. Ten giant buildings within a three-block circumference nearly collapsed, three hundred and forty-eight more were damaged, and the license plate dangling from the Mercury Marquis blew off as it raced down I-235. The blast rocked the ground forty miles away.

WORKERS, CHILDREN, AND BYSTANDERS KILLED

Hundreds of men, women, and children were caught in the vacuum-vortex of the explosion inside the Murrah Building. In less than a second, concrete, glass, steel, dust, and gas fumes mixed with mangled bodies, burned flesh, and severed limbs.

On the ninth floor, five drug enforcement agents were immediately killed. One of them, a fifty-three-year-old career officer with a wife and five children, plunged all the way to the bottom, where he was buried in a maze of ragged metal, pipe, and concrete.

Fifty people were instantly killed between the eighth and sixth floors. One uniformed marine was crushed while sitting at his desk. He fell six floors and was still sitting at his desk when he hit bottom.

Twenty people were immediately killed between the fifth and fourth floors. One man, who had a desk facing the north windows, was ripped apart by the glass blizzard. A forty-year-old single mother was crushed to death beneath a huge concrete girder.

Twenty-seven people were slaughtered on the third floor. One fifty-seven-year-old man was sitting at his desk when his legs were blown off. He looked out the window for a brief moment, as if in peace. Then he died soon after.

The second floor took the full force of the explosion. The blast hit most of the youngsters in the face, blowing them backward, instantly killing fifteen children and their three teachers. One toddler had his brain blown out of his head. A two-year-old girl was hit with a blast of glass ten times more powerful than a rifle bullet, embedding thick shards in her body and blowing a hole in her skull the size of a baseball. The infants resting in their cribs never had a chance. Their human remains, tiny arms and legs, were found a block away.

Another eighteen workers instantly died on the first floor. Twenty-four bystanders also were killed. They included a sixty-one-year-old milk truck driver who had gone to the Murrah Building to sign up for his retirement pension, his fifty-six-year-old wife, and their four-year-old granddaughter. Like the other victims, they had been annihilated.

Firefighters from Oklahoma City Station 1 arrived at the scene first. As they began picking through the still-cascading wreckage, a firefighter found a woman's blood-soaked right hand in the concrete rubble. Overcome with emotion, he knelt down and squeezed it. Remarkably, he said that the farewell gesture was returned. The hand squeezed back. . . .

STAGGERING THROUGH THE RUINS

The Murrah Building had been demolished, its stately columns shattered, its massive windows splintered. The center of its roof rested at the level of what was once the third floor; the top seven floors had pancaked one into another, then been met by the upward shot of the first two floors. Because the blast had pushed the first floor into the second, and simultaneously pushed seven floors of concrete and steel downward onto the second floor, America's Kids became the epicenter of human suffering.

The bomb had torn a giant pit through the bottom floor that was now filled with marble slabs, concrete rubble, broken glass, and human flesh. The shell left standing looked monstrous. Ducts, cables, shorn girders, and chunks of concrete spilled onto the street; gas, smoke, and dust filled the blue sky above. The Journal Record parking lot was strewn with burnt, mangled chassis, fenders, hoods, glass, and burning tires. Broken gas lines had caught fire and 5th Street was now engulfed in a huge blanket of black smoke.

From the east and west corners of the pancaked floors, survivors staggered from the ruins. Some were half naked, others were in their underwear, and still others had their shoes blown off. They came with their skin torn and shredded, their bones broken, barefoot, walking over glass, covered in blood, dust, and plaster. Many screamed with fear, waving frantically for help. Others were silent, stunned.

Below, one man lay dead in a twelve-foot-deep, thirty-foot-wide crater where the Ryder truck had "vaporized," his body engulfed in flames. In the middle of 5th Street lay a woman, screaming as she burned to death. Hundreds of people were running through the streets, crying uncontrollably, glass shards embedded in their faces and splinters lodged in their eyes. People stumbled out of the nearby buildings, confused and crying. A young, panic-stricken woman ran up and down 5th screaming, "Where's my baby? My baby's in there!" A middle-aged man staggered down the sidewalk, blood on his face, saying that he was "going home now. It's time to go home now." Two elderly women walked down 5th toward Harvey in a daze, their faces, eyes, hair, and coats covered in blood and glass.

Others wandered around in shock, unaware that they were seriously injured until they felt their shoes filling with blood. A forty-eight-year-old woman crossing 5th was blown back, wrapped around a parking meter, and thrown into a car, breaking her jaw and arm. One man entering the front door of the Murrah Building was walking around with his left arm blown off; another, on what was left of the third floor, was missing his right arm. A woman sat on the 5th Street curb holding a blood-soaked shirt against her head while a stream of blood ran down her chest.

Across the street at the YMCA, a six-foot-two, 240-pound man, lying in bed, was picked up by the blast and thrown through the window. Some children from the Y's day-care center tumbled onto the street in such shock that they could not speak. Others were crying and screaming. All of them had been sliced by the flying glass, the sailing fence, the plaster, and insulation.

SEARCHING FOR CHILDREN, TREATING THE WOUNDED

Terrified parents descended on America's Kids to find crushed toys, highchairs, and cribs scattered everywhere, mingled with tiny arms, legs, and fingers. One of them was Aren Almon, a twenty-two-year-old single mother. The day before, her daughter, Baylee, had celebrated her first birthday. Ms. Almon was working her second day as a clerk at a downtown insurance company when the bomb went off. Together with her supervisor, she raced to the Murrah Building and began frantically asking people if they had seen a baby girl with light brown hair wearing yellow overalls.

Anthony Cooper and his wife, Dana, both twenty-four, were the parents of two-year-old Christopher and closely connected to the day-care center. Dana was its director; Anthony had just brought three gallons of milk to the center. As Cooper was returning to his car in the Journal Record lot, the bomb knocked him off his feet.

The children who survived were deeply traumatized. They wandered amid the rubble, covered in blood and dust so that it was impossible to tell if they were girls or boys, black or white.

The sirens brought police, bomb squads, firefighters, doctors and nurses, paramedics and priests, medical students, off-duty cops, National Guard troops, and anyone else who could help. Fire crews rushed to shut off underground gas lines, and medical teams established a system of triage—the treatment of battlefield wounded—and set up first-aid sites along 4th and Harvey. Victims were given priority according to their condition. If they were able to talk, they were tagged "minor." If they were bleeding severely, they were tagged "moderate." The unconscious were tagged "critical" and the rest were tagged dead. This quickly assembled system led to relief efforts that are unprecedented in the annals of American crime and justice.

There was crying and screaming from inside the building. Hoping to find survivors, the rescuers plunged into the waist-deep rubble, risking their own lives. They began digging with nothing more than their hands, catching their breaths at the sight of body parts and babies burned and mutilated beyond recognition. Some wept when they found living children, as they cradled them, limp and weightless. Dozens of untrained volunteers also rushed into the wreckage in an attempt to save the injured. One of the first was a nurse named Rebecca Anderson, who was almost instantly knocked unconscious by falling concrete.

One rescuer found a baby's fingers lying beside an American flag, but no body. Another, medical technician Terry Jones, found a two-year-old boy in the rubble who was still breathing, but his brain was hanging from his head. Amid the cascading concrete, Jones performed brain surgery on the child.

Near the ruins of the day-care center, Don Hull, a homicide detective from the Oklahoma City police department, spotted a small foot protruding from the rubble. He dug the concrete away and found twenty-two-month-old Joseph Weber with his left arm folded behind his back, a compound fracture below his shoulder, and a large cut on the left side of his face. Yet the boy was not bleeding. Hull gently moved Joseph's arm around his body and Joseph gasped and began crying. Then he started bleeding profusely. The detective held the small body tightly against his chest to slow the bleeding and made his way toward the entrance. As he approached the triage station, Joseph stopped breathing. Hull gave the boy CPR and he responded. Hull took several more steps and the boy quit breathing again. Hull again administered CPR and Joseph started breathing again. Hull ran to a waiting ambulance and just then the boy's head fell back and his eyes rolled into his head. Once more, Hull administered CPR, begging the child to breathe, and again Joseph responded as he was given oxygen and rushed to the Children's Hospital.

At the same time, Oklahoma City police sergeant John Avera and his partner had just returned to the pit after pulling out two women when Avera heard a baby crying. He went to the sound and removed several man-size chunks of concrete. There, in the dark, lay two baby girls, crying in horror and bleeding from the head. Avera bent down, lifted the first baby in his arms, and handed it to his partner who ran toward the triage station. He knelt and gently picked up the second baby. Just then, she quit crying and her body went limp.

Avera carried the baby to the street, where he laid her in the arms of firefighter Chris Fields, a thirty-year-old officer from Station 5. As Fields turned from the hellish jumble of glass, steel, and concrete, an amateur photographer captured an image that would soon become an American emblem for the sorrow of April 19.

Officer Fields is cradling the infant in his arms, the bright Oklahoma sun shining off his red helmet. The color of his helmet matches the blood streaming from the baby's head, arms, and legs. His brown firefighter's jacket matches the baby's light brown hair, now covered with dust and insulation. And the yellow stripes in his jacket, bold and clear, seem to correspond with the soft yellow in the baby's tiny overalls. But perhaps it is the look of profound sorrow on his face that is so moving, for this fireman is staring into the face of death.

BOSNIA, SOMALIA, AND HAITI: U.S. INTERVENTIONISM IN THE POST–COLD WAR WORLD

MICHAEL MANDELBAUM

The early years of the 1990s marked a difficult transition period for U.S. foreign policy. President Bill Clinton entered office in 1993 challenged with leading the world's only remaining superpower. Prior to the end of the cold war, U.S. foreign policy had been played much like a chess match against the Soviet Union, with each side reacting to the other's military interventions abroad with a delicate but clearly defined diplomatic strategy. The goal was to contain the influence of the Soviet Union while avoiding nuclear conflict at all costs. Following the collapse of the Soviet Union, the United States was cut adrift from this decades-long approach to foreign policy.

In the following viewpoint, Michael Mandelbaum describes how the Clinton administration directed military interventions in Bosnia, Somalia, and Haiti strictly for humanitarian purposes during the first nine months of 1993. According to Mandelbaum, the new administration believed that the end of the cold war had ushered in an era of virtuous humanitarian intervention in Third World nations. The failure of these three interventions, however, pointed to a miscalculation in the administration's conception of "foreign policy as social work": The American public was not willing to support military actions in far-flung nations where no national security interests were at stake. By the end of 1995, according to Mandelbaum, the administration's continued emphasis on "helping the helpless" and its failure to establish clear priorities for post–Cold War foreign policy had come at the expense of U.S. relations with far more important international powers, such as China, Japan, and Russia. The author is a professor of American foreign policy at Johns Hopkins University.

T he seminal events of the foreign policy of the [Bill] Clinton administration were three failed military interventions in its first nine months in office: the announced intention, then failure, to lift the arms embargo against Bosnia's Muslims and bomb the Bosnian Serbs in May 1993; the deaths of 18 U.S. Army rangers at the hands of a mob in Mogadishu, Somalia, on October 3; and the turning back of a ship carrying military trainers in response to demonstrations in Port-au-Prince, Haiti, on October 12. Together they set the tone and established much of the agenda of the foreign policy of the United States from 1993 through 1995.

A Failed Vision

These failed interventions expressed the view of the worldwide role of the United States that the members of the Clinton foreign policy team brought to office. Their distinctive vision of post–Cold War American foreign policy failed because it did not command public support. Much of the administration's first year was given over to making that painful discovery. Much of the next two years was devoted to coping with the consequences of the failures of that first year.

Bosnia, Somalia, and Haiti were not, as the administration claimed, problems it had inherited. The Bush administration had sent troops to Somalia for the limited purpose of distributing food and not, as the Clinton administration's ambassador to the United Nations (UN), Madeleine Albright, put it, "for the restoration of an entire country." As for Bosnia and Haiti, during the 1992 presidential campaign Clinton promised to change the Bush policies by using air power to stop ethnic cleansing in the Balkans and by discontinuing the repatriation of Haitian refugees fleeing to the United States.

The Clinton campaign promises, however, cannot be properly understood merely as tactical maneuvers designed to secure electoral advantage. Although they certainly were that, they also reflected the convictions of W. Anthony Lake, the campaign's foreign policy coordinator who became President Clinton's national security adviser. The campaign commitments may have been expedient, but they were not cynical. Nor were they challenged by Warren Christopher, who became the secretary of state, the office from which American foreign policy has generally been directed.

The abortive interventions shared several features. Each involved small, poor, weak countries far from the crucial centers that had dominated American foreign policy during the Cold War. Whereas previous administrations had been concerned with the powerful and potentially dangerous members of the international community, which constitute its core, the Clinton administration turned its attention to the international periphery.

FOREIGN POLICY AS SOCIAL WORK

In these peripheral areas the administration was preoccupied not with relations with neighboring countries, the usual subject of foreign policy, but rather with the social, political, and economic conditions within borders. It aimed to relieve the suffering caused by ethnic cleansing in Bosnia, starvation in Somalia, and oppression in Haiti. Historically the foreign policy of the United States has centered on American interests, defined as developments that could affect the lives of American citizens. Nothing that occurred in these three countries fit that criterion. Instead, the Clinton interventions were intended to promote American values.

Lake characterized this approach, incorrectly, as "Pragmatic neo-Wilsonianism." While Woodrow Wilson, like Bill Clinton, favored the spread of democracy, so has every other president since the founding of the republic. While Wilson sought to promote democracy in Europe to prevent a repetition of World War I, the absence of democracy in Bosnia, Somalia, and Haiti was not going to lead to World War III. And while Wilson had a formula for spreading democracy—the establishment of sovereign states on the basis of national self-determination—that principle was precisely what the Clinton administration was determined to prevent the Serbs from applying in the Balkans.

Lake himself supplied a better analogy. "I think Mother Teresa and Ronald Reagan were both trying to do the same thing," he said in suggesting that the Clinton foreign policy encompassed both, "one helping the helpless, one fighting the Evil Empire." In fact, they were trying to do different things. Reagan conducted a traditional foreign policy with a strong ideological overlay. He was in the business of pursuing the national interest of the United States as he understood it. Mother Teresa, by contrast, is in the business of saving lives, which is what Lake and his colleagues tried in 1993 to make the cornerstone of American foreign policy. They tried, and failed, to turn American foreign policy into a branch of social work.

While Mother Teresa is an admirable person and social work a noble profession, conducting American foreign policy by her example is an expensive proposition. The world is a big place filled with distressed people, all of whom, by these lights, have a claim to American attention. Putting an end to the suffering in Bosnia, Somalia, and Haiti would have involved addressing its causes, which would have meant deep, protracted, and costly engagement in the tangled political life of each country.

When the time came to carry out the commitment to do so at the risk of American lives, the president balked. He refused to bomb in Bosnia, withdrew U.S. troops from Somalia, and recalled the ship from Haiti, thereby earning a reputation for inconstancy that haunts his presidency. In each case, however, he did not have, nor was he likely to get, the political support in the United States necessary to rearrange the political and economic lives of the three countries so as to end their misery and uphold American values.

THE COLD WAR DIFFERENCE

The new American foreign policy that surfaced and sank in the first nine months of 1993 was the product of an unusual set of circumstances that created a void: a public and a president less interested in international affairs than at any time in the previous six decades combined with the disappearance of the familiar foreign policy guideposts of the Cold War. Into that void stepped a group of people who, during the [Jimmy] Carter administration, had been uncomfortable with and unsuccessful at waging the global conflict with the Soviet Union but who believed they could take the political capital the public had furnished for 40 years to oppose the Soviets and put it to uses they deemed more virtuous.

In this they were wrong. The American public had supported intervention in poor, distant reaches of the Third World during the Cold War, and would no doubt do so again, but only on behalf of traditional American national interests.

This was the great lesson to emerge from the fiascoes of Clinton's first year. It can be illustrated by comparing two Caribbean invasions, ten years apart, in which the United States sought to remove an unfriendly government: the Reagan administration's dispatch of forces to Grenada in 1983 and the Clinton administration's efforts to intervene in Haiti in 1993 and 1994. By most criteria Haiti is the more important of the two: larger, closer, a source of refugees, and a country that the United States had occupied from 1915 to 1934. Yet the invasion of Grenada was less controversial.

The reason was that the first invasion was part of the Cold War. The radical Grenadan government was aligned with Cuba, an ally of the Soviet Union, with which the United States was locked in a mortal struggle. The intervention in Grenada could thus be portrayed as an act of self-defense, albeit at several removes, and self-defense is a cause for which Americans have always been willing to sacrifice. The invasion of Haiti could not be presented in that light. Grenada could be seen as affecting American interests. With the end of the Cold War, Haiti could not. It was the conflict with the Soviet Union that connected the international periphery to American interests.

In the wake of their initial failures, administration officials lamented that the conduct of foreign policy had been easier for their predecessors. This is not true. There has never been a formula for deciding on military intervention, and Cold War presidents had to make that decision with the specter of nuclear conflict with the Soviet Union hovering in the background, an experience the Clinton administration was spared.

But if the decision to intervene was not easier during the Cold War, it was simpler: U.S. presidents did not necessarily know when to use force, but they always knew why—to come at the Soviet Union, its allies, and its clients, and thus defend American interests. The argument for intervention was not always universally persuasive, but it was always plausible. In Bosnia, Somalia, and Haiti in 1993 it was not even plausible.

Lake provided an epitaph for the foreign policy of Mother Teresa, one that captured the motive for its rise and the reason for its demise: "When I wake up every morning and look at the headlines and the stories and the images on television of these conflicts, I want to work to end every conflict, I want to work to save every child out there," he said. "But neither we nor the international community have the resources nor the mandate to do so."

COMEDY, TRAGEDY, AND HAITI

While the [Clinton] administration withdrew from Somalia, the problems of Haiti and Bosnia lingered on, pieces of unfinished business, reminders of the humiliations of 1993.

In both, the administration followed the same pattern. First it adopted policies that made things worse. Then, in 1994 in Haiti and in 1995 in Bosnia, it finally used force. But the motivation was not, as in 1993, to "help the helpless," in Lake's words. Rather it was to bolster the administration's political standing, which was suffering from the failure to resolve these problems. Both interventions achieved a measure of success, but in each case the success was provisional, fragile, and reversible.

In Haiti, the Clinton administration first tried to dislodge the junta led by Brigadier General Raoul Cedras by imposing an ever-tighter trade embargo, ultimately cutting off almost all Haitian contact with other countries. The embargo devastated Haiti, destroying its small manufacturing sector and leading to predictions of starvation by the end of 1994. That prospect, combined with the continuing exodus of refugees, the insistence of the Congressional Black Caucus that the elected Haitian president Jean-Bertrand Aristide be restored to power, and a hunger strike protesting the failure to do this by American political activist Randall Robinson, persuaded the administration to use force. Finally, in October 1994, troops from the United States landed in Haiti, the junta's leaders departed, and Aristide returned.

The triumph, however, was conditional. For the administration had promised not simply to return Aristide but to restore (or, to put it more accurately, create) democracy and help the country lift itself out of destitution, which required the establishment of a stable political system, the rule of law, and a freely functioning market economy.

Because Haiti lacked all three, the administration's goals could not be accomplished overnight. To give Haiti a chance to reach them required a substantial American commitment. This the Clinton administration was not able to give. The stay of the American and U.N. troops was to be short, ending in February

1996. Their mission was limited; they did not make a serious effort to disarm the country. Financial aid would not be long-term.

All this reduced the capacity of the United States to help ensure that Aristide would leave office, as he promised, in February 1996, that an orderly democratic succession would take place, and that economic reforms would be carried out. At the end of 1995, therefore, Haiti's long-term prospects for democracy and prosperity were uncertain. The administration lacked leverage in Haiti because it lacked political support in the United States. The American public was opposed to the dispatch of troops. The president did not ask for congressional approval of the operation because he would not have received it. Economic assistance to the country was unpopular with the Republican congressional majority.

The weakness of the administration's political position was demonstrated by the unusual role accorded former President Jimmy Carter. Along with retired General Colin Powell and Senator Sam Nunn (D-Ga.), he negotiated an agreement with the Haitian junta for U.S. troops to enter the country peacefully and for the junta to leave. Carter's function was to negotiate terms and make concessions that the Clinton administration, because of its political weakness, found it impolitic to make publicly.

The Clinton administration tried to make a case for invading Haiti, falling back on the kinds of arguments that had justified the use of force during the Cold War. J. Brian Atwood, the director of the U.S. Agency for International Development, attempted to connect autocratic rule in Haiti with American interests by asserting that it was "an assault on the progress toward democracy that has been made throughout the hemisphere."

The argument was inappropriate in a way that was both comic and tragic: comic because it was ludicrous to contend that the fate of a small, impoverished half of a Caribbean island would affect Mexico, Argentina, or Brazil; tragic in that it was precisely because Haiti was so isolated that its political and economic conditions had become—had been allowed to become—so miserable.

That appeal to national interest failed because the United States had no interest in Haiti. Haiti was, however, one place where an appeal to values might have generated support. Because it was nearby, poor, weak, had once been occupied by the United States, and was populated by descendants of African slaves, the United States had reason to be concerned about its fate. A serious effort to put Haiti on a path toward decent politics and rational economics could have been presented as a good deed in the neighborhood at manageable cost and justified by the fact that America is a rich, powerful, and generous country. The Clinton administration, however, did not try to make that case.

THE EXIT IS THE STRATEGY

Bosnia was more complicated than Haiti because it involved relations with America's European allies, Britain and France, with whom for 30 months the Clinton administration was at odds. The Europeans deemed the conflict a civil war, to be ended as soon as possible even at the cost of a settlement unfavorable to Bosnia's Muslim government in Sarajevo. They supported the three proposed peace accords of the period: the Vance-Owen Plan of 1993, the Owen-Stoltenberg Plan of 1993, and the Contact Group Plan of 1994. The Clinton administration, in contrast, viewed the war as Serbian aggression against Bosnia. Its goal was justice for the Bosnian government even at the price of prolonging the war. It favored air strikes against the Serbs.

The Americans and the Europeans were each able to veto the policy the other wanted. The United States prevented the implementation of the peace plans; the Europeans blocked all but token bombing. The war dragged on. More and more people were killed or displaced, transatlantic acrimony mounted, and the gap between bellicose pronouncements and timid actions made the Western powers look increasingly inept.

In the summer of 1995 the United States launched a diplomatic initiative in the Balkans. The motive, as it had been with Haiti the previous year, was concern about the damage the war was doing to President Clinton's domestic political standing. The House and Senate voted, against the president's wishes, to end the arms embargo against the former Yugoslavia, but delayed a vote to override the president's veto to give diplomacy a chance. The president would have suffered embarrassment if, as seemed likely, his veto had been overridden. Moreover, the end of the embargo would likely have provoked the withdrawal of the British and French peacekeepers in Bosnia, triggering the dispatch of U.S. troops to the war zone to help extricate them and risking American casualties.

The course of the war turned out to favor American diplomacy. Bosnian Serb ethnic cleansing in eastern Bosnia and mil-

Refugees from Bosnia-Herzegovina find shelter in a gymnasium in Croatia.

itary victories by the Croatian army in the west removed the U.N. peacekeepers from easy reach of the Bosnian Serbs—who on occasion had held U.N. troops hostage—paving the way for a compromise between the Americans and the Europeans. With their peacekeepers no longer at risk, the Europeans consented to a vigorous campaign of bombardment against the Bosnian Serbs in late August and early September of 1995. At the same time, the United States accepted the European preferences on the division of territory between the three contending groups in Bosnia—ethnic cleansing had made different parts of the country more homogeneous. Bosnian Serbs' demand that they be permitted to federate with Serbia, just as the Bosnian Croats had been allowed to federate with Croatia under the terms of the American-brokered Croat-Muslim alliance of the year before. Perhaps because of the American bombing, certainly because of the American concessions, a cease-fire was achieved, and a conference convened in Dayton, Ohio, in November 1995 that produced a peace settlement.

Where flimsy political support had forced the Clinton administration to compromise on the implementation of its goals in Haiti in 1994, in Bosnia in 1995 political weakness compelled compromise on the goals themselves. Indeed, the principles that the administration had said were at stake in Bosnia were all but abandoned: the settlement rewarded what the administration had termed Serb aggression and ratified the results of ethnic cleansing. The United States negotiated directly with Serbian President Slobodan Milosevic, whom the administration had initially considered a war criminal. Bosnia was partitioned along ethnic lines, subverting the principles of undiluted sovereignty and ethnic pluralism that members of the Clinton administration had insisted, in 1993 and 1994, were inviolable.

The single indisputable American accomplishment in the Balkans between 1993 and 1995 was to assist Croatia in gaining control of some additional territory in Bosnia and all the territory it had included as a Yugoslav republic. This, however, was hardly a victory for American values. The Croats had practiced ethnic cleansing on a scale comparable to the Bosnian Serbs and were just as ardent about ethnic homogeneity and intolerance of Muslims. The federation between Croats and Muslims in Bosnia that the United States had brokered in 1994 was a partition between the two groups in all but name.

Prior to the Dayton negotiations, the administration had promised to send as many as 25,000 American troops to Bosnia as part of a peace settlement, and, as it had with the invasion of Haiti, struggled to find a rationale for this. As with Haiti, interests were said to be at stake, specifically the interest in avoiding a larger conflict. "If war reignites in Bosnia," President Clinton said, "it could spark a much wider conflagration. In 1914, a gunshot in Sarajevo launched the first of two world wars."

The conditions that had led to World War I, however, were absent eight decades later. The assassination of the heir to the Hapsburg throne in 1914 was the occasion for rival great powers to settle their differences by war. There is no such rivalry for the Balkan conflicts of the 1990s to ignite. Indeed, post–Cold War Europe lacks great European military powers to prosecute such a rivalry: Russia is not great, Germany is not military, and the United States is not European. The people of the former Yugoslavia were allowed to fight over its territory precisely because their wars did not pose a threat to the rest of Europe.

The United States, its European allies, and the Soviet Union would not have allowed Yugoslavia to disintegrate during the Cold War, the end of which had made Europe safe for war in the Balkans. Because Bosnia could not plausibly be connected to interests the American public would consider worthy of sacrificing blood and treasure to defend, the support for dispatching American troops to enforce the Dayton accords was bound to be weak. As in Haiti, therefore, the chief purpose of an American expeditionary force in Bosnia would be to leave as soon as possible, with as few casualties as possible, rather than to do whatever was necessary, for as long as necessary, to keep (or make) peace.

At the end of the Cold War, General Powell proposed a set of precepts for the use of force abroad that included the need for both a clear mission and a clear exit strategy. The Clinton interventions in Haiti in 1994 and prospectively in Bosnia in 1996 modified the Powell doctrine by conflating the two: the exit strategy became the mission. . . .

THE FOREIGN POLICY PRESIDENT

After three years the Clinton administration had not articulated a clear foreign policy doctrine for the post–Cold War world, but it had compiled a foreign policy record. How good was it?

During the Cold War, the yardstick was straightforward: how well the nation was doing in the worldwide struggle against the Soviet Union. In the wake of the Cold War, three different criteria for judgment are available: the one important to the Clinton foreign policy team, the one important to the country, and the one of most immediate importance to President Clinton himself.

By the standards of Mother Teresa, the Clinton foreign policy could claim modest success. At the end of 1995 Haitians and Bosnians were better off, or at least less likely to be killed, than had been the case 15 months earlier. Of the administration's three abortive interventions in 1993, the one in which the United States may have accomplished the most was Somalia, where, by some estimates, American intervention saved half a million lives. That had been the aim and was thus partly the achievement of the Bush administration.

On the other hand, the Clinton team did not succeed in establishing Lake's commitment to "helping the helpless" as the dominant principle of American foreign policy. Meanwhile, political support for the organization it had hoped would be an instrument of its new foreign policy, the United Nations, fell sharply, in part because the administration sought to deflect responsibility for its own failures in Bosnia and Somalia onto the international organization.

The more traditional standard by which the foreign policy of a great power is evaluated is its relations with the most important members of the international system. Here the Clinton performance could not be judged a success. The real legacy of the Bush administration was not Bosnia, Somalia, and Haiti. It was, instead, unprecedentedly good American relations with all the other major centers of power: Western Europe, Japan, China, and Russia. Three years later, those relations were worse in every case. . . .

Between the beginning of 1993 and the end of 1995, relations with Russia deteriorated sharply, but this was largely unavoidable, the result of Russians' delayed anger at their reduced international status and economic disintegration. However, the clumsy exclusion of Moscow from much of the diplomacy surrounding Bosnia and the commitment to expand NATO made the inevitable deterioration unnecessarily worse.

NATO expansion had the potential to alienate Russia from the post–Cold War settlement in Europe and make the goal of overturning that settlement central to Russian foreign policy, even as the infamous Clause 231 of the Versailles Treaty, assigning guilt for World War I to Germany, helped set the Germans on the course that led to World War II. In that worst case, the Clinton policy would rank with America's two greatest twentieth-century foreign policy blunders: the failure to remain politically engaged in Europe after World War I and the Vietnam War.

Still, at the end of 1995, while relations with the major centers of power were worse than they had been when the Clinton administration took office, they were not catastrophically or irretrievably worse. That meant that in 1996, for the president and the country, the immediate test of the Clinton foreign policy would be its impact on his prospects for reelection.

Polls consistently showed that the administration's foreign policy performance was held in low esteem by the American public. The same polls showed that, in the public's ranking of issues important to the country, those having to do with foreign policy were consistently at the bottom. Nonetheless, foreign policy was likely to be part of the 1996 election in a way unhelpful to the president.

Clinton's political difficulties, as he entered the election season, could be divided into two parts. On the ideological spectrum he had drifted too far to the left for many voters during his first two years. A gifted, energetic politician, he subsequently devoted himself to moving nearer to the center. But another problem afflicted him: doubt about whether he measured up to the job of chief executive and commander in chief. The conduct of foreign policy was only one part of this problem, but it was likely to prove more convenient as a metaphor for issues of character and leadership than the details of his personal life.

In this sector of the political battlefield, therefore, his early vacillation on military intervention, his dispatch of troops abroad without political support at home, his failure to spell out a clear set of priorities for post–Cold War American foreign policy, his visible discomfort in dealing with international issues, and his choice of senior foreign policy officials who proved unable to establish their authority either at home or abroad, were likely to come back to haunt him. As election day approached, his political opponents would have every reason to portray Bill Clinton as what he had never wanted to be and had gone to great lengths to avoid becoming: a foreign policy president.

1995–1998: Technology and Scandal

CHAPTER 2

THE UNABOMBER: TERROR AGAINST TECHNOLOGY

KIRKPATRICK SALE

Beginning in 1978, a terrorist dubbed "the Unabomber" by the FBI began to carry out mail bombings against targets connected to modern technology, including university professors, business leaders, and a computer store. By 1995, the Unabomber had killed three people and injured over two dozen. The FBI's long and expensive search for the Unabomber had proven fruitless, but events in the summer of 1995, initiated by the Unabomber himself, led to a startling break in the case.

The Unabomber had written a thirty-five-thousand-word treatise titled "Industrial Society and Its Future," which he sent to the *New York Times* and the *Washington Post* in late June of 1995. He demanded that the two papers publish the treatise in its entirety within three months or he would commit another deadly bombing. If the treatise were published, the Unabomber claimed that while he might bomb again, he would try not to kill people. After consulting with the FBI, the two papers agreed to publish the treatise, which appeared as an insert in the *Washington Post* on September 19, 1995. The Unabomber's thirst for notoriety, however, soon became his downfall. The writing style of the treatise seemed oddly familiar to David Kaczynski, based on letters he had received from his reclusive brother, Ted, who lived in a remote cabin in Montana. Kaczynski alerted the FBI to the possible connection, and Ted Kaczynski was later arrested at his cabin in early April 1996. In 1998, he was sentenced to life in prison.

From "Is There a Method in His Madness?" by Kirkpatrick Sale, *Nation*, September 25, 1995. Copyright © 1995 by The Nation Company L.P. Reprinted with permission.

In the following analysis of the treatise written shortly before its publication, Kirkpatrick Sale argues that "Industrial Society and Its Future" should be published. According to Sale, who makes no apologies for the Unabomber's murderous campaign, the treatise ultimately delivers an important message about the negative impact of technology on society. Sale is the author of *Rebels Against the Future: The Luddites and Their War on the Industrial Revolution.*

A ny day now the powers at the *New York Times* and the *Washington Post* will have to decide whether they will print the full 35,000-word text of the document sent to them in late June 1995 by the man the Federal Bureau of Investigation is calling the Unabomber. In the letter that accompanied the text, he gave each paper three months to publish his screed, upon which he promises to "desist from terrorism," but he warned that if they refused he would "start building [his] next bomb." That deadline is September 29.

PUBLISHING A CHALLENGE TO THE "INDUSTRIAL-TECHNOLOGICAL" SYSTEM

Naturally the decision has been somewhat complicated for the two papers, since they don't want to seem to "give in to terrorist demands" and don't particularly like giving such publicity to the Unabomber's decidedly anti-establishmentarian opinions. They are especially perturbed by his demand to be allowed to publish additional 3,000-word pieces for the next three years to rebut any critics of the original, thus prolonging the Damoclean threat. And yet they obviously don't want to give the man an excuse to send out more of his mail bombs, two of which have killed and two wounded their recipients in the past three years.

I have read the full text of the Unabomber treatise—the F.B.I. sent along two young female agents with copies of it for me to peruse—and I would recommend that either one of the papers publish it and trust the man will keep his word about ending the mad, unconscionable bombings. They should forget about the "giving in to terrorism" excuse, which is mostly meaningless in this case since there are no grand causes to be satisfied, no hostages to be freed and no reason to think that the threat would be repeated because it then becomes laughable. They needn't worry about the propaganda effect of printing it, since it is a woodenly written term paper, full of academic jargon and pop psychology, repetitive and ill-argued, that will keep only the most dedicated readers awake beyond its opening paragraphs.

Which, I would say, is a shame. Because the central point the Unabomber is trying to make—that "the industrial-technological system" in which we live is a social, psychological and environmental "disaster for the human race"—is absolutely crucial for the American public to understand and ought to be on the forefront of the nation's political agenda. I say this, of course, as a partisan. The Unabomber stands in a long line of anti-technology critics where I myself have stood, and his general arguments against industrial society and its consequences are quite similar to those I have recently put forth in a book on the people who might be said to have begun this tradition, the Luddites. Along with a number of people today who might be called neo-Luddites—Jerry Mander, Chellis Glendinning, Jeremy Rifkin, Bill McKibben, Wendell Berry, Dave Foreman, Langdon Winner, Stephanie Mills and John Zerzan among them—the Unabomber and I share a great many views about the pernicious effect of the Industrial Revolution, the evils of modern technologies, the stifling effect of mass society, the vast extent of suffering in a machine-dominated world and the inevitability of social and environmental catastrophe if the industrial system goes on unchecked.

We disagree, to be sure, about what is to be done about all this and the means by which to achieve it. In the course of his career, at least as the F.B.I. has reconstructed it, [since 1978] the Unabomber has carried out sixteen bombings, killing three people and injuring twenty-three others, apparently choosing targets in some way connected to modern technology—a technological institute at Northwestern University, the University of Utah business school, a Salt Lake City computer store, a University of California geneticist, and a Yale computer scientist, among others—to try to "propagate anti-industrial ideas and give encouragement to those who hate the industrial system." That strikes me as simple madness. Maiming and killing people does not normally propagate ideas, and in this case no one knew what ideas were in the Unabomber's mind until he started writing letters this past year and then delivered his treatise in June. As for getting the message across, the only message that anyone got for sixteen years was that some nut was attacking people associated with universities and computers (hence the F.B.I.'s tag, *Una*bomber).

But the bombings are going to get his document published, right or wrong, one way or another, and sooner rather than later. If the two newspapers don't publish it, *Penthouse* has offered to, and failing that, someone is sure to try to get it out as a pamphlet or send it over the Internet. That is what moves me to try to assess the treatise now, because I believe it would be a good idea to sort out its sound ideas from its errant ones, and to find the areas that ought not be discredited simply because of the agency that puts them forth—and as a service to all those who would fall asleep over the document itself.

SUMMARIZING THE UNABOMBER'S TREATISE

"Industrial Society and Its Future" is the modest-enough title, and it is labeled as "by FC," which the author describes as a "terrorist group" though there is no sign from the writing style here that more than one person is behind it, and the F.B.I. believes that the Unabomber is acting alone. (The fact that he has escaped detection for seventeen years—especially during this past year, when he has become the target of the largest manhunt in the agency's history—would tend to support that.) "FC" is variously cited as the initials for "Freedom Club" or "Freedom Collective," although it is popularly thought to stand for a vulgar comment about computers; it is not explained in his text.

The sixty-six pages that follow begin with two pages of trivial typo corrections, showing the kind of fastidiousness ("sovle" should be "solve:" "poit" should be "point") one might expect from a craftsman whose bombs the F.B.I. has described as "meticulously" constructed; then come fifty-six pages of argument divided into twenty-four subtitled sections and 232 numbered paragraphs; and it all ends with thirty-six footnotes, mostly qualifying statements in the text. That form, plus the leaden language and stilted diction, the fondness for sociological jargon and psychobabble, and the repeated use of "we argue that" and "we now discuss" and the like, make it certain that this was written by someone whose writing style, and probably whole intellectual development, was arrested in college.

The F.B.I. has said that it believes he was a student of the history of science, but on the evidence here he was a social psychology major with a minor in sociology, and he shows all the distressing hallmarks of the worst of that academic breed. He spends twelve pages, for example, on a strange and somewhat simplistic explanation of "something that we will call the power process," consisting of four elements "we call goal, effort and attainment of goal" plus "autonomy," all in an effort to explain why people today are unhappy and frustrated. Only someone trapped in the social sciences would talk that way.

Various professor types have been quoted in the papers saying how "bright" this fellow must be, but the arguments here are never very original and the line of reasoning is often quite convoluted. He has read a lot in certain areas—no poetry, though, I'll bet—and has thought a lot about the particular things that concern him, but aside from a few flashes there is no suggestion of anything more than a routine mind and a dutiful allegiance to some out-of-the-ordinary critics of modern society. I'm sure he makes good bombs, but grading him on his intellect I wouldn't give him more than a C+. I venture to say he didn't make it to his senior year.

The opus isn't helped by the fact that at least a third of it is essentially irrelevant, social-psych padding and scholarly back-and-forthing, one-hand-and-the-othering. Two long sections attacking "modern leftism" and "leftish" academics have nothing to do with his thesis, and I suspect they are offered because he had a bad time with certain sectarian groups in the early 1970s—no surprise—and with certain progress-minded, pro-technology Marxists he met in the academy.

Any good editor would have cut it.

But as near as I can fathom it after three careful readings, the Unabomber's argument would seem to be this:

• "Industrial-technological society" has succeeded to the point where, because of its size and complexity, it has constricted human freedom, meaning one's power to "control the circumstances of one's own life." Such freedoms as we do have are those permitted by the system consistent with its own ends—economic freedom to consume, press freedom to expose inefficiency and corruption—and do not in fact give individuals or groups true power, in the same sense that they have control over satisfying "life-and-death issues of one's existence: food, clothing, shelter and defense." "Today people live more by virtue of what the system does FOR them or TO them than by virtue of what they do for themselves. . . . Modern man is strapped down by a network of rules and regulations, and his fate depends on the actions of persons remote from him whose decisions he cannot influence."

• Industrial society *must* perform this way in order to succeed—"the system has to regulate human behavior closely in order to function"—and cannot be reformed to work differently. "Changes large enough to make a lasting difference in favor of freedom would not be initiated because it would be realized that they would gravely disrupt the system."

• Industrial society must increasingly work to constrict freedom and control behavior since "technology advances with great rapidity" and on many fronts: "crowding, rules and regulations, increasing dependence of individuals on large organizations, propaganda and other psychological techniques, genetic engineering, invasion of privacy through surveillance devices and computers, etc."

• But the problem of "control over human behavior" continues to bedevil this society, and right now "the system is currently engaged in a desperate struggle to overcome certain problems that threaten its survival," primarily social (the growing numbers of "rebels," "dropouts and resisters") but also economic and environmental. "If the system succeeds in acquiring sufficient control over human behavior quickly enough, it will probably survive. Otherwise it will break down. We think the issue will most likely be resolved within the next several decades, say 40 to 100 years."

• Therefore, the task of those who oppose the industrial system is to advance that breakdown by promoting "social stress and instability in industrial society," which presumably includes bombing, and by developing and propagating "an ideology that opposes technology," one that puts forth the "counter-ideal" of nature "in order to gain enthusiastic support." Thus, when the system becomes sufficiently stressed and unstable, a "revolution against technology may be possible."

A BARROOM CRITIQUE OF SOCIETY

Now, this is a reasonable enough argument—the Unabomber is not irrational, whatever else you can say about him—and I think it is even to some extent persuasive. There is nothing wild-eyed or rabble-rousing about it (it could actually use a lot more Paine-ist fomentation and furor) and the points are most often buttressed with careful arguments and examples—though nowhere, interestingly, a single statistic. It is too slow, too plodding, too repetitive; but you have to say its case is made in a competent, if labored, fashion. His critique of industrial society today is most telling, I think, and reads as if he'd spent a lot of time defending it in the back rooms of bars. . . . Just picking at random, I find these examples:

> The system does not and cannot exist to satisfy human needs. Instead, it is human behavior that has to be modified to fit the needs of the system. This has nothing to do with the political or social ideology that may pretend to guide the technological system. It is not the fault of capitalism and it is not the fault of socialism. It is the fault of technology, because the system is guided not by ideology but by technical necessity.

> If the use of a new item of technology is INITIALLY optional, it does not necessarily REMAIN optional, because new technology tends to change society in such a way that it becomes difficult or impossible for an individual to function without using that technology. . . . Something like this seems to have happened already with one of our society's most important psychological tools for enabling people to reduce (or at least temporarily escape from) stress, namely, mass entertainment. Our use of mass entertainment is "optional ". . . yet mass entertainment is a means of escape and stress-reduction on which most of us have become dependent.

> The technophiles are hopelessly naive (or self-deceiving) in their understanding of social problems. They are unaware of (or choose to ignore) the fact that when large changes, even seemingly beneficial ones, are introduced into a society, they lead to a long sequence of other changes, most of which are difficult to predict. . . . In fact, ever since the industrial revolution technology has been creating new problems for society far more rapidly than it has been solving old ones.

Not inspired, but thoughtful, perceptive enough, when abstracted from its labored context.

What's surprising about all this, though, is that it reads as if the Unabomber thinks he's the first person who ever worked out such ideas. It is hard to believe, but he seems woefully ignorant of the long Luddistic strain in Western thought going back at least to William Blake and Mary Shelley, and he does not once cite any of the great modern critics of technology such as Lewis Mumford, Jacques Ellul, Paul Goodman, Max Weber, E.F. Schumacher or Rachel Carson, nor any of the contemporary laborers in this vineyard. In one of his letters to the *Times* he does say that "anyone who will read the anarchist and radical environmentalist journals will see that opposition to the industrial-technological system is widespread and growing," so he must know something about the current critics, although he does not mention specific articles or authors or particular periodicals. (If I had to guess which has been most influential on him, I'd say the *Fifth Estate,* a feisty anti-technology paper published out of Detroit for the past thirty years, but he does not name it anywhere.)

That failure to ground himself in the Luddistic tradition, where both utopian and dystopian models proliferate, may be the reason that the Unabomber is so weak on envisioning the future, particularly the kind of revolution he seems to want.

I would agree with the Unabomber's general position that "to make a lasting change in the direction of development of any important aspect of a society, reform is insufficient," and I might even agree that in certain circumstances therefore "revolution is necessary." But I can't figure out at all what kind of revolution this is to be. He says that "a revolution does not necessarily involve an armed uprising or the overthrow of a government," a conviction he is so certain of he repeats it twice more, adding that "it may or may not involve physical violence," and in two footnotes he suggests that it might be "somewhat gradual or piecemeal" and might "consist only of a massive change of attitudes toward technology resulting in a relatively gradual and painless disintegration of the industrial system."

This is a somewhat peculiar position for a man who has been killing and injuring people in service to his dream of a new society, and I'm not sure what he thinks revolutions are or how they are achieved. If he has in mind something more like the Industrial Revolution or the Copernican revolution, he doesn't suggest how that might come about, and the sorts of strategies he ends up advocating—promoting social instability, destroying and wrecking "the system," seeing "its remnants . . . smashed beyond repair"—sound an awful lot like a revolution with a good deal of violence. He even suggests at one point that the models are the French and Russian revolutions, both pretty bloody affairs.

The whole question of violence indeed is confused in the Unabomber's mind, oddly enough after seventeen years during which he must have been thinking about it a little. He never once addresses the reasons for his own string of bombings or explains what he thinks he has been accomplishing, other than to say that this was the way to have "some chance of making a lasting impression." He is critical of "leftists" who commit violence, because it is only "a form of 'liberation'" they justify "in terms of mainstream values . . . fighting against racism or the like," and later is critical of leftists because they are "against competition and against violence." His revolution is not necessarily to be violent, yet he never confronts the idea of a nonviolent revolution or how it would be strategically carried out.

The one task of revolutionaries the Unabomber is clear about is the business of producing an anti-technology "ideology," although he doesn't anywhere concern himself with the hard business of saying what that would consist of. But it doesn't much matter to him, since the primary purpose of this ideology is "to create a core of people who will be opposed to the industrial system on a rational, thought-out basis," an intellectual cadre who can then dish it out "in a simplified form" for the "unthinking majority" who "like to have such issues presented in simple, black-and-white terms." "History is made by active, determined minorities," you see, and "as for the majority, it will be enough to make them aware of the existence of the new ideology and remind them of it frequently." Lenin couldn't have put it better.

The Unabomber's idea of a systemic breakdown is, I think, more plausible than his concept of revolution; one could see how, as the system was breaking down of its own weight and incompetence, unable to manage the problems its technology creates, this might be "helped along by revolutionaries." Just how the breakdown would come about is not spelled out. The Unabomber gives only a passing glance to the multiple environmental disasters the system is producing for itself and never mentions the likelihood, as chaos theory predicts, that the complex industrial house of cards will not hold. At least he does posit a "time of troubles" after which the human race would be "given a new chance."

A Vision Not Necessarily Inspired by Nature

I should note that the Unabomber, on the evidence here, does not have any special vision of an ecologically based future, as the newspapers have suggested. Indeed, he is no environmentalist, and I'd say he has only the faintest grasp of the principles of ecology. It's true that he refers to nature at one point—"That is, WILD nature!"—as a "positive ideal," but this is almost entirely cynical, nature as a concept that he figures will be useful in propaganda terms because it is "the opposite of technology," because "most people will agree that nature is beautiful" and because "in many people, nature inspires the kind of reverence that is associated with religion." He shows no real understanding of the role of technology in enabling industrial society not only to exploit nature but to pass that off as legitimate, and not one individual environmental problem is addressed here, except overpopulation. . . .

It's clear enough that the Unabomber counts "radical environmentalists" as among those rightly opposing technology, and his use of wood in some of his bombs and his killing of a timber lobbyist in California suggests a further affinity. But he indicates no sympathy for the kind of biocentric "deep ecology" and bioregionalism espoused by most of them, and his concerns are exclusively anthropocentric, his appreciation of other species and natural systems nil. He also mocks those who believe in the "Gaia theory" of a living earth, common in many environmental groups: "Do its adherents REALLY believe in it or are they just play-acting?"

In short, it feels to me that his appeal to nature is entirely utilitarian (like adding another little mechanism to your bomb to make sure it works) rather than a heartfelt passion, of which he seems to have very few in any case. But if nature does not inspire his vision of the future, it is hard to tell what does. Presumably he would want, as a self-described anarchist, some kind of world where "people live and work as INDIVIDUALS and SMALL GROUPS," using "small-scale technology . . . that can be used by small-scale communities without outside assistance." But he nowhere bothers to hint at how this future society would operate (other than to say it would burn all technical books), nor does he refer to any in the long line of anarcho-communal writers from Peter Kropotkin to Murray Bookchin who have given a great deal of thought to the configurations of just such a society.

It's true that the Unabomber offers the defense at one point that "a new kind of society cannot be designed on paper" and when revolutionaries or utopians set up a new kind of society, it never works out as planned." That gives him leeway to avoid discussing what kind of world he wants (even in a three-page section called "THE FUTURE"); unfortunately, it also leaves a gaping hole in his treatise. Even those who agree that the industrial system should be torn down will want to get some idea of what is supposed to replace it before they are moved to endorse the cause, much less become the revolutionaries the Unabomber wants.

A "CRUCIAL MESSAGE" DELIVERED BY A TERRORIST

So, in sum, what are we to make of this strange document? So important to its author that he is prepared to kill people (even though he has written that he is "getting tired of making bombs") to get it published in a major newspaper. So embarrassing to those newspapers that they don't know what to do with it.

It is the statement of a rational and serious man, deeply committed to his cause, who has given a great deal of thought to his work and a great deal of time to this expression of it. He is prescient and clear about the nature of the society we live in, what its purposes and methods are, and how it uses its array of technologies to serve them; he understands the misery and anxiety and constriction this creates for the individual and the wider dangers it poses for society and the earth. He truly believes that a campaign of social disorder led by misfits, rebels, dropouts and saboteurs (and presumably terrorists), coupled with the concerted propaganda work of a dedicated intellectual elite, has a chance to cause or hasten the breakdown of industrial society, and this motivates him in his grisly work.

The document is also the product of a limited and tunnel-visioned man, with a careful and dogged but somewhat incoherent mind, filled with a catalogue of longstanding prejudices and hatreds, academically trained, occasionally inventive, purposeful and humorless. He is amoral, not to say cold-blooded, about acts of terrorism, which are regarded as an effective tactic in service to the larger cause. He is convinced enough in his cause to have produced this long justification for it, complete with numerous bold assertions and his own "principles of history," but he repeatedly finds qualifications and reservations and indeed ends up calling the article no more "than a crude approximation to the truth," as if to suggest that somewhere within he is not quite confident.

All in all, I think despite its flaws it is a document worth publishing, and not only because that could presumably help stop the killing. There is a crucial message at the core of it for those with fortitude enough to get through it, and unless that message is somehow heeded and acted on we are truly a doomed society hurtling toward a catastrophic breakdown. I can't expect the *Times* and the *Post* to give much credence to that idea—and they can lard it with their own dissents and denials if they choose—but they might just realize that there is a growing body of people these days beginning at last to understand the increasing perils of the technosphere we have created. For, as the *New Yorker* recently put it, there's a little of the Unabomber in all of us.

TELEVISION COMEDY EMBRACES IRONY

MICHAEL RUST

In the 1990s, the television comedy *Seinfeld* was a pop culture phenomenon, attracting millions of viewers each week. The show's creator, Jerry Seinfeld, described it as "the show about nothing," an apt assessment of a comedy that steered clear of the usual sitcom formulas. The show depicted a circle of friends in New York City, often conniving against coworkers, strangers, and one another. *Seinfeld* eschewed the phony moralizing and political correctness of previous sitcoms in favor of ironic humor that pushed the boundaries of good taste.

The success of *Seinfeld* and the pioneering animated series *The Simpsons* encouraged the development of riskier television comedies in the mid-1990s that embraced satire and irreverence. *South Park*, an animated program featuring foul-mouthed third graders, took the new comedic ethos to an extreme, antagonizing cultural conservatives. In the following commentary written shortly after the final episode of *Seinfeld* aired on May 14, 1998, Michael Rust describes the rise of irony-laden "postmodern" humor on television. Rust maintains that the nation's fondness for raunch and satire is the result of shifting cultural mores. The author is a reporter for the weekly *Insight on the News*.

H umor always has played a critical role in American history, shaping the national character. As *Seinfeld*'s exit demonstrates, Americans take their humor seriously. The normal response to it might be: "Oh my God! They've killed Western civilization!" But no, this alarming cry doesn't

From "Laughs, Culture, Yadda, Yadda," by Michael Rust, *Insight on the News*, June 8, 1998. Copyright © 1998 by News World Communications, Inc. Reprinted with permission.

echo throughout the country each Wednesday evening when the Comedy Channel broadcasts *South Park*, a weekly animated chronicle of the adventures of some foul-mouthed third-graders in South Park, Colorado. Of course, it well might. The show, which has become the new cult hit on cable television, and which has been featured on the covers of *Newsweek, Rolling Stone* and *Entertainment Weekly*, features each week the untimely demise of a silent young character named Kenny. The response of his cohorts to Kenny's death always is the same and has become a staple of youth discourse: "Oh my God! They killed Kenny!"

THE RISE OF POSTMODERN HUMOR

South Park is not a sign of impending apocalypse, although regular viewers do occasionally watch an animated Jesus and animated Satan square off in a kung-fu match. But it is another sign of yet another turn of the page in the ongoing saga of American humor. In her classic 1936 work, *American Humor: A Study of the National Character,* critic Constance Rourke argued that the American comic spirit had helped the fledgling nation spread across a continent and assume a national character. American humor, she said, had a single, all-important function, namely creating "a sense of unity among a people who were not yet a nation and who were seldom joined in stable communities." Humor, she said, developed "ideal images, those symbols which peoples spontaneously adopt and by which in some measure they live."

In other words, what a nation laughs at helps determine what kind of nation it is. When Rourke wrote in the 1930s, there was a long tradition of written humor, transmitted through print and stage. *The New Yorker* was then home to the urbane humorous sketch; on the other side of the country in Hollywood, the "screwball comedy" was in its golden age.

Now, "the idea of the humorist seems to me to have been dead for quite a long time," [says] Terry Teachout, columnist for *Civilization*. . . . There seems little room for it in a culture that has been labeled "postmodern." This adjective has been tossed around quite freely in academe and journalism, but that doesn't mean it isn't useful.

"It is a terrible and irritating word," says Teachout. "But it hasn't been leached of meaning in the sense that the word 'racism' has. If you use 'postmodern' carefully, it really does refer to a kind of exhausted nihilism."

And whether humor will be used to combat that nihilism or contribute to it remains to be seen, but postmodern is definitely the flavor of choice for cutting-edge comedy as the millennium approaches. *Seinfeld*, "the show about nothing" finished its highly successful nine-year run on NBC with a five-month countdown to the final episode, which [aired on May 14, 1998, and] drew an estimated 70 million viewers. At the same time, much of the TV humor that merges cult status with mainstream success has been animated. *The Simpsons*, cartoonist Matt Groening's brilliant takeoff on the television culture that spawned it, now is the longest running sitcom on television. After *Beavis and Butthead* [a show featuring two animated teenaged heavy metal fans] finished its MTV run, creator Mike Judge found new success with Fox's *King of the Hill*. *Daria*, on MTV, and the Comedy Channel's controversial *South Park* have achieved critical—and with *South Park*, popular—success in their first year on the air.

Daria, MTV's animated take on a highly intelligent, socially isolated adolescent girl's sometimes-strained relationships with family, school and life, may be typical of the best appeal of this new comedy, suggests Teachout. "Daria's out there, but it's not nihilist. It is, like much else emerging from generation X, a very shrewd critique of the baby boomers. That's really what it's about—all these kids moving and living in postmodern culture, and they don't seem too terribly impressed with it, either."

IRONY-LADEN TV HAS ITS CRITICS

Not everyone has been happy, of course. Russ Smith, editor of the weekly *New York Press* blasts the New York media for its saturation coverage of [the final episode of *Seinfeld*] "the Titanic of TV finales," which included daily countdowns and front-page coverage in the *New York Post*. Noting that *Seinfeld* is produced in Los Angeles, Smith scores *Post* editorial page editor John Podhoretz for claiming that the antics of Jerry, Elaine, Kramer and George were "partly responsible for the rejuvenation of New York. It was just absurd."

And, in fact, this new wave of irony-laden TV comedy has drawn a mixed reaction from conservatives. One conservative cultural critic privately refers to some of the right-wing response as "the grandma approach." This is perhaps best embodied by the annual parent's guide to television, produced by the conservative Media Research Center, or MRC. Of *Seinfeld*, the guide primly notes that "topics have included oral sex, homosexuality, impotence, masturbation, accompanied by in-depth discussions of birth-control methods."

At the same time, television producer Rob Long, a regular contributor to *National Review,* wrote in the conservative magazine that *Seinfeld* "is gleefully free of cant. There are no messages, positive or otherwise, delivered in an episode except the only one that matters: Laugh! Enjoy! And tune in next week. We are the kings; they are the clowns. Implicit in the series is the understanding that our moral and spiritual life is our own affair. Jerry and friends are strictly for laughs."

And, in fact, Long says part of *Seinfeld*'s success is because "after years of pious liberal nonsense, the American viewing public relished the naughty pleasure of apolitical laughter." The show "isn't a show about nothing; it's a show about nothing pompous," Long concluded. And, in fact, the episode where Jerry and George are mistakenly identified as homosexuals became legendary for its finessing of politically correct bromides. Every time a character would explode with terror and anger about being thought of as gay, he would add the caveat, "not that there's anything wrong with that." Likewise the legendary episode about masturbation, "The Contest," went through 21 minutes of dialogue without once actually mentioning the name of the solitary indulgence.

Likewise, the MRC's take on *The Simpsons,* praised by conservative editor and columnist Fred Barnes and lauded by *National Review*'s David Klinghoffer as "the most brilliant show on television," seems equally dour: "This show has ridiculed entrepreneurs, educators, religion, and law enforcement officials, and has occasionally incorporated foul language into the dialogue." But the animated Fox hit show "offers rather sophisticated humor," points out conservative media critic Tim Graham. "Satire can be very subtle and maybe my eight-year-old won't understand it. *The Simpsons* is one of those cartoons where I sit and watch it with my son and I'm like barreled over laughing and my son doesn't know why. It will make fun of TV in real subtle ways. I think it's a work of genius."

FILTERING AMERICAN CULTURE THROUGH THE TV SCREEN

Certainly, conservative critics of modernity who fail to appreciate the nuances of much of modern culture may find their vision of the political landscape hindered. For much of the electorate, the future electorate, and the nonparticipating electorate, the TV screen is more comforting than reality. For over four decades, American culture, for good or bad, has been filtered through television. The explosive growth of television in the 1950s is one of the defining features of postwar American culture. Between 1948 and 1955, television sets were installed in two-thirds of the homes in the United States. By 1960, 90 percent of American households contained at least one set, which was on for nearly five hours every day. Nearly forty years later, that has been expanded to over seven hours, and the choices available to TV consumers have gone from three networks and a smattering of local channels to hundreds of cable offerings.

In her book, *Make Room for TV: Television and the Family Ideal in Postwar America,* historian Lynn Spigel described how television, viewed initially as an intrusion into the home, quickly became the arbiter of routine for the entire household. Rather than a novelty item, TV became a key factor in scheduling work and play and determining when the family would interact with the outside world. As Americans focused in on the tube, the comedy presented there began to displace the written word.

Milton Berle held America's biggest spotlight as the star of *Texaco Star Theater,* which debuted June 8, 1948. Berle helped make TV an essential part of many American lives and, as his popularity rose, so did sales of television sets. Similarly, on *Show of Shows,* the burly Sid Caesar and Imogene Coca, that most ingenious of ingenues, wowed huge Saturday night audiences with an hour-and-a-half of live, no retake, sketches that skewered everything from nutty professors to arty movies.

Life with Luigi, The Life of Reilly, and *Mama* were ethnic sitcoms that might never see the light of day today, featuring, respectively, Italian-Americans, Irish-Americans and Norwegian-Americans. Later, *I Love Lucy* and *The Honeymooners* defined the modern situation comedy and became hallmarks of baby-boomer culture. *Amos 'n' Andy,* in retrospect, the omega point of political incorrectness was, for years, virtually the only place blacks could be seen on television; it has never appeared in syndication because the stereotyping of African Americans would be too offensive to modern viewers.

TV, once Hollywood's shabbier stepsibling, now has become the medium of choice among many aspiring comic actors and writers. Alums of the venerable *Harvard Lampoon* have gone on to writing and producing spots at prominent shows such as *Seinfeld* and *The Simpsons.* ("Where they are never heard of again," cracks Teachout.) The most famous, Conan O'Brien, went from *Simpsons* producer to host of his own late-night show. The two creators of *South Park,* twentysomethings Matt Stone and Trey Parker—who, perhaps predictably, cite talk-show host Jerry Springer as a major influence—have become major players in Hollywood, and have been signed to write the sequel to [the hit movie] *Dumb and Dumber.*

RAUNCH, SATIRE, AND WIT

At the same time, their show has achieved a unique status, being the only regular television series to boast a TV-MA rating (the strictest, for programs not suitable for anyone under 17.) Parents armed with the v-chip can program their televisions not to show any TV-MA rated show. If parents embrace the v-chip, this could be trouble for Comedy Central, since children under 17 make up around one-fifth of the *South Park* audience.

The controversial cartoon has, according to the network, helped sell more than a million T-shirts and close to $30 million worth of merchandise since its debut last August. "If *Seinfeld* made television history by positing that adults are petty, nasty, self-serving beasts," opined *Rolling Stone,* "*South Park* has, during its (history) suggested that such lousy behavior doesn't begin at the age of 18." It does this through such episodes as "Big Gay Al's Big Gay Boat Ride," "An Elephant Makes Love to a Pig" and "Mr. Hankey—the Christmas Poo," the latter a happy holiday ode to a talking stool sample. Alien anal probes, the passing of fiery gas, a child dressing as Hitler for Halloween—all have been fodder for the series which has become must-see viewing on many college campuses.

"That does not strike me as funny," says Graham. "I don't think it's humorless to find unfunny a show where the same character gets killed every week in grostesque ways. It makes *Beavis and Butthead* look like *I Claudius.*" Many share this understandable view, particularly those responsible for children. And the shows that garner the most applause across the board are those that transmit their often-sardonic message with intelligence and wit rather than a shock-filled taste for the jugular.

"*Seinfeld* is the most intricately plotted, self-conscious situation comedy ever broadcast on American television," wrote Long. "In 21 minutes of storytelling time, *Seinfeld* could cram 20 or more scenes, some barely five seconds long, to keep the story moving." At the same time that *Seinfeld* was heading into the endless sunset of syndication, HBO's *The Larry Sanders Show* was also approaching its finale. Created by star Gary Shandling, *Sanders* was a unique combination of sitcom and cinema verite, using the backdrop of a late-night talk show to utilize real celebrities interacting with the fictional characters, all in a weekly half-hour format. Like *The Simpsons, Sanders* spoofed the very television culture which had created and nurtured it and, in this, it may represent a wave of the future, as children of the 1960s approach their own version of cancellation and syndication.

"To me, the interesting thing about generation X is that it doesn't have as much garbage to clear away," says Teachout. "It's starting with nothing, which means it might be able to get to something faster than someone from the baby-boomer generation, who has to start by a 1990s clearing away his own cultural garbage first."

TIGER WOODS MAKES GOLF HISTORY

RICK REILLY

In the summer of 1996, twenty-year-old Tiger Woods announced that he was joining the professional golf tour instead of returning to Stanford University for his junior year. Woods had distinguished himself as a golfer by winning three straight national junior golf titles followed by three U.S. amateur titles over a six year period. Golf fans soon found themselves in awe as Woods met with unprecedented success within his first two months on the professional tour. Out of seven tournaments, Woods won two and finished in the top five in the others, tying long-standing records and pocketing $734,794 in earnings.

Woods's performance on the golf course was in and of itself a remarkable achievement. But Woods also came from a mixed-race background and appeared African American to onlookers. The sight of a minority dominating what had long been considered the sport of wealthy white men was inspiring to non-whites, who had previously felt excluded from the game and unwelcome at the country clubs where the tournaments were held. In the following profile, written during the first few months of Woods's pro career, Rick Reilly remarks on Woods's rising popularity and the diverse crowd of new fans he is drawing to golf tournaments. Reilly contends that Woods is providing the pro golf circuit with a much needed infusion of diversity and excitement. The author is a reporter for *Sports Illustrated* magazine.

To understand what golf is now, don't watch Tiger Woods. Watch who watches Tiger Woods. Young black women in tight jeans and heels. Tour caddies, back out on the course after hauling a bag 18 holes. White arbitrageurs with cell phones. Giant groups of fourth-graders, mimicking their first golf swings. Pasty golf writers who haven't left the press tent since the days of Fat Jack [Jack Nicklaus]. Hispanic teens in Dallas Cowboys jerseys trying to find their way around a golf course for the first time in their lives. Bus drivers and CEOs and mothers with strollers catching the wheels in the bunkers as they go.

MAKING SPORTS HISTORY

History will do that. History will suck you into places you have never been. Woods is making history almost daily. Last week at Disney World in Orlando, the throngs following him turned every tee box into the line at Space Mountain, and he gave them still more history, winning for a cereal-spoon-dropping second time in his first seven starts—the greatest professional debut in golf history—and bankrolling his way to 23rd on the Tour's money list and the pole position in this week's gaudy Tour Championship at Southern Hills in Tulsa. The way things were supposed to work, Tiger was to tee it up at the PGA Tour Qualifying Tournament in December to try to earn his card. He even sent in the $3,000 entry fee. He can void the check now. From Tour school to Tour Championship in seven weeks. The kid's a quick study.

They will show up in Tulsa, too, this tsunami of Tiger Tailers, dipping their big toes into the game for the first time, hoping to answer the question, Is this really happening? At the Walt Disney World/Oldsmobile Classic, where Woods won another $216,000 to get him to nearly three quarters of a million, attendance tripled from the year before. For his seven-week scorched-divot tour since he became a professional on August 28, 1996, tournament directors conservatively estimate that he has drawn an extra 150,000 fans. And this is not Chicago and Los Angeles. This is Coal Valley, Illinois, and Endicott, New York. No wonder that when Woods committed to play the Disney, the tournament director jumped into a swimming pool.

Whoo-boy. Maybe those Nike ads had it right. Is golf ready for this? Golf used to be four white guys sitting around a pinochle table talking about their shaft flexes and deciding whether to have the wilted lettuce soup. Now golf is Cindy

Crawford sending Woods a letter. A youngster who'd been promised a round of golf with Woods was bouncing all around his Orlando home two weeks ago, going, "When is Tiger coming? When is Tiger coming?" The kid's name? [Professional baseball player] Ken Griffey Jr.

Australian reporters are demanding a press conference the minute Woods's feet touch Australian soil in November for the Australian Open. At the Quad City Classic in Coal Valley, they had to print up more tickets. Teens in Milwaukee screamed his name so loud and for so long that he had to come to the window and wave to get them to calm down. "It was like he was the pope!" says Tiger's mom, Tida.

He's not the pope. More like a god. "I don't think we've had a whole lot happen in what, 10 years?" says golf's last deity, Jack Nicklaus. "I mean, some guys have come on and won a few tournaments, but nobody has sustained and dominated. I think we might have somebody now."

When was the last time a 20-year-old showed up and grabbed an entire sport by the throat? The Disney [tournament] was Woods's fifth top-five finish in five starts. Not only has no rookie ever come within a moon shot of doing that, but also no player has done it since Curtis Strange 14 years ago. . . .

What else? A scoring average as a pro that, at 67.89, would be the lowest in Vardon Trophy history if Woods had enough rounds to qualify, lower by almost a stroke than Greg Norman's record 68.81, set in 1994. Woods would also be this year's leader in three other statistical categories: driving average (302.8, 14 yards better than John Daly's), birdies per round (4.68) and eagle frequency (one every 55 holes). He has finished, in order, 60th, 11th, fifth, third, first (at Las Vegas), third and first, and he goes to Tulsa to play the big boys as "the best player on our Tour," says veteran Jay Haas.

Want to hear something scary? "I really haven't played my best golf yet," Woods says. "I haven't even had a great putting week yet."

Could it be that this remarkable streak is not a streak at all? "Oh, god," says Peter Jacobsen, who would have loved to have had one top-five this year. "If this is how he is every week, then it's over. He's the greatest player in the history of the game."

Want to hear something scarier? Woods won while being sick all week. Last Saturday night he did not look much like a god at all but just a homesick kid praying for the Nyquil to kick in.

He had a sore throat, bags under his eyes and sneezes backed up and holding. He was sprawled on rented furniture in a rented condo next to the one he will move into soon, stuck with a courtesy car out front because he hasn't had time to buy his own wheels yet and is too young to rent. You think it's easy throttling an entire sport before you're old enough to drink?

Take women, for instance. "Women don't seem that interested because I'm so young," he has said. "Think about it. Most of the women my age are in college."

Money. For a kid who has signed $60 million in endorsement deals, won three quarters of a million playing and just signed a $2.2 million book deal, why does he always have only three bucks in his pocket? His agent, Hughes Norton, is fond of telling him—usually while Norton is taking a couple of hundreds out of his wallet and handing them to Woods—"For a rich guy, you sure are poor." His mother keeps bailing him out too. "What kind of damned millionaire are you?" she says.

Norton says he has gotten none of the money back, but we figure Woods is good for it, what with a spring-loaded bomb of a swing that may soon make the term par 5 obsolete. For Woods there are no par-5s. At the 595-yard 14th on Saturday at Disney's Magnolia Course, Woods still had 284 yards to go over trees and a green-guarding lake. He cold starched a three-wood—over the green. In his seven starts he has birdied 68 of the 128 par-5s he has played, including 12 of 16 at the Disney.

It has been a kind of blister bliss for Woods's caddie, Mike (Fluff) Cowan, who is having to pace off ponds and trees and Haagen-Däzs stands that until now have never been in play in his 20 years on Tour. Last week Fluff may have become the first caddie in history to utter this sentence: "It's 290 to clear that bunker. I like three-wood."

"Man, you should have seen how Tiger was hitting it," Paul Goydos was saying in the locker room last week after having to play directly behind Woods and his moving city of fans. "You'd have been humbled."

"C'mon," said John Cook. "What's so humbling?"

"How 'bout he reaches number 8 [614 yards] in two?"

Silence.

"Now that," said Cook, O-mouthed, "is humbling."

In Tiger Woods 21st-Century Golf, all bets are off. At the Disney nobody else had security guards. Woods had four. On a Tour where top 25 gets you into all the tournaments you want and a second home on the beach besides, Woods is turning up the attitude. "There are a lot of guys out here who come into a tournament thinking, Well, eight under will get me top 25. That'll be all right," says Cook. "Now here comes this kid who's ripping and shaking from the 1st tee."

What is so charming about this historic ride is the tournaments where it has all played out—Milwaukee, Quad City, the Texas Open, British Columbia—the end-of-the-year-liquidation-sale events that nobody enters unless he's hurting for his card or took a wrong turn at Doral [a prestigious golf tournament in Miami, Florida]. But for this one magic stretch, these places were the Rainbow Rooms. They will have to make do with that memory for a good long while. Elvis will probably never play the club lounges again.

Taking on Seasoned Pros

Still, it's not as if Woods beat nothing but club pros on the Tiger Tour. Of the Top 20 players on the Sony World Ranking, he has beaten Ernie Els (No. 3), Fred Couples (5), Corey Pavin (8) twice, Phil Mickelson (9), Davis Love III (10) twice, Mark O'Meara (11), Vijay Singh (16), Loren Roberts (17), David Duval (19) and Scott Hoch (20) twice. On Sunday at the Disney he matched a rejuvenated Payne Stewart, who needed to win to make Tulsa, birdie for birdie. Woods did him one better, firing a 66 to Stewart's 67 to win.

Is this the same kid whose best finish in a pro event as an amateur was an underwhelming 22nd? "You guys don't understand," Woods says. "When I played in those tournaments, I was either in high school or college. I'd get dumped into the toughest places to play, and I usually was trying to study, get papers done and everything else. I knew if I came out here and played every day, I'd get into a rhythm, and I have."

But it's how he wins that's eerie. He seems to have a Psychic Friends thing going about what exactly it will take to get the job done. Last Friday morning, as he was having his cereal at his rented breakfast table with his father, Earl Woods, he put down the sports pages and made an announcement. "Pop," he said. "Got to shoot 63 today. That's what it will take to get into it."

"So go do it," droned Earl, half awake.

The little condo they share in Orlando does not get the Golf Channel, the only network that showed the Disney, so Earl heard nothing more about the tournament until that afternoon when his son got home from his new job. "Whaddya shoot?" said Pop, blandly.

"Sixty-three," said Sonny.

"Oh, my god," said Pop.

Hey, aren't kids supposed to have fun at Disney World?

Things are going so well for Woods these days that he wins playoffs by default. His 21-under-par score of 267 (69-63-69-66) was actually tied by fellow rookie Taylor Smith, but Smith was disqualified because his split putter grips were not round. Smith is about as far from Woods as he can be. He and his pregnant wife, Nicole, rent a $450 apartment in Waycross, Georgia. When Smith was one shot out of the lead on the 8th hole, Nicole was bouncing up and down saying, "We're going to buy a house now. We are going to buy a house!" But at the turn the ruling was made, and when Smith's appeal was denied after the round, the house was gone and Nicole was in tears. "I'm going to find something positive out of this," said Smith. "I just haven't found it yet."

INSPIRING A DIVERSE CROWD

Woods is finding positives all around him, like in the new, throbbing gallery he is inventing: school teachers and Little League teams and whole black families like the McCorveys of Merritt Island, Georgia, the kind of family that golf never saw except waiting outside the caddie tent. "They used to say this was a white man's sport," says Carolyn McCorvey, a Lockheed employee and mother of a six-year-old who's taking up the game. "Well, not anymore. They used to say it was boring, too. But not with all the money this young man is making."

Listen to how new the sounds are too.

"You go, T!" a young black man yelled at Woods on Sunday. "Take care of bizness!"

There was this from two teenage African-American girls—a sight seldom seen in pre-Woodsian golf—just after Tiger had ripped a shot that sounded like a Scud taking off.

"And that ain't nothin' yet!" one said.

As Woods passed, they smiled at him and he smiled back.

"Lorrrrd!" said the other. "He is just too cute!"

Woods understands what he is doing to the game. "To look out here and see so many kids, I think that's wonderful," he says. "They see someone they can relate to, me being so young. It's not like Jack Nicklaus. It's really nice seeing more minorities in the gallery. I think that's where the game should go and will go."

Woods seems as charged by the voltage from his enormous crowds as everybody else. He will high-five kids, look fans in the eye and actually respond "Thanks" when they holler out, "Kill 'em, Tiger!" ("Tiger Woods just thanked me," said one high school boy in hightops and a Charlotte Hornets jersey with his cap on backward. "My year is made, dude!") Woods doesn't have Fluff hand out unwanted balls at the end of a round; Woods throws them to kids while he's playing. "I remember when I was a kid, I always wanted to be a part of it," Woods says. "I always wanted to be connected somehow."

Who doesn't? At the Disney a young black man was wandering around with his buddies trying to follow Woods but looking lost. Finally he discreetly approached a black cameraman. "Brother," he said, "can I ask you something?"

The cameraman leaned over the ropes to hear him. "Sure."

"Well," the young man said, "what do we do?"

He'll have an entire era to learn.

CLONING: A SCIENTIFIC BREAKTHROUGH CHALLENGES MEDICAL ETHICS

GINA KOLATA

In 1997, scientists in Great Britain announced the ground-breaking news that they had successfully cloned an adult sheep. The creation of "Dolly" the lamb, as the clone was named, raised fears that the technology might eventually be used to clone humans, an application that many scientists and layper-sons consider unethical. Since the birth of Dolly, the controversy over cloning has grown with the rapid advance of cloning tech-nology. In 2001, a group of U.S. scientists announced that they had cloned a human embryo, furthering concerns that human cloning may become a common practice. In the following article, written in 1997, Gina Kolata describes the feelings of dis-belief and surprise held by other scientists upon receiving the news of Dolly's birth. The scientists responsible for Dolly assert that cloning has important research applications, but they fore-see troubling ethical questions as cloning becomes more effi-cient. Gina Kolata is a reporter for the *New York Times*.

From "Scientist Reports First Cloning Ever of Adult Mammal," by Gina Kolata, *New York Times*, February 23, 1997. Copyright © 1997 by The New York Times, Inc. Reprinted with permission.

I n a feat that may be the one bit of genetic engineering that has been anticipated and dreaded more than any other, researchers in Britain are reporting that they have cloned an adult mammal for the first time.

A SUCCESSFUL CLONING: DOLLY THE SHEEP

The group, headed by Dr. Ian Wilmut, a 52-year-old embryologist at the Roslin Institute in Edinburgh, has created a lamb using deoxyribonucleic acid (DNA) from an adult sheep. Their achievement shocked leading researchers who had said it could not be done. The researchers had assumed that the DNA of adult cells would not act like the DNA formed when a sperm's genes first mingle with those of an egg.

In theory, researchers said, the same techniques could be used to take a cell from an adult human and use the DNA to create a genetically identical human—a time-delayed twin. That prospect raises the thorniest of ethical and philosophical questions.

Dr. Wilmut's experiment was simple, in retrospect. He took a mammary cell from an adult sheep and prepared its DNA so it would be accepted by an egg from another sheep. He then removed the egg's own DNA, replacing it with the DNA from the adult sheep by fusing the egg with the adult cell. The fused cells, carrying the adult DNA, began to grow and divide, just like a perfectly normal fertilized egg, to form an embryo.

Dr. Wilmut implanted the embryo into another ewe; in July, the ewe gave birth to a lamb, named Dolly. Though Dolly seems perfectly normal, DNA tests show that she is the clone of the adult ewe who supplied her DNA.

"What this will mostly be used for is to produce more health care products," Dr. Wilmut told the Press Association of Britain early today, according to the Reuters news agency.

"It will enable us to study genetic diseases for which there is presently no cure and track down the mechanisms that are involved. The next step is to use the cells in culture in the lab and target genetic changes into that culture."

Simple though it may be, the experiment, to be reported this coming Thursday in the British journal *Nature,* has startled biologists and ethicists.

Dr. Wilmut said he was interested in the technique primarily as a tool in animal husbandry, but other scientists said it had opened doors to the unsettling prospect that humans could be cloned as well.

SCIENCE FICTION BECOMES FACT

"It's unbelievable," said Dr. Lee Silver, a biology professor at Princeton University who said the announcement had come just in time for him to revise his forthcoming book so the first chapter will no longer state that such cloning is impossible.

"It basically means that there are no limits," Dr. Silver said. "It means all of science fiction is true. They said it could never be done and now here it is, done before the year 2000."

Dr. Neal First, a professor of reproductive biology and animal biotechnology at the University of Wisconsin, who has been trying to clone cattle, said the ability to clone dairy cattle could have a bigger impact on the industry than the introduction of artificial insemination in the 1950's, a procedure that revolutionized dairy farming. Cloning could be used to make multiple copies of animals that are especially good at producing meat or milk or wool.

Although researchers have created genetically identical animals by dividing embryos very early in their development, Dr. Silver said, no one had cloned an animal from an adult until now. Earlier experiments, with frogs, have become a stock story in high school biology, but the experiments never produced cloned adult frogs. The frogs developed only to the tadpole stage before dying.

It was even worse with mammals. Researchers could swap DNA from one fertilized egg to another, but they could go no further. "They couldn't even put nuclei from late-stage mouse embryos into early mouse embryos," Dr. Silver said. The embryos simply failed to develop and died.

As a result, the researchers concluded that as cells developed, the proteins coating the DNA somehow masked all the important genes for embryo development. A skin cell may have all the genetic information that was present in the fertilized egg that produced the organism, for example, but almost all that information is pasted over. Now all the skin cell can do is be a skin cell.

Researchers could not even hope to strip off the proteins from an adult cell's DNA and replace them with proteins from an embryo's DNA. The DNA would shatter if anyone tried to strip it bare, Dr. Silver said.

Last year, Dr. Wilmut showed that he could clone DNA from sheep embryo cells, but even that was not taken as proof that the animal itself could be cloned. It could just be that the embryo cells had DNA that was unusually conducive to cloning, many thought.

Dr. Wilmut, however, hit on a clever strategy. He did not bother with the proteins that coat DNA, and instead focused on getting the DNA from an adult cell into a stage in its normal cycle of replication where it could take up residence in an egg.

DNA in growing cells goes through what is known as the cell cycle: it prepares itself to divide, then replicates itself and splits in two as the cell itself divides. The problem with earlier cloning attempts, Dr. Wilmut said, was that the DNA from the donor had been out of synchrony with that of the recipient cell. The solution, Dr. Wilmut discovered, was to, in effect, put the DNA from the adult cell to sleep, making it quiescent by depriving the adult cell of nutrients. When he then fused it with an egg cell from another sheep—after removing the egg cell's DNA— the donor DNA took over as though it belonged there.

Dr. Wilmut said in a telephone interview that he planned to breed Dolly next fall to determine whether she was fertile.

PRACTICAL APPLICATIONS AND RESEARCH

Dr. Wilmut said that the method could work for any animal and that he hoped to use it next to clone cattle. He said that he could use many types of cells from adults for cloning but that the easiest to use would be so-called stem cells, which give rise to a variety of other cells and are present throughout the body. In his sheep experiment, he used mammary cells because a company that sponsored his work, PPL Therapeutics, is developing sheep that can be used to produce proteins that can be used as drugs in their milk, so it had sheep mammary cells readily available.

For Dr. Wilmut, the main interest of the experiment is to advance animal research. PPL, for example, wants to clone animals that can produce pharmacologically useful proteins, like the clotting factor needed by hemophiliacs. Scientists would grow cells in the laboratory, insert the genes for production of the desired protein, select those cells that most actively churned out the protein and use those cells to make cloned females. The cloned animals would produce immense amounts of the proteins in their milk, making the animals into living drug factories.

But that is only the beginning, Dr. Wilmut said. Researchers could use the same method to make animals with human diseases, like cystic fibrosis, and then test therapies on the cloned animals. Or they could use cloning to alter the proteins on the surfaces of pig organs, like the liver or heart, making the organs more like human organs. Then they could transplant those organs into humans.

Dr. First said the "exciting and astounding" cloning result could shake the dairy industry. It could allow the cloning of cows that are superproducers of milk, making 30,000 or even 40,000 pounds of milk a year. The average cow makes about 13,000 pounds of milk a year, he said.

"I think that if—and it's a very big if—cloning were highly efficient, then it could be a more significant revolution to the livestock industry than even artificial insemination," Dr. First said.

ETHICAL QUESTIONS ABOUND

Although Dr. Wilmut said he saw no intrinsic biological reason humans, too, could not be cloned, he dismissed the idea as being ethically unacceptable. Moreover, he said, it is illegal in Britain to clone people. "I would find it offensive" to clone a human being, Dr. Wilmut said, adding that he fervently hoped that no one would try it.

But others said that it was hard to imagine enforcing a ban on cloning people when cloning got more efficient. "I could see it going on surreptitiously," said Lori Andrews, a professor at Chicago-Kent College of law who specializes in reproductive issues. For example, she said, in the early days of in vitro fertilization, Australia banned that practice. "So scientists moved to Singapore" and offered the procedure, Professor Andrews said.

"I can imagine new crimes," she said.

People might be cloned without their knowledge or consent. After all, all that would be needed would be some cells. If there is a market for a sperm bank selling semen from Nobel laureates, how much better would it be to bear a child that would actually be a clone of a great thinker or, perhaps, a great beauty or great athlete?

"The genie is out of the bottle," said Dr. Ronald Munson, a medical ethicist at the University of Missouri in St. Louis. "This technology is not, in principle, policeable."

Dr. Munson called the future possibilities incredible. For example, could researchers devise ways to add just the DNA of an adult cell, without fusing two living cells? If so, might it be possible to clone the dead?

"I had an idea for a story once," Dr. Munson said, in which a scientist obtains a spot of blood from the cross on which Jesus was crucified. He then uses it to clone a man who is Jesus Christ—or perhaps cannot be.

On a more practical note, Dr. Munson mused over the strange twist that science has taken.

"There's something ironic" about the study, he said. "Here we have this incredible technical accomplishment, and what motivated it? The desire for more sheep milk of a certain type." It is, he said, "the theater of the absurd acted out by scientists."

In his interview with the Press Association of Britain, Dr. Wilmut added early today: "We are aware that there is potential for misuse, and we have provided information to ethicists and the Human Embryology Authority. We believe that it is important that society decides how we want to use this technology and makes sure it prohibits what it wants to prohibit. It would be desperately sad if people started using this sort of technology with people."

THE BOMBING OF U.S. EMBASSIES IN AFRICA

NEW REPUBLIC

In a simultaneous attack on the U.S. presence in Africa, the American Embassies in Nairobi, Kenya, and Dar es Salaam, Tanzania, were bombed by terrorists on August 7, 1998. The Nairobi bombing killed twelve American diplomats, thirty-four Kenyan embassy employees, and 167 citizens who were near the embassy at the time of the blast; over five thousand people were injured. In Tanzania, ten people were killed and over seventy were injured. Osama bin Laden, a wealthy Saudi exile, was connected to the bombings. Bin Laden had taken refuge in lawless Afghanistan after instigating Islamic fundamentalist opposition to Saudi Arabia's royal family. Once there, he funded the training camps of the al-Qaeda terrorist network, which had established a significant presence in Afghanistan.

At the time of the bombings, the American public and political leaders were preoccupied by the sex scandal involving President Bill Clinton's relationship with White House intern Monica Lewinsky. On August 17, 1998, the president delivered grand jury testimony before Office of the Independent Counsel prosecutors, who were aggressively seeking his impeachment. Three days later, in retaliation for the embassy bombings, the president ordered a missile attack directed at a pharmaceutical plant in North Khartoum, Sudan, under the assumption that it was producing biological weapons. In addition, al-Qaeda training camps in the Kowst region of Afghanistan were targeted. The

U.S. response was regarded as ineffective and met with widespread skepticism both at home and in the Middle East; critics maintained that the president was merely distracting attention from his domestic troubles. In the following editorial, which appeared in the *New Republic* magazine in late August 1998, the authors assert that President Clinton has wrongly followed other U.S. presidents in making threats against terrorists that are not followed by effective and appropriate force. As a result, terrorists have received the message that they will face no serious consequences for their actions, in the opinion of the authors.

T he bombings in Nairobi and Dar es Salaam caught the leader of the free world taking care of other business. He was everywhere, Bill Clinton, when this terrible assault on American sovereignty and embassies—this terrible slaughter of Americans and non-Americans—took place: one fund-raiser in San Francisco, two in Los Angeles, a luncheon in Louisville, Kentucky, a dinner in Chicago for Senator Carol Moseley-Braun. Then back to Washington for more meetings with his lawyers. He promised retribution against the perpetrators; he invoked his favorite cant about the "global society" threatened by these bombings. But there was an oddly feeble and perfunctory ring to what he said.

The president was hardly alone in his moral and political distraction. At one White House press briefing in the aftermath of the bombings, the story about terrorism barely held the attention of the guild. Once the obligatory questions about the bombing had been asked and answered, it was back to what we have been gorging on: the Lewinsky affair, the dress bought at the Gap, and the stain on it. There was no way that Sam Donaldson and Wolf Blitzer could be diverted from what has been their obsession for seven months now.

A FREE RIDE FOR TERRORISTS

Grant the world's wholesalers of terror their due: They can see into our condition and priorities and span of attention. They can divine our passions and our interests. They are astute enough to attack America abroad at a time when the moral authority of the president of the United States is under attack at home. Thus did they minimize the chances that the United States would hit back.

Not that those chances were very great anyway. For a generation now, ever since the April 1983 bombing of the U.S. Embassy in Beirut, one American president after another has threatened retribution against outrages aimed at our embassies and barracks and airliners, but the threats have never really been made good. The sole exception was that big raid that Ronald Reagan ordered against Libya in 1986 as retaliation for a Libyan-backed murder of two American servicemen in a Berlin nightclub.

Otherwise, it has been a free ride for the terrorists; even Reagan tried to bargain with their Iranian sponsors over hostages in Beirut. Under Clinton, the United States has opted not to hit Qaddafi again for his refusal to hand over the two Libyan operatives who carried out the bombing of Pan Am Flight 103 over Lockerbie, Scotland, in 1988. Instead, we have kept economic sanctions in force—despite European complaints—and attempted to wait Qaddafi out. Now even that policy has been vitiated by the administration's recent decision, in tandem with Tony Blair's British government, to drop the demand that the Libyans stand trial in Scotland; instead, we may now accept a trial under British rules in a third country such as Holland. The administration says this is "calling Qaddafi's bluff." But what's the plan if the Libyan dictator, having achieved this much give in the American position, decides to raise the stakes?

There was a brazen challenge to our power in Saudi Arabia two years ago [1996]. Nineteen U.S. servicemembers lost their lives in a gigantic truck bomb blast at the Khobar Towers in Dhahran. Nothing came of the Clinton administration's threats to bring the killers to justice. Evidence points to Iran as the sponsor of the attack, but Saudi Arabia has prevented the United States from obtaining information the FBI needs to seal the case. Apparently, the Saudis are frightened of doing anything to offend the Iranians—who are nearby and could bring even more terror to their realm if the United States takes action. The Clinton administration has decided it had no choice but to acquiesce in the timidity of our Saudi allies.

WEAKENING U.S. RESOLVE

Saudi sensibilities also appear to account for the fact that one Imad Mughniyah, of the Lebanese Party of God, is still free to operate in Beirut (a city which is, to be sure, under the political and military influence of Hafez al-Assad's Syria). American intelligence and law enforcement officials consider Mughniyah a suspect in the April 1983 bombing of the U.S. embassy in Beirut that killed 16 people; in the slaughter of 241 U.S. Marines in Beirut in October 1983; and in the June 1985 hijacking of TWA Flight 847, in which an American Marine was murdered. According to *The New York Times*, the FBI nearly arrested Mughniyah in 1995 when it learned that his flight was about to make a stopover in Saudi Arabia. But, rather than permit the arrest on their soil, the Saudis redirected the plane to Beirut. The Clinton administration sent Riyadh a strong letter of protest.

Meanwhile, the Clintonites have articulated a new policy toward Iran, based on the notion that the recent election of President Mohammed Khatami augurs a moderate turn in the direction not only of Iranian domestic politics but also of Iranian foreign policy. Whatever its other rationales, this policy shift may have signaled to Iran's hard-liners that terror has succeeded in weakening U.S. resolve, even as it gives them a new motivation—disrupting any U.S.-Khatami rapprochement—to strike.

The bombings in East Africa are yet another reminder that, even in the modern world, there is still such a thing as radical evil. There are certain people who kill Americans just because they believe it is the right thing to do—indeed, a blessed thing to do. Yet it bears repeating that the vast majority of those killed in these attacks on American targets were not Americans; indeed, *The New York Times* carried a picture of a Muslim funeral for one of the victims. (The religion and race of the victims were fortunately a matter of indifference to Israel, whose military rescue team was on the scene almost immediately, professionally taking charge of the search for survivors.)

The president and his foreign policy advisers often speak as if they appreciate the meaning of what national security adviser Sandy Berger last week duly labeled "unadulterated evil," but their policies and actions are not truly commensurate with their words. The threat of indictment does not strike fear in the hearts of those who plan attacks like those in East Africa—much less does it deter them. The only language international terrorists, and the nations that sponsor them, understand is the language of effective and appropriate force; yet force is precisely the instrument of national power with which the Clintonites are most uncomfortable. Meanwhile, out there, in the shadows, the plausible conviction spreads that you can attack American embassies with murderous results and pay no serious price.

A PRESIDENT IMPEACHED: BILL CLINTON AND THE LEWINSKY SCANDAL

WASHINGTON TIMES

On December 19, 1998, based on evidence presented by independent counsel Kenneth W. Starr, the U.S. House of Representatives voted to impeach President Bill Clinton for committing perjury and obstructing justice. Starr's report to Congress asserted that the president had lied under oath about a sexual relationship with White House intern Monica Lewinsky in a deposition given for the Paula Jones sexual harassment suit. It was also alleged that the president had obstructed justice by encouraging Lewinsky to lie about their relationship, concealing evidence, and interfering with Starr's investigation.

Once the House votes to impeach a president—concluding that his actions constitute "high crimes and misdemeanors"—the Senate must conduct a trial to determine whether the president should be removed from office. Clinton was acquitted of the impeachment charges by the Senate in February 1999, but the Lewinsky scandal and impeachment proceedings tarnished the president's reputation and diminished his stature as a world leader. In the following editorial, written one day prior to the House's vote for impeachment, the editors of the conservative *Washington Times* argue that the president's criminal conduct has delegitimized his presidency, leaving no doubt that he should be impeached.

Today marks only the second time in the history of the Republic that the House of Representatives will gather to debate whether to impeach a president. Sadly, it is a debate that will take place in the most poisonous atmosphere in memory. The debate would have been acrimonious in any case, but now that President Clinton has started dropping bombs on Iraq, the argument is no longer merely about presidential crimes and whether they meet the standards of impeachment. Members of the president's party now charge that any debate on impeachment is itself a high crime—the treasonous offense of giving aid and comfort to the enemy. This is the ugly and inexorable result of Mr. Clinton's tenure. This is the low and dangerous place to which the president's dishonesty has brought us. That is why there can be no doubt: President William Jefferson Clinton should be impeached.

LYING UNDER OATH: IMPEACHMENT ARTICLES I AND II

Four articles of impeachment will be presented today. They are not, however, all created equal.

"Article I. . . . William Jefferson Clinton willfully provided perjurious, false and misleading testimony [on August 17, 1998] to the grand jury concerning one or more of the following: (1) the nature and details of his relationship with a subordinate Government employee; (2) prior perjurious, false and misleading testimony he gave in a Federal civil rights action brought against him; (3) prior false and misleading statements he allowed his attorney to make to a Federal judge in that civil rights action; and (4) his corrupt efforts to influence the testimony of witnesses and to impede the discovery of evidence in that civil rights action. . . ."

It is obvious to any reasonable person that the president is guilty as charged. Mr. Clinton and his lawyers have lamely asserted that "details of his relationship with a subordinate" can never be known because it is a "he-said, she-said" situation. That doesn't wash. Caught in lie after lie, Mr. Clinton has only admitted to those things that were already proven. And where the president has yet to admit lying, he instead argues that he was only misleading people.

Then there are the specifics of the relationship. Monica Lewinsky's account of her encounters with Mr. Clinton may be sordid, but they have the detail and internal coherence one expects from truthful testimony. Her description of events also fits with contemporaneous accounts given to friends and therapists. If that weren't enough, there is the fact that Mr. Clinton's description of hands-off trysts is peculiar enough to insult credulity.

The president's men would have us dismiss these lies as mere trivialities. But the lies cannot be so easily shunted aside, having been told under oath to a federal grand jury. In any case, those lies were no mere quibbles about details. They were essential if Mr. Clinton was to maintain the ludicrous fiction that he had, strictly speaking, told the truth in his Paula Jones [sexual harassment suit] deposition. Mr. Clinton said he had no sex with Miss Lewinsky, and points to the convoluted definition [of sexual relations] for cover.

In February 1998 President Bill Clinton was acquitted of impeachment charges, however, his reputation had been permanently tarnished.

Mr. Clinton lied to the grand jury and did so in an effort to cover up lies he had already told under oath. That is why the lies to the grand jury were not about sex; they were about perjury. The president committed a crime in August in an effort to escape accountability for a crime he committed in January. The facts are clear and damning. Lawmakers should approve Article I.

"Article II. . . .(1) On December 23, 1997, William Jefferson Clinton, in sworn answers to written questions asked as part of a Federal civil rights action brought against him, willfully provided perjurious, false and misleading testimony. . . . (2) On January 17, 1998, William Jefferson Clinton swore under oath to tell the truth, the whole truth, and nothing but the truth in a deposition given as part of a Federal civil rights action brought against him. Contrary to that oath, William Jefferson Clinton willfully provided perjurious, false and misleading testimony. . . ."

Mr. Clinton lied under oath in the Paula Jones deposition. Various excuses, explanations and distractions have been offered in an effort to paper those lies over. None is even remotely persuasive. Mr. Clinton maintains that he never exactly lied, instead outsmarting Mrs. Jones' counsel with misleading and unhelpful, but true, responses. Not even the president's defenders stick with that story anymore. They have fallen back on the "Yes, but" defense. Yes, Mr. Clinton lied in the deposition, but it was just an effort to protect his family. Yes, Mr. Clinton lied in the deposition, but it was only a civil case. Yes, Mr. Clinton lied in the deposition, but that civil case was politically motivated, was thrown out and has since been settled. None of these caveats change the fact that Mr. Clinton lied under oath. The president committed perjury. It is an offense that disqualifies him from the high office he holds. Lawmakers should approve Article II.

OBSTRUCTING JUSTICE: IMPEACHMENT ARTICLES III AND IV

"Article III. William Jefferson Clinton . . . has prevented, obstructed, and impeded the administration of justice, and has to that end engaged personally, and through his subordinates and agents, in a course of conduct or scheme designed to delay, impede, cover up, and conceal the existence of evidence and testimony related to a Federal civil rights action brought against him. . . ."

The third article is a sort of grab-bag containing the various elements of the conspiracy Mr. Clinton wove in his effort to bamboozle the lawyers for Paula Jones. This article focuses on the scheme the president devised to keep his affair with Monica Lewinsky a secret. (1) He encouraged Miss Lewinsky to sign a false affidavit. (2) He encouraged Miss Lewinsky to give false testimony if she were deposed. (3) He organized the effort to recover gifts from Miss Lewinsky's, presents that had been subpoenaed as evidence in the Jones suit. He is responsible for [White House secretary] Betty Currie taking the gifts and hiding them under her bed. (4) He helped in a job search to keep

Miss Lewinsky silent. (5) He had his lawyer employ the false affidavit he had requested of Miss Lewinsky. (6) He coached potential witnesses in false testimony. (7) He lied to his aides so that they would (innocently) repeat the lies to a grand jury.

The conspiracy outlined in Article III is plausible and persuasive. But unlike Articles I and II, the evidence is not undeniably overwhelming. The article charges that Mr. Clinton encouraged Miss Lewinsky to lie in her affidavit, but Miss Lewinsky quite explicitly told the grand jury that Mr. Clinton never instructed her to lie. The same difficulty is posed with regard to the second charge of the article. The third charge in the article alleges that Mr. Clinton directed Mrs. Currie's gift-retrieving sortie. As with the first two charges of the article, there is conflicting testimony: Miss Lewinsky says that it is Mrs. Currie who called about the gifts; Mrs. Currie testified that it was the other way around. The fourth charge also suffers from the direct testimony of Miss Lewinsky, who insists that no one "promised" her a job for her silence. (Indeed, there is reason to believe that the notion of a job-for-silence quid pro quo originated with Linda Tripp.) The fifth charge is the most potent— but that is because it flows out of the devastating perjury charges in Articles I and II. The sixth and seventh charges allege that Mr. Clinton told copious lies to everyone around him in an effort to muddy the waters, an offense that is not in the same ball park with the lies spoken while under oath.

The House Judiciary Committee might have sorted out these discrepancies in testimony by calling Miss Lewinsky, Mrs. Currie and others to testify. Instead, much of the committee's time was wasted on the pedantry of historians and legal scholars. Even though it is reasonably apparent that Mr. Clinton engaged in an ad hoc conspiracy to obstruct justice, when it comes to impeachment, reasonably apparent is not good enough. The president's defenders warn against lowering the bar of impeachment by including offenses that are somehow less than "high crimes and misdemeanors." They are sorely mistaken if they think perjury is not a high crime. But they are correct that impeachment should not be invoked lightly. The way to respect the severity of the sanction is to demand that the evidence of the crime be more than compelling. Unless the House wants to develop and discover evidence that resolves the ambiguities in the evidence of a conspiracy, lawmakers should reject Article III.

"Article IV. . . . William Jefferson Clinton refused and failed to respond to certain written requests for admission and willfully made perjurious, false and misleading sworn statements in response to certain written requests for admission propounded to him as part of the impeachment inquiry authorized by the House of Representatives of the Congress of the United States. . . ."

Mr. Clinton's response to the 81 questions put to him by the Judiciary Committee was arrogant, smug and dishonest. The answers helped convince a majority of lawmakers that the president was neither contrite nor would ever be. The president's reply to the committee's query helped steel legislators' resolve; but it should not be a grounds, in and of itself, to remove Mr. Clinton. Presidents, in their role as the head of the executive branch of government, should have room to spar with the legislative branch. Lawmakers, even in the context of impeaching Mr. Clinton, can show their deference to proper presidential power by overlooking the insult delivered to them in the president's answers. In any case, those lies were merely repetitions of the lies already underpinning Articles I and II. Lawmakers should reject the redundant Article IV.

PROTECTING THE CONSTITUTION, SETTLING QUESTIONS

The president says he is willing to accept some sort of punishment, be it a rebuke, censure or perhaps a sizable fine. The advocates for censure say his transgressions do warrant punishment, but not impeachment. The president's apologists continue their quest for "the proper proportional punishment," a quest rooted in a fundamental mistake about the Constitution. They view impeachment as a form of punishment—indeed, they regularly refer to it as a political death sentence. Crimes that fall short of the necessity of jail time are often dealt with by a fine and a stern judicial talking-to: shouldn't Congress do the political equivalent in this case? The answer is No. The whole notion that the president should be punished is mistaken. It is not the business of Congress to punish anyone for anything. But it is the business of Congress to protect the Constitution from a president who commits felonies.

Impeachment is about the presidency; its purpose is to defend the honor and dignity of the office; its purpose is to check abuses of power; and most of all, its purpose is to protect the nation from a president whose contempt for the Constitution makes him unfit. Alas, Mr. Clinton is such a man.

The president's partisans on Capitol Hill argue there should be no debate on impeachment while the nation is engaged in hostilities. Sadly, their arguments lend credence to the suspicion that the bombing in Iraq was begun in an effort to delay the president's day of reckoning. To the contrary, the Democrats' claim only amplifies the reasons for holding a vote on impeachment. If a president is unfit to hold the office, then he is unfit to put the lives of brave warriors at risk. By the timing of his strike at Saddam Hussein, Mr. Clinton has raised the question of the legitimacy of his command. By his criminal dishonesty, Mr. Clinton has raised the question of the legitimacy of his presidency. The questions must be settled. They must be settled now.

1999–2001: Youth Violence, an Election Dispute, and Fleeting Dot-Coms

CHAPTER 3

THE COLUMBINE MASSACRE

DALE ANEMA

In the late 1990s, deadly shootings at schools across the country involving perpetrators as young as eleven years old shocked the nation. Between February 1997 and May 1998, thirteen students and teachers were killed and scores more wounded in five separate school shootings. Americans, however, were unprepared for the tragedy that unfolded at Columbine High School in Littleton, Colorado, on April 20, 1999. Two students armed with guns and homemade bombs stormed the school, killing twelve students and a teacher and wounding twenty-three before taking their own lives.

The Columbine massacre raised troubling questions about the forces in American culture that compel some children to act out their anger with deadly violence. The often ruthless social hierarchy of high school was cited as one possible cause. The shooters, seventeen-year-old Dylan Klebold and eighteen-year-old Eric Harris, had considered themselves social outcasts at the high school and had targeted athletes and preppies in their assault. Easy access to guns, violent rock lyrics, and video games were also blamed for the shootings. In the following recollection of the events of April 20, Dale Anema, the father of a Columbine student, describes the desperate wait for news of his son's whereabouts. Anema expresses anger at the media, which he says used the tragedy to promote an agenda of gun control and big government solutions to violence. The author is a businessman who travels the West from his home in Colorado.

From "A Father at Columbine High," by Dale Anema, *American Enterprise*, September 1999. Copyright © 1999 by American Enterprise Institute for Public Policy Research. Reprinted with permission.

On a business trip to Trinidad, Colorado, I'm driving to the local Pizza Hut a few minutes after noon, when suddenly the radio's regular programming is interrupted by a news bulletin: Two or three gunmen with hand grenades and/or pipe bombs are attacking Columbine High School— where my son Nathan attends.

FRANTIC PHONE CALLS

I pull over and call my wife, Roxane, on a payphone. She's already heard from most of Nathan's friends, but not from Nathan. One friend, Tyler, says Nathan was in the crowd ahead of him running out of the cafeteria. Tyler says the kid next to him was shot and went down, and a bullet whizzed by his head. He's sure Nathan got out, but hasn't seen him since.

Roxane and I frantically call all of Nathan's close friends. No one except Tyler has seen him since the gunfire erupted. Roxane rushes in the car to the three locations where they're holding the kids who've escaped so far. Nathan is nowhere to be found. The news says the shooters are targeting minorities and athletes. Nathan, though only a freshmen, is in very good shape and obviously an athlete. We're frantic. I don't want to be away from the phone and television for the three-hour drive home. The minutes seem like hours. By 1:15 we are sure Nathan is in the building.

Just this morning I was thinking how lucky I am that both the kids are getting As, are superior athletes, and are very sweet and caring. Suddenly their grades and athletic prowess seem totally meaningless. I think of the times when Nathan, as young as three, defended friends against older bullies. I pray Nathan hasn't done something stupid. I have often joked with him that no one can run faster than a bullet. I hope he remembers that.

I pray for the best but accept the reality that there is a good chance Nathan is dead. Recently I've worried about his having to go to a protracted war in [the former] Yugoslavia, but maybe he was gunned down in school. What would I do? He is far better than I deserve, and now he may be gone.

Judy Shipman, our next-door neighbor, has come over to coordinate the calls. Roxane and I are still phoning everyone we can think of, but we're beginning to lose hope. The television is reporting many bodies in the school. I bark at Roxane that she should revisit the holding sites and drive around the police lines to see if Nathan is there observing things. I call back a few minutes later and talk to Judy. She says Nathan is very considerate and would have called home if he could. I both love her and hate her for saying that.

Each of the past five summers Nathan and I have climbed two or three 14,000-foot peaks. I'm wondering if he'd like to have his ashes scattered over one of them. I pray I'll be able to carry on for his mother and sister.

Nathan has his learners permit and a few weeks ago he was driving to a soccer game. I was in the passenger seat and two of his teammates were in the back, chattering away with him. I wanted to be one of the guys and thought hard for something interesting to say. Waiting until a lull in the conversation, I repeated something amusing I'd heard on Paul Harvey. His friends ignored me and talked loudly, but Nathan said, "Hey guys, listen; this is really funny." I repeated the joke and they all laughed. Now who will listen to see if I have anything worth hearing?

Just after 3:00, I am watching the news. A telephoto shot from a helicopter shows the latest group of students a SWAT team is leading from the building. The figures are about the size of bees, but one seems to run like Nathan and has a red backpack like his. I go limp. The figures are too small to tell anything. The phone rings; it's Roxane. She's been watching a channel with a closer view of the kids—it was definitely Nathan!

Praise the Lord! I feel heartsick for the parents of the deceased, but my son is alive! I run down the motel walkway to tell a guy I hardly know that my son is alive, he was in Columbine High School but is alive and well! The guy has been watching a movie and at first doesn't know what I'm talking about. I don't care: I have to tell somebody.

Nathan calls Roxane 20 minutes later from a holding area. She says he is very calm. The police keep him for two and a half more hours, questioning him and making him write down everything he saw.

I talk to him for about an hour as soon as he gets home. He gives an account of what he saw in a calm, precise manner. Roxane and I decide it would be best for him to spend as much time as possible with his school friends for the next several days. He spends that night and the next day with several of his closest pals.

THE AFTERMATH: MEDIA HYPE AND FINGER-POINTING

The next week Nathan spends mornings and nights with different groups of friends and the afternoons with us. His friends' parents agree that the kids need to spend as much time together as they want. Trying not to impose my prejudice against therapists, I ask Nathan a couple of times if he'd like to have counseling sessions. He looks askance and says, "Thank you, but I think that would do much more harm than good."

Before the shootings, Nathan would joke around when I hug him and pull away from me after a few seconds. These days he eagerly hugs back. If he doesn't know exactly where his mom or sister are, he anxiously asks, "Where's Mom?" "Where's Paige?"

The community is in shock. Families and neighbors huddle together and, in my neighborhood at least, avoid the media events as much as possible. Everyone has some connection with at least one victim. Dazed, we talk to each other in low tones on the sidewalk or at the store. Sympathy for the victims' families floods us, but everyone is dumbfounded by the actions of the police. Why did they wait three and a half hours to get the kids out? Why did they leave the wounded teacher, Dave Sanders, the only real hero during the assault, inside to die while they got the kids out? The more we learn, the more incredulous we become. This is a neighborhood of conservatives, staunch supporters of law enforcement, but everyone I talk to is stunned by the indifference or incompetence of our supposed protectors.

The Columbine High School district is entirely in unincorporated Jefferson County. Some of us now wonder if we should have incorporated into a city government. Perhaps a city police department would be better defenders than a county sheriff's office? But we quickly dismiss the thought: There were police and SWAT teams from several area forces. One was as bad as the other. In fact, the SWAT teams are now referred to as SQUAT teams. Giving the police every benefit of doubt, we can find no Braveheart in the bunch.

Everyone I talk to also finds the media hype contemptible. There are constant interviews with Wellington Webb, the mayor of Denver, and with the mayor of Littleton. What do they have to do with anything? The attempts by some reporters to wheedle the kids and the victims' parents into calling for more counselors or more gun control are particularly despicable.

Two pending gun bills are immediately dropped by the Colorado legislature. One is a proposal to make it easier for law-abiding citizens to carry concealed weapons; the other is a measure to prohibit municipalities from suing gun manufacturers. I wonder: If two crazy hoodlums can walk into a "gun-free" zone full of our kids, and the police are totally incapable of defending the children, why would anyone want to make it harder for law-abiding adults to defend themselves and others?

The cultural elite is using our own tragedy to thrash us soundly. Televisions and newspapers echo with the causes of the carnage, all failures of us Colorodans: Lack of gun control, insufficient number of mental health workers, meanness of jocks. The cultural elite sense this is a golden opportunity, much like the Oklahoma City bombing. They now have the upper hand and can whittle away at the First and Second Amendments. After all, if they could control the content of movies and video games, they could better brainwash our youth. And if all kids had to periodically see government mental health workers, think what influence they would have! Not to mention that the elites, or at least many of their friends, would have a lot more well-paying government jobs.

And so the choruses of trendy ideas ring out: Gun rights are indefensible in the wake of slaughter. Promoting athletics in schools is archaic; it increases testosterone, adrenaline, and self-confidence, making jocks more independent and less likely to submit to community goals. Besides, it's unfair that some kids are naturally more athletic than others. (The shooters are said to be targeting athletes and minorities, but the media utterly separate those groups: The minorities are lambs, the athletes, goats.)

The social conservatives have been typically silent in response. The National Rifle Association is successfully browbeaten into shortening their annual convention in Denver to one day. Of course, nobody on TV mentions that perhaps gun-free zones are potential magnets to crazed killers, or that concealed-carry laws have invariably lowered crime rates everywhere they've been tried. Or that earlier school shootings have in fact been stopped by armed citizens, long before police arrived.

I don't hear any call for private groups to organize national boycotts of companies that produce and advertise smut and senseless violence; only governmental solutions are being suggested. Even some conservative leaders seem to think all efforts must come from the federal government, which bans even the mention of God in our schools, passes out condoms to our kids, and refuses to enforce existing gun laws. Certainly no one has voiced the possibility that shooter Eric Harris's watching the nightly bombing of Yugoslavia might have added to his aggression.

Other undiscussed angles on the horror: A psychiatrist prescribed an anti-depressant for Harris. Did the drug or withdrawal from it increase Harris's sense of isolation or anger? Could a mental health worker have played some part in this carnage? On the other hand, do athletic programs perhaps increase self-reliance and camaraderie, and offer incentives to do better academically? Apparently this is not the time to talk about such possibilities.

My neighbors and I feel the shooters' parents were unbelievably negligent, but most of our comments place much blame on government actions: banning prayer and the Ten Commandments in schools, having a President devoid of morality, no parental choice or control of schools, prohibitions on expulsions of bad kids, incompetence and indifference by the police and school administrators in dealing with the would-be killers.

We're all very careful not to discuss our views of the police in front of the kids, so as not to make them more fearful. A bogus copycat e-mail is circulating, warning there will be more carnage at Chatfield High School where the Columbine students are to finish the school year. Nathan is a bit leery. I tell him because of what happened it will be the safest school in the world. He laughs nervously and says, "Yeah, right. The cops couldn't keep armed kindergartners out of the building."

Our daughter Paige is in sixth grade at a charter school. Since that fateful Tuesday she has been badgering Roxane to homeschool her next year. She's scared of some very disruptive kids in her class whom the school is not legally permitted to expel. We haven't made a final decision, but are leaning toward granting her request.

I hear one commentator say, "Well, the people of Littleton have a different view of guns now." I don't know what the people of Littleton think, but the people in my neighborhood think that overbearing government controls are the problem, not part of the solution. The contempt my family feels for the posturing of President Clinton and Vice-President Gore is vehemently echoed by many. Even some of my most moderate neighbors are livid.

The media parades one psychological expert after another saying the shooters were as much victims as anyone—they were bullied and just snapped. Somehow these experts are also transferring the racism of the shooters onto the entire student body, which dared to "ostracize" the murderers. This really up-

sets Nathan. Roxane, the most easygoing person I know, is beside herself: The shooters were neo-Nazis at best. They chose to
be different. They were largely ignored by their classmates because they were hateful racists who created their own weird
subculture, which had no appeal to normal kids.

Nathan and his friends seem to be doing fine. They are very
sad over their fallen comrades and talk with surprising openness about how their friends' deaths won't be forgotten, how
the memory of their friends will make them strive harder to
make a positive difference in the world.

All of our lives have been disrupted by the actions of two very
sick hoodlums, the incompetence of local government, and in-
trusive, mindless babble from outside politicians, analysts, and
reporters. Our little cul-de-sac has been very tight knit since we
moved in 11 years ago, but nothing like the way it is now. We're
under siege in many ways. The gentleness shared is impossible
to describe—we love each other for our tears. The deaths of the
children won't be for naught; at least not on our block.

THE DEATH OF JOHN F. KENNEDY JR.

NEAL GABLER

In mid-July 1999, a thirty-six-year-old John F. Kennedy Jr. was killed while piloting a small private aircraft to the island of Martha's Vineyard off the Massachusetts coast. His wife, Carolyn, and his sister-in-law Lauren were also killed. JFK Jr. was the most famous living member of the Kennedy political dynasty. Millions of Americans remembered watching an infant "John-John" salute the casket of his father, who served as president from 1961 until his assassination in 1963. As a result, JFK Jr. grew up entirely in the public spotlight. The media were fascinated with JFK Jr.'s life and good looks, and many observers hoped that one day he would continue his father's political legacy and run for office. Undecided about a political career at the time of his death, Kennedy worked as editor of the political magazine *George*, which he had launched in 1995.

It took nearly a week for the search conducted by the coast guard and the navy to locate the plane's wreckage and the three bodies. During that time, media coverage of the event was enormous, and the story dominated newspaper headlines and television newscasts. Weeks later, a minor backlash against the excessive coverage ensued, with critics questioning why the death of a young man, albeit a Kennedy, had elicited so much attention. In the following essay, Neal Gabler explains that in the midst of the media frenzy, millions of Americans were profoundly affected by JFK Jr.'s death. According to Gabler, Americans appreciated the sense of dignity and humility that JFK Jr. exhibited in the midst of a life that compelled him to play the role of celebrity from birth. Neal Gabler is the author of *Life the Movie: How Entertainment Conquered Reality.*

The tragedy that befell John F. Kennedy Jr., his wife, Carolyn, and her sister Lauren last week in the waters off Martha's Vineyard seemed eerily familiar—and not just because the alleged Kennedy family curse had descended yet again. It seemed familiar because the media used the occasion to reprise their saturation coverage of terrible events as different as the Columbine High School massacre and Princess Diana's death. Once again, we got the correspondents keeping watch over the family, taking the pulse of the public, and staking out the spontaneously erected memorial with its votive offerings. We got experts parsing the incident with the assiduousness of Talmudic scholars, the talking heads delivering encomiums, the proffered condolences and prayers from the first family, the solemn TV anchors groping for appropriately sententious expressions of sorrow. Only the names and places had changed.

Some Holocaust historians have argued that any representation of the Shoah necessarily trivializes the horror and that it is better left unrepresented, hence literally unimaginable. One might make the same case here: that reducing a public tragedy to a series of media conventions, a special-event TV extravaganza, similarly trivializes the event and converts the viewers, whether they realize it or not and whether they like it or not, into actors mourning for the cameras as part of a global festival of grief.

A DEATH THAT AFFECTED MILLIONS

Still, the grief is no less real for the fact that it has been routinized, and I am sure that, if pressed, the media chiefs would claim that they provided this sort of wall-to-wall coverage precisely because the public needed a ritual through which to channel its pain. They may be right. JFK Jr.'s death clearly affected many Americans, myself included, in ways that seem profound and mysterious. Why he elicited these feelings, beyond the tragedy of a life cut short long before fruition and of a family repeatedly afflicted, is a question worth pondering—a question whose answer may tell us as much about ourselves as about JFK Jr.

To understand our reaction to him one must first understand that, inasmuch as he was a Kennedy, his name enabled him to enter another, even more powerful fraternity than the Irish

Catholic political dynasty into which he was born: celebrity. At birth he was immediately dragooned into that national repertory company of the famous, and, like each of its members, he enacted an ongoing saga for us, recorded in the media. His education, his romances, his career plans, his bar exams, his designation by *People* magazine as the "sexiest man alive," and his marriage to Carolyn Bessette were all scenes for our viewing pleasure. Or, put another way, his life had become a movie, and he had become its star.

Moreover, the continuity of the movie over nearly four decades created for the public a sense of familiarity with its protagonist that was practically, well, familial. Like soap opera aficionados who weep at soap weddings and keen at soap funerals, the nation watched JFK Jr.'s own soap opera, suffered his tragedies, and relished his successes. In effect, by making his life so public, the media had, despite his own resistance, made him an intimate—"America's son," as Kennedy biographer Ed Klein referred to him on CNN's "Larry King Live."

As part of the much-loved Kennedy family, John F. Kennedy Jr., (far left), spent his entire life in the public spotlight.

But to see JFK Jr. as a familiar celebrity commodity does not quite do justice to the Jungian force of his celebrity. The Greeks long ago appreciated the power of heroes to transmit values that could help one contend with the world. In Homeric times, myth was deemed the best vehicle to perform this function because life itself was thought to be too arbitrary, too artless. One of the things we have learned to do in this century, courtesy of celebrity journalism, is to take the arbitrariness of life and treat it as art. Thus the lives of celebrities—their affairs, divorces, illnesses, addictions, peccadilloes, binges, and epiphanies—become the modern equivalents of epics. And celebrities, more often than not, are the modern-day equivalents of mythic heroes.

But they are heroes in a very special sense. What classical heroes did was demonstrate man's possibilities and limitations. Joseph Campbell, in his famous study of cross-cultural myths, *The Hero with a Thousand Faces,* describes just how this process works by identifying three basic stages through which virtually all mythic heroes pass. They emerge from ordinary reality, enter a wondrous world where they undergo a series of trials, and then, having been transformed by the experience, they return to tell us what they have learned, making their heroism a function of both their deeds and their gifts to us. The hero, then, has to negotiate between the ordinary and the godly, the temporal and the otherworldly, keeping a foot in each camp so that he can show us how to adapt ourselves to a world that is half spiritual, half material—a world of wonder but also of pain.

This is almost exactly what celebrities like JFK Jr. do in contemporary culture. They emerge from our quotidian reality; they survive the celebrity maelstrom of romance, drugs, infidelity, media scrutiny, et al. into which they are plunged; and then they return, via the media, to tell us what they have learned there—usually the pacifying bromide that the benefits of celebrity are nothing compared to the benefactions of a good family, good work, and knowing who you really are. As a result, they provide us with something important, perhaps even necessary. They give us the vicarious thrill of the divine while reinforcing our sense of self-worth.

If this, in our culture, is an important job, it is also a tenuous one. Half god, half man, the celebrity, like the hero, is always poised between our identification with him, which makes him one of us, and our idolatry of him, which makes him better than we. If he lists too far in either direction, he loses his Olympian perch: too far toward the godly and we must reel him back in; too far toward the ordinary and we lose interest. Thus the constant push and pull between Oprah Winfrey's huge salary and her struggles with her weight, between Julia Roberts's great beauty and her botched romances, between Elizabeth Taylor's fame and her constant illnesses. In fact, the fascination most celebrities hold for us is the tension between these halves that becomes the plot points in their life movies.

LIFE AT THE JUNCTION OF CELEBRITY AND POLITICS

For JFK Jr., the extremes were indeed extreme—the promise of his life and the tragedy of his death. Unlike most celebrities, he was born of gods—the son of an improbable marriage between the Apollo and Aphrodite of American politics and the grandson of the Zeus and Hera of twentieth-century America, Joseph and Rose Kennedy. Hubris, the bane of the classical hero and the occupational hazard of the modern celebrity, was in his blood, though in the case of the Kennedys the sense of ease and entitlement, the feeling that there were absolutely no limits to their dreams, presented itself less often as overbearing arrogance than as confident charm.

One suspects JFK Jr. couldn't possibly have imagined that he wouldn't be able to fly safely through blackest night. Yet, while this utterly American and decidedly underweening pride was a major factor in the Kennedy appeal, it was also an integral part of their drama—yin and yang all wrapped up in one package. Like Icarus, the Kennedys always seem to be flying close to the sun, teasing fate. And, watching them, we have always been caught up in the suspense of their enterprise. As they rise, they carry us with them to the highest highs until mortality pulls them back to earth and brings us to our lowest lows. It is as if the entire Kennedy family is a memento mori.

What made JFK Jr. so captivating was that he lived within this hubris, but what made him so endearing was that he clearly understood celebrity and the role he was compelled to play. From his father, he seemed to have inherited or intuited a kind of ironic detachment that let him survey the distance between the JFK Jr. of the media and the JFK Jr. of real life. He seemed to take pleasure in the idea that the former bore so little resemblance to the latter, and he was said to be honestly self-effacing, even self-deprecating, qualities not generally attributed to celebrities.

From his mother, JFK Jr. seemed to have been imbued not only with dignity at a time when many other celebrities were retailing their lives for profit, but also with a sense of the fatuousness of the whole celebrity circus. He was bemused by the idea that his life was a movie and that he was its star. That is the expression one sees in his photos: the look of barely stifled astonishment at the idiocy of his own celebrity. And it is the ironic metaphor of his death as well. A man who so clearly had his bearings in life most likely died by losing his bearings in the air.

His legacy, *George* magazine, is also his sly commentary on the public lust for celebrity. What JFK Jr. understood from his father's life and from his own was that even the sacrosanct church of politics had become another celebrity showcase, that politics was essentially entertainment and that what the electorate wanted was not ideology or policy but excitement. In short, he established *George* at the very junction where he himself lived since the day he was born—the junction of celebrity and politics.

If this makes JFK Jr. the first postmodernist politico in America, the first to discover that politics is inseparable from popular culture, it is certainly apt. He was not, in the old Kennedy mold, a political hero come to smite social ills. He was a famous young man who graciously accepted center stage without ever forgetting it was a performance we wanted and a performance he was, however reluctantly, obligated to give.

WOODSTOCK '99: PEACE AND LOVE REPLACED BY VIOLENCE

LARRY FLICK ET AL.

Thirty years after the original Woodstock festival, legendary for its music and peaceful crowd, Woodstock '99 was held in late July in Rome, New York, drawing 200,000 young people for three days of rock music. Unlike its predecessor, Woodstock '99 was marred by violence and sexual assaults against women. Rioting erupted on the last night of the festival, as mobs set fires, looted concession stands, and vandalized vehicles. Following the event, allegations arose that several women had been raped in the "mosh pit" near the front of the stage. Some participants argued that the crowd, enduring intense summer heat, had grown irritated with the overpriced food and water and unsanitary conditions. Other observers asserted that the festival's organizers had erred in booking too many hard rock acts, encouraging an atmosphere of macho aggression. In the following article, Larry Flick and colleagues interview performers and the festival's organizers to determine why Woodstock '99 deteriorated into violence. Flick is a reporter for *Billboard* magazine.

From "In Woodstock's Wake. Hard Questions," by Larry Flick, Carla Hay, Melinda Newman, and Chris Morris, *Billboard,* August 14, 1999. Copyright © 1999 by BPI Communications. Reprinted with permission.

Howevever else it's ultimately remembered, this year's
edition of Woodstock will be viewed through the long
lens of history as a case study of some of the baser instincts within popular culture and human nature, circa the century's close.

Feeding off of one another, these instincts bubbled up under
a blazing sun July 23–25 in Rome, New York, scarring what was
planned as a 30th anniversary celebration of the landmark 1969
festival of peace, love, and music. The sad triumvirate marking
Woodstock '99 will be allegations of rape, looting, and serious
reflection on just what went wrong—and what larger lessons
might be taken from the fallout.

TOUGH QUESTIONS LINGER

"There are certainly things that I and my partners would like to
go back and redo," says John Scher, who co-produced the event
with Michael Lang and Ossie Kilkenny. "We will systematically
go through every single problem, and to the degree that you can
fix it after the fact and make it better, we will."

Performer Sheryl Crow, veteran of Woodstock '94, left the '99
event with some tough questions. "I don't know if these kids
haven't been raised to have pride in themselves, but I've just
never seen that kind of anger [in an audience]. I think the implications of it are more than it just being about kids coming together for the weekend for a rock show. I think it's how they feel
about their situation, and my question is, 'What made them so
mad?' I just thought it was very demoralizing. I would absolutely not play Woodstock again."

Most who were in attendance argue that it was the combination of assorted elements that made for a pressure-cooker-like
environment—some out of the promoters' control, such as excessive heat and widespread drug and alcohol use mixed with
expensive food and drink prices and the aggressive nature of
some of the performers.

These elements contributed to what some describe as an "otherworldly" atmosphere wherein seemingly anything could—and
did— happen. The event was tainted by random acts of violence
that included at least four alleged rapes and a wild looting spree
sparked by a series of fires set by 200 to 500 members of the estimated audience of 200,000. Additionally, the crowd grew inordi-
nately rowdy during Limp Bizkit's July 24 set and began tearing
apart the wooden fence surrounding the mixing platform.

"When you get a crowd of 200,000 people together, some of them will let their morals slip—and they'll slip into an anonymity of numbers," says Dave Sirulnick, the executive producer of MTV's on-site coverage of Woodstock '99. "In a scenario like this, you're likely to have a 22-year-old kid do something he might not normally."

"It was like the rules of the real world went out the window," says festival attendee Daniel Levine, 22, a college student from Buffalo, N.Y. "After a while, there was a 'mob rules' mentality. My friends and I got knocked around a little by a bunch of guys who were just ranting around, acting wacked just because they felt like they could get away with it."

Lee Cole, 24, another college student from Buffalo, agrees. "The longer we were there, the crazier people got. It didn't help that there was no escape from the heat. Even for four bucks, you couldn't get a cold bottle of water. Everything was baking hot. I think even the quietest guy in the world would go a little nuts in a scene like that."

MISOGYNY AND SEXUAL ASSAULTS

In the end, however, an overriding tone of misogyny—and the four sexual assaults reported to authorities by press time in connection with Woodstock '99—is what leaves the ugliest aftertaste of the event.

After leaving the festival, Crow continued to watch some of the pay-per-view footage and was disturbed by much of what she saw. "The pay-per-view cameras were on the naked women three-fourths of the time and only showing music one-fourth of the time," she says. "I've never watched TV and saw so many women completely nude and dancing in front of the camera."

Given what she witnessed, Crow says the four charges of alleged sexual assault "seems like a low number. There were topless girls on guys' shoulders who were constantly being groped. These kids were out of control."

While Crow says she felt a sense of misogyny coming from the audience, "I also had a sense of conflicting feelings. You had these women who were being groped, and they were doing nothing to stop it. And you had women, porn-shaved, dancing for the camera. . . . The message that was coming across in the music was self-loathing, and that's what the kids were there to hear. And I felt like I was a fish out of water. . . . From watching on TV, I kept thinking there had to be deaths and rapes, and if there were only four [rapes], that's incredible."

One manager of an act that performed at Woodstock says, "I couldn't wait to get out of there.

He says that the kind of lawlessness witnessed at the festival was understandable when many state troopers patrolling the

Unlike its peaceful predecessor, Woodstock '99 was characterized by violence and sexual assaults against women.

site were having their pictures taken with topless or nude women, referring to media reports about such things.

"If you've got cops saying [that kind of behavior is] OK, pretty soon we're base animals," the manager says. "You throw alcohol and drugs on top of that, you've got a fucking recipe for disaster. . . . Dude, it's 'Lord Of The Flies.' It's a B.F. Skinner experiment in survival of the fittest."

He says he saw widespread instances of mistreatment of women: "Chicks were just getting fucking thrashed. I've never seen girls at such a disadvantage. I've never seen a situation where girls should be afraid. It was just gnarly. Can you imagine being a fucking girl in all that? Un-fucking-believable!"

For attendee Karen Marcello, 22, personal safety became a key issue by the event's second day. "Guys, in general, were getting real pushy to girls who were alone," she says. "I was afraid to leave my cluster of friends for more than a few minutes at a time."

Performer Kid Rock acknowledges that women are "not always treated the way they should" at events like Woodstock— or at concerts in general.

"The guys just don't always show the kind of respect they should," he says. "The ladies will show their breasts, in keeping with the free spirit of our shows, and the guys will get out of control and start grabbing them, which is not at all cool."

He adds, "I've started having to yell from the stage, 'Don't grab the chicks.' If a girl wants to walk around naked, she should be able to do so without some idiot treating her like a rag."

Everclear's Art Alexakis adds that he saw no performers condoning or egging on assaults. "Do I think anyone spurred on the rapes? Absolutely not. I didn't see anyone from any band trying to get anyone violent. Did I see anyone saying anything to the point of stepping over the line? Absolutely not. If they did, I'd be ripping their throats out, literally and figuratively."

FROM THE STAGE: AN AGGRESSIVE SITUATION

"I'm embarrassed for my generation that [the violence] happened," says Scott Stapp, lead singer of Creed, which was the second-to-last act on the Woodstock '99 main stage. "We've become a barbaric society, and the violence was so unnecessary, and it made no sense at all. It's sad to think that people had to ruin the festival for others."

Crow says her stage experience was so bad that "within the

second song, I thought about walking off. I've never been in a situation where people were throwing mud and fecal matter from the latrines at the stage. It was happening to everybody, not just me. People were out there just flipping me off, I thought, 'Let me get off this stage so these kids can see DMX and Offspring,' but they treated them the same way."

Remarking on a picture she saw of festival opener James Brown standing onstage holding a clump of mud that had been tossed at him, Crow says she thinks that the crowd possibly arrived angry and was further riled by heat, the difficulty some people had in getting water, and "probably some drugs."

Crow says the music "exacerbated" the aggressive situation, "but I don't think the music is to blame. I think it's just the state these kids are in."

For many bands, playing the festival was a positive experience. Godsmack vocalist Sully Erna says the vibe was all good from the stage. "We felt a very positive intensity" says Erna. "The audience was aggressive but not out to harm anyone."

Collective Soul played at both Woodstock '94 and '99. According to the band's guitarist, Dean Roland, Woodstock '99 was more organized. "It seemed more laid-back this year and more organized internally" he says. "We really enjoyed it."

He also says that compared with some of the band's other gigs this year—including one at which lead singer Ed Roland was knocked out onstage after someone threw a lighter at him—the audience was "way more attentive than I thought they'd be. We were really pleased with the audience. I will say I've never seen quite that many breasts. We started calling it Breastfest."

Tony Park, lead singer of Pushmonkey says that during his Sunday-evening set, he and his band-mates "didn't feel threatened at all." However, he adds that as he strolled the grounds during the Red Hot Chili Peppers' set, "I felt a little more threatened. It was basically like I was in a landfill: mud, trash, vomit, urine, piles of stuff."

Pushmonkey came straight to Woodstock from Ozzfest, where, Park says, crowds knew how to behave. "I respect the Ozzfest crowds," he says. "They have pit etiquette. You can tell they take care of each other, and that's something that I didn't see at Woodstock. I saw people doing mean things and obnoxious things: just debauchery, sweat, and flesh. It felt very evil."

Slotting one aggressive band after the next on Saturday night may not have been the smartest move, says Park. "If you take the Woodstock of the '60s," he says, "there was a lot of hippie chill-out. Smoke some weed, relax. But this is a modern world, and this is an aggressive world. And to try to apply some of the ideals to what we have now in our world is a risky situation at best. You didn't have mosh pits in the '60s. It's crazy now."

TOO MUCH?

Looking back, event organizer Scher concedes that perhaps he shouldn't have programmed Saturday night as he did. The night featured Limp Bizkit, Rage Against The Machine, and Metallica.

"I got a little too hung up, too excited, about what I'm calling the battle of the bands," he says. "In hindsight, I did take into account that they'd play off each other, but I didn't take into account how that would affect the audience."

Scher says he watched the first half-hour of the Limp Bizkit set before getting called away to attend to other matters. "I wasn't there when people started tearing stuff down," he says. "I got called on the radio, and by the time I got back [to the stage], it was resolved."

Scher says he was told that Limp Bizkit's Fred Durst tried to say something to the crowd members to calm them, but the audience didn't hear because the public-address system had been momentarily turned off.

"Some wayward fans started to dismantle some of the wooden barricades that surrounded the mixing position, and it scared the [sound company's] technician. And for some reason I'm still not clear on, he decided to turn off the P.A. By the time I got there, the P.A. was up, and they were playing again. It was probably off a minute or so, but it was off at a critical time."

Jeff Kwatinetz, manager of Limp Bizkit, declined to be interviewed for this story.

Following Limp Bizkit's performance, Scher says, he had a conversation with Rage Against The Machine's Zack de la Rocha. "There's no question that we needed to do something," Scher says. "Limp Bizkit finished their show, and the audience was unquestionably in a state of arousal. I had a very positive conversation with Zack. He was incredibly concerned. He wanted to know what I and our security people felt the situation was. We said it was a situation that needed to be brought down a level, so we let the set change go on a little bit longer than we had done earlier.

"We all believed the intensity quieted down a bit," Scher continues. "Zack said, 'Let me measure the situation when I get out there. I don't want anyone to get hurt.' I think he acted responsibly. He was prepared to talk to the audience if they needed a talking-to. By the time his set was under way it was back under control."

Scher feels that the evening was handled well, given the circumstances. "At no point did I feel like we needed to pull the plug on the show; that was never discussed. Although we might have walked to the edge during the Limp Bizkit set, I think everybody backed away. I think we might have had a different strategy if Zack hadn't been as responsible. I believe with the knowledge that I have now, the acts acted as responsibly as they could have."

Kid Rock adds, "There was a sense among the bands that I saw that we each have a responsibility to the kids. If you see shit going down, you have to acknowledge it from the stage and tell 'em to knock it off."

For Peter Mensch, co-manager of participating acts Metallica, the Bruce Hornsby Group, and the Red Hot Chili Peppers, the Woodstock crowd never seemed particularly menacing or out of hand.

"I watched a little bit of Limp Bizkit and Rage Against The Machine, and it was mostly guys; there were a few women there," he says. "I didn't have any concerns. I didn't feel that in any way, shape, or form that people in the front of the stage were being overcrowded. Nothing in the least struck me as being dangerous."

Although he remembers seeing one bonfire while the Chili Peppers were onstage on Sunday he says that by the time the other fires broke out, "we had left the building. The other stuff [fires, looting] just doesn't make any sense to me."

He also says that the fuss over the aggressive nature of the bands playing Saturday night is pointless and that the music had nothing to do with people's actions. "If after a show of Jewel, Creed, and Red Hot Chili Peppers people decide to break things, how can you say it's the music?"

TAKING RESPONSIBILITY

Indeed, most of the artists involved place the blame of the violence squarely on the attendees who committed it, not the music.

"People better not blame it on the music," says Godsmack's

Erna. "I think it's very weak what the people did. It's a shame that people don't know how to have a good time and party anymore without tearing stuff down. I saw some interviews on TV where people were saying they had lousy campsites and were starved for water, and they're charging $5 for a hot dog. [According to Scher, hot dogs were $3.] It seemed like tension was just building up and just exploding toward the end of the weekend. But if you're having such a bad time, just leave. Go home; take a shower. There's no reason to be destructive."

Alexakis believes that it was simply a mindless segment of the festival population that spawned the violence and lawlessness, rather than any combination of factors present at the site.

"When you get that many people out in the sun, pissed off, no sunscreen, burned badly paying $4 for a bottle of water—that's still no reason to loot," he says. "People wanted to be lazy, and you get that mob-rules mentality when you get together people who don't want to think."

At one point during the Saturday-night show, MTV's crew and on-air personalities had to retreat from the 16-foot tower from which they were broadcasting due to what Sirulnick describes as a "shower of objects hurled at us by the crowd."

He adds, "People went berserk. And there we were, right in the middle of a field. We became a target. No one was hurt, but it was scary."

Two weeks after the festival, Scher says that he hasn't been served any lawsuits. While he adds, "I don't want to threaten a lawsuit or anything," it's clear that he's doing some investigation of his own into certain events. "We're certainly very disturbed to have heard the information about the fire department turning back and not putting out the initial fires on Sunday for reasons we still don't understand. If the fire department had the opportunity to put these fires out, it may have solved a lot of problems. Based on the information that has come out, we'd like to know their reasoning [for not coming in]."

THE EVENT LIVES ON

The violence of Woodstock '99 hasn't affected the event's marketing plan. On August 3, 1999, Epic announced that it's forging ahead with plans to release a double CD and longform home video of performance highlights from the event this fall.

Also, a two-hour recap of the event aired as scheduled August 3 on Fox-TV. According to a Fox spokeswoman, the network didn't consider pulling the special after negative reports about the festival came forth. "We never thought about not airing it," she says. "We mention the negative stuff, but for the most part, it's a two-hour special on the positive stuff. We highlighted 17 of the acts that played.". . .

One veteran concludes, however, with what may be the final lesson of Woodstock '99: Whatever the circumstances, no one can escape personal responsibility.

Says Willie Nelson, whose group opened the show on Woodstock's east stage on Sunday, "It's possible for somebody onstage to control the crowd. Leon Russell once had a crowd at fever pitch at a show. He said, 'Be careful who you let put you into this type of euphoria.'

"There is the responsibility of the artist, or anybody if they have a lot of people they're talking to. If they raise [the audience's] emotions, they're obligated to do it positively."

GLOBALIZATION SPREADS DISSENT: PROTESTING THE WORLD TRADE ORGANIZATION IN SEATTLE

CLIVE CROOK

In early December 1999, thousands of protesters from environmental groups and labor unions descended on Seattle to protest the meeting of the World Trade Organization (WTO). The WTO is an international organization created in 1995 to regulate commerce among 135 countries and reduce international trade barriers. Many protesters accused the WTO of being an undemocratic body that conducted its meetings in secret and exercised excessive power over governments. The protesters saw the WTO as an agent of globalization, spreading capitalism and consumerism across the globe with little concern for its effect on local populations or the environment.

On the first morning the WTO was scheduled to meet, a violent group of self-described anarchists broke off from the throngs of peaceful protesters, smashing store windows and covering storefronts in graffiti. The melee in the streets trapped visiting dignitaries in their hotel rooms and caused the cancellation of the meeting's opening ceremonies. By late afternoon,

From "Brainless in Seattle, Also Spineless, Witless, Hopeless, and Shameless," by Clive Crook, *National Journal,* December 11, 1999. Copyright © 1999 by National Journal Group, Inc. Reprinted with permission.

Seattle's mayor had called in the National Guard, imposed a dusk-to-dawn curfew, and designated a no-protest zone in the downtown area surrounding the WTO's meeting place. Over five hundred protesters were arrested. Due to the disrupted meetings, the WTO delegates failed to reach an agreement on scheduling the next round of trade talks.

In the following essay, Clive Crook contends that the protesters were wrong to attack free trade and the WTO. According to Crook, the WTO was not set up as a rival to national governments, as asserted by the protesters, nor does the promotion of free trade conflict with the interests of the world's poor. Crook is deputy editor of the *Economist* magazine.

T he collapse of the trade talks in Seattle is among the worst failures of American political leadership of recent years. That, you may say, is quite a claim—but consider: The Clinton Administration pressed for this meeting. It was keen, it said, to launch a drive toward global trade liberalization in the American city that best symbolizes the boundless opportunities of the "new economy." As it turned out, the effort was so comprehensively wrecked that it not merely failed to start a new round of talks, but also undermined previous advances in the cause of liberal trade. Better if there had been no meeting at all.

GOVERNMENT CONCESSIONS WEAKEN TALKS

For most of this, the protesters are not to blame. Their marches and rallies had long been planned and advertised. Governments knew what to expect. They should have been ready to deal with the issues that the peaceful majority was raising. As for the idiotic violence of a small minority, perhaps that came as a surprise—but it should not have, and in any case, tactically speaking, it should have been helpful. There is no sympathy among the great majority of Americans or people anywhere for the kind of protester who says, "I demand democracy and justice, and to show I mean it, here's a brick through your window." Opponents like that ought to be a godsend for any government with a jot of intellectual self-confidence or integrity. There was nothing of either to be seen last week.

It was not what the protesters did that caused real damage, but what the assembled rich-country governments—and the Clinton Administration, above all—said in response. The protesters attacked the World Trade Organization (WTO) as though it were an international executive agency (which it isn't), as though it had independent powers (which it hasn't), as though it has set itself up as a rival to national governments (which is ridiculous). And how did governments answer? They conceded that the protesters had a point: "Yes, we must have a look at how the WTO operates."

Not content with assaulting this one institution, the protesters also deplored capitalism and free trade, the most powerful engines for improving human welfare the world has ever known. Most people understand that, of course. How many votes are there in the United States for the draconian suppression of economic and political freedoms that would be required to meet the protesters' demands (insofar as it is possible to make sense of them)? Yet how did governments answer? They admitted that there is a problem: "Yes, we agree, free trade must be fair trade."

The protesters, in their most outrageous lie, purported to be defending the interests of the poor—a line of reasoning that scandalizes governments all across the developing world, whose best hope of attacking poverty is through stronger trade and other economic links with the rich West. And how did (rich-country) governments answer? They said this, too, must be looked at: "Yes, there's more to progress than money and markets."

Altogether, it was an astounding and shameful cop-out—and nowhere more cynical than in the tacit endorsement of the view that the problem resides in the WTO itself. The protesters' charges against that body are genuinely puzzling, in that they seem to be inspired not by tactical considerations (such as the view that the WTO is a soft target, which is perfectly true) but by a genuine conviction that the institution is an evil usurper of democratically elected states.

ATTACKS ON WTO UNFOUNDED

Yet, unlike the International Monetary Fund, for instance, the WTO does nothing on its own initiative: The term "organization" in its name refers not to the modest entity with offices in Geneva, but to the assembly of governments that constitute the membership. Moreover, all those decisions of member governments that are misleadingly called decisions of the WTO are reached by consensus: Every government, in effect, has a veto. The WTO's director-general, Mike Moore, is therefore quite right when he says that the system is "ultrademocratic."

Indeed, in the past, one of the main complaints that the United States made about the WTO (and its predecessor, the General Agreement on Tariffs and Trade) was that it was too democratic. That a consensus of every government was needed before anything could be done stymied progress, it was argued. This was the rationale for the regional path to freer trade, through the North American Free Trade Agreement, the Asia Pacific Economic Cooperation forum, and similar initiatives.

The idea was to let smaller groups of like-minded governments get together and make faster progress than the WTO as a whole was capable of. Whether this regional approach makes sense—and it does, in fact, have big drawbacks—the perceived need for such an alternative underlines the fact that the WTO goes nowhere without the unanimous consent of the governments that constitute it. In what sense, then, is this mere forum for collective decision-making usurping the role of national governments? The accusation is nonsense.

The protesters complain, in particular, about the WTO's dispute-settlement procedures. One charge made by protesters, and repeatedly cited in the press, is that a WTO panel once ruled America's Clean Air Act to be illegal; another is that the WTO likewise struck down the Endangered Species Act. Rarely have these accusations been answered in the press—even though the U.S. Trade Representative, at any rate, knows them to be groundless. Officials at the WTO have answered them, but their statements have gone virtually unreported.

The first point in both these cases is that the WTO initiates no action against any government; under its rules, only other governments can do that. The second point is that the disputing governments must agree to the composition of the dispute panels. Again, nothing is imposed at WTO discretion. Turning to the specifics, the WTO panel did not find the Clean Air Act to be illegal: It found that it was being applied more leniently to domestic producers than to foreign ones, which violated an agreement that the United States had voluntarily entered into. In the shrimp-and-sea-turtles case, another panel affirmed that the United States was within its rights to protect endangered species: Its complaint was that the government, again in violation of the agreement it had signed, was discriminating against Asian suppliers in favor of Caribbean ones.

Not all of the protesters are as dimwitted or ignorant of the facts as their claims tend to suggest. Some know what's what and ignore or suppress the truth out of a desire to make mischief. Others, though, and maybe the majority, are simply associating themselves with an argument they do not understand out of a vague foreboding at the current pace of economic change.

Enlightened, responsible political leadership ought surely to regard it as a duty to deal with both sorts of critic—the unscrupulous as well as the anxious and confused. False arguments about the crimes of the WTO should be shot down. And vaguer concerns about the pace of globalization, to the extent that they are valid, should be answered with proposals that are seriously addressed to the issues.

On this second point, take a specific example. One of the few American industries that still enjoy strong protection from imports is textiles and clothing. The WTO cannot force America to liberalize these imports until America is good and ready. So the issue is for Americans to decide: Does the country want access to cheaper clothes and a more competitive clothing-export industry, at the cost of fewer jobs for American workers in textiles, or not?

Plainly, the economy as a whole would be better off if America used its manpower where it was most productive. As for which course is better for America's poor, this is not obvious: Textile workers are better off (in the short run, at least) with import protection, but a lot of poor people in America would, presumably, be grateful for cheaper clothes. Beyond question is that America's textile-protection regime stops some of the poorest people in the Third World from getting any less so.

It is quite right that advocates of free trade should be made to confront the issue of the losers from liberalization. They should come forward with ideas for cushioning the impact on the rich-country workers who lose from freer trade—perhaps with more generous plans for compensation or with assistance in retraining and relocation, or both. What is unconscionable is to claim that import protection in the rich countries has anything to do with the search for global equity. And it is almost as bad when governments that claim to favor free trade writhe and prevaricate at the first sign of opposition—and then try to make a scapegoat of an institution of their own devising, regardless of the cost to any future ambitions they once entertained for further trade reform.

What the world clearly saw in Seattle was a squirming abdication of political leadership.

THE Y2K COMPUTER BUG: APOCALYPSE NOT

LESLIE MIZELL

By the close of the 1990s, the technology revolution had introduced computers into nearly every facet of American life. From businesses to governments to homes and schools, U.S. society had become dependent on computers for countless daily transactions and activities. The approach of the year 2000, however, stoked fears that a computer software glitch, known as the "Y2K" computer bug, would crash computer systems around the world. Experts warned that computers would read January 1, 2000, as January 1, 1900, triggering financial chaos, power and water shortages, airplane crashes, and the launch of nuclear weapons. Many governments and businesses around the country embarked on costly campaigns to correct the software problem before the close of the 1990s. Those efforts were not enough to assuage the fears of some Americans, who headed for the hills and stockpiled provisions to ward off the approaching apocalypse. Leslie Mizell describes in the following analysis how the Y2K computer bug, hyped to excess in the media, was in large measure a nonevent, as the overwhelming majority of computer systems entered the year 2000 without incident. Mizell is the former editor of *Game Players* magazine and the author of computer-game strategy books.

From "A Look Back at Y2K and the Millennium Bug," by Leslie Mizell, *Office Solutions*, December 2000. Copyright © 2000 by Quality Publishing. Reprinted with permission.

T here were three results of the Y2K [year 2000] apocalypse the media promised us for 12:00:01 a.m. Jan. 1, 2000—you either made a lot of money; lost a lot of money; or got an extra $100 out of the bank, bought some batteries and canned hash, and kept your fingers crossed.

MEDIA-GENERATED FRENZY

The frenzy surrounding the idea that the world's computers would recognize the 1/1/00 date as Jan. 1, 1900 and malfunction was great for software companies, computer manufacturers, and consultants of all shapes and kinds. But Y2K turned out to be primarily a media-generated story, and New Year's Day dawned—anticlimactically—virtually problem free.

Don't say the experts didn't tell us.

"I still don't see any evidence of a likelihood of serious disruptions," said Nicholas Zvegintzov, president of the Software Management Network, back in December 1998. "Being afraid isn't evidence."

But we were afraid—or at least our leaders and officials were. Worried that electricity, water, and sewer service would break down; that computer glitches would disrupt worldwide telecommunications; that global stock markets and banking systems would crash.

Blame the fear on computer consultant Peter de Jager, who wrote the 1993 *ComputerWorld* article "Doomsday 2000" that's credited with sending up the first red flag about the "millennium bug." In the months leading up to January 1, de Jager fielded more than 2,000 interviews. "Every time I spoke to reporters," de Jager says, "I repeated 'If we don't fix it, then we have a problem.' And it was reported: 'Peter de Jager says we have a problem.' There's a difference."

With its catchy "Y2K" moniker and end-of-the-world hype, most newspapers, magazines, and TV shows focused on the sensational aspects and drowned out the voices of reason with tales of survivalists stocking up on canned food and ammunition.

"The software systems were either fixed, ignored, turned off, or never had a problem to begin with," says William Ulrich, author of *The Year 2000 Software Crisis.*

ACTUAL Y2K BUGS

Surprisingly after all the hype, the actual systems which suffered Y2K problems received only limited press. The exception was a Department of Defense (DOD) satellite system that failed as the New Year hit Greenwich Mean Time—the DOD was unable to process information from the satellite's ground-processing station for two days. Ironically, the Pentagon later reported the outage was triggered by software designed to prevent Y2K failure.

Other problems included:

• About 50,475 Medicare claims that were returned because they were dated 1900 or 2099. The bug was traced to providers who hadn't upgraded their systems.

• The Federal Aviation Administration's air-traffic control system reported inaccurate date displays that had no effect on safety issues. A Low Level Wind Shear Alert System failed to operate at eight sites, but was back to normal within two hours. A Kavouras Graphic Display System rejected weather data because it believed the year was 2010; 13 automated flight-service stations couldn't update weather data until the glitch was repaired.

• Processing daily updates of Oregon's food-stamp system failed, resulting in the installation of a new system the next business day. Data-tracking systems for the state's Child Support Enforcement, Temporary Assistance for Needy Families, and other social agencies reported glitches that were fixed by January 7, but resulted in a one-day delay in payment to clients.

• Louisiana reported a 10-hour service interruption on Leap Day when its Medicaid Eligibility Verification System didn't recognize the February 29, 2000, date as valid. Alternate systems were available until the problem was fixed.

• Sunquest Information Systems filed a lawsuit against the investment firm Morgan Stanley Dean Witter for selling them a company—a $5 million Compucare database division—that was riddled with Y2K bugs, despite assurances to the contrary. The case was settled out of court for an undisclosed amount.

MONEY SPENT AND THE Y2K HANGOVER

No one doubts the Y2K problem could have created nationwide or worldwide problems had the date approached unforeseen. But almost everyone agrees the $600 billion spent on compliance was too large a chunk of change and was primarily used to ease people's minds.

Congressman Stephen Horn, chairman of the Subcommittee on Government Management, says the potential impact of the Y2K problem made the federal government designate it a high-risk area in February 1997. "Our purpose was to stimulate greater attention to assessing the government's exposure to Y2K risks and to strengthen planning for achieving Y2K compliance for mission-critical systems. We produced a series of guides and reports [to provide] approaches to enterprise readiness, business continuity and contingency planning, testing, and day-one planning. In addition, we issued over 160 reports and testimony statements detailing specific findings and recommendations."

The Website for the President's Council on Year 2000 Conversion (www.y2k.gov) averaged more than 45,000 hits per week—with 3 million in the week of the rollover date—and its toll-free number averaged 15,000 callers per month.

Of course, the money, in general, was well spent, since the nation's computers are now not only more modern and maintained, but also more integrated. And the investment continues to pay off. For example, Detroit was hit in mid-June with a massive power failure, as its century-old municipal system failed. It took two days to restore electricity to all the 4,500 buildings affected, but the power provided in the outage's early stages came from generators bought—you guessed it—in case of Y2K emergencies.

"Y2K turned out to be this big nothing," says Gregory Bowens, Detroit mayoral spokesman. "But the $1.5 million the city spent on generators turned out to be money well spent."

Far more severe than any problems in January was the way the Y2K bug bit the stock market this autumn. The technology market had long been overvalued, but the balloon finally burst when artificially inflated sales of software, computers, appliances, and other industries that did well during the Y2K scare fell off in 2000, resulting in drastically reduced profits.

Sunbeam, for example, reported an $80 million loss in the second quarter, and company officials blamed the drop on the late-1999 consumer demand for gas grills, stoves, lamps, and power generators. "It cannibalized 2000 sales," says chief executive officer Jerry Levin.

But Sunbeam's problems pale in comparison to Compuware's, a software company specializing in custom applications for mainframe computers—the same mainframes that needed extensive, expensive retooling for Y2K compliance. Throughout the 1990s, Compuware was able to double profits every year, culminating in $2 billion in revenues and $352 million in profits in 1999.

Although most Y2K spending ended late in 1999, Compuware, nonetheless estimated its revenues would grow 35–40 percent in 2000 because it was training its Y2K experts as e-commerce consultants. But clients who were afraid to change software vendors in 1999—a time when Compuware raised its rates—bolted in 2000, and retraining employees proved more time-consuming than the company had thought.

In April, Compuware announced it would earn only 13–15 cents a share for its fiscal fourth quarter, less than half the estimate, and its stock dropped 40 percent in one day. The price never recovered: Its 52-week low at press time was $5.62, and its average is more than 80 percent below where it was a year ago.

Of course, Compuware is only one example, and other mainframe software providers, such as Computer Associates and BMC, have also dropped. Computer sales as a whole are way down, since anyone even considering upgrading an old computer did so last year. PC sales have also been impacted by the slow adoption of the Windows 2000 application.

THE UPSIDE

The good news as we approach the real end of the millennium is that never before have the nation's computers been as compatible and as well maintained, and never before have there been so many contingency plans for system failures.

"It was a really boring New Year's Day," says Dave Wennergren, the Navy's deputy chief information officer for e-business and security. "But that meant all our preparations paid off."

The men and women serving on the Navy's U.S.S. Topeka, stationed in the Pacific, were the first to enter the year 2000, but the Navy has 800,000 personnel inhabiting every time zone in the world. Y2K compliance was a particular problem. Some 2,000 information systems had to be examined, and rollover scenarios were extensively tested.

"For every Y2K problem we found, there were four or five other interoperability problems we wanted to fix," Wennergren says. "Now the Navy knows where every computer is and where its interdependencies lie."

The same is true of the government. "Y2K was a wake-up call," says David McClure, an associate director for information technology management issues at the General Accounting Office. "It showed us how integrated information technology is into everything the government does. [And it] made us get a grip on how vulnerable government information systems are to disruptions. Y2K focused the debate over what would happen if systems were tampered with or brought down or even destroyed. Cyber security came to the forefront as a result of the dialogue about Y2K."

So whether or not your stock portfolio has taken a hit, you can rest assured that your government is in better shape this December than it was last December. And you can also be glad you're not Gary Britt of Tampa, Fla. To prepare for Y2K, he and five friends bought $35,000 worth of dehydrated food—400 cases worth. In August, the forty-something Elvis impersonator started placing classified ads to sell the food, hoping to recoup 75 percent of the group's money, and, one assumes, reclaim their basements and garages.

GORE VS. BUSH: THE 2000 ELECTION DISPUTE

AL GORE

Voters went to the polls on election day, November 7, 2000, anticipating a close race between then-vice president Al Gore and Texas governor George W. Bush. The candidates had their ideological differences, but often sounded more alike than not on several well-publicized issues. In addition, a third party candidate, Ralph Nader of the Green Party, was running on a liberal platform that was expected to take votes away from Al Gore, a moderate Democrat.

As election night progressed, it became apparent that the outcome would hinge on the state of Florida and its twenty-five electoral votes. At 8:00 P.M., the major television news networks declared Gore the winner of Florida. Two hours later, the networks retracted their announcement, stating that the race in Florida was still undecided. The uncertainty continued until after 2 A.M., at which time Fox News declared Bush the winner in Florida and the next president of the United States. Once again, the other networks repeated this announcement, only to retract it two hours later at 4 A.M. Bush held a lead of only 1,784 votes out of the 6 million votes cast in Florida. Early in the morning of November 8, the media's take on the election was that it was too close to call.

The election entered a new phase of controversy and contention that would last for the next five weeks. The Gore campaign faulted confusing "butterfly" ballots for over nineteen thousand votes being disallowed in Palm Beach County for reasons of voter error. Many voters protested that the ballots had

Excerpted from Al Gore's Concession Speech, December 13, 2000.

led them to accidentally vote for two candidates or the wrong candidate. In addition, some Democratic black voters claimed that they had been turned away from the polls. The Gore campaign requested a hand recount in several Florida counties, which the Bush campaign quickly filed suit to prevent. According to the Bush campaign, the intent of the voter would be impossible to determine from the "hanging" and "dimpled" chads, or ballot indentations, in counties that had used punch card ballots.

After much legal wrangling and confusion, on December 12, 2000, the U.S. Supreme Court overruled a Florida Supreme Court decision allowing a state-wide manual recount. In the following speech delivered the day after the U.S. Supreme Court ruling, Al Gore conceded the election to George W. Bush. Gore maintained that while he strongly disagreed with the ruling, he was prepared to put aside the partisan divisions of the campaign and accept Bush as the nation's next president. He also asserted that the peaceful resolution of the contested election demonstrated the strength of American democracy.

G ood evening.

Just moments ago, I spoke with George W. Bush and congratulated him on becoming the 43rd president of the United States—and I promised him that I wouldn't call him back this time.

I offered to meet with him as soon as possible so that we can start to heal the divisions of the campaign and the contest through which we just passed.

Almost a century and a half ago, Senator Stephen Douglas told Abraham Lincoln, who had just defeated him for the presidency, "Partisan feeling must yield to patriotism. I'm with you, Mr. President, and God bless you."

PUTTING ASIDE "PARTISAN RANCOR"

Well, in that same spirit, I say to President-elect Bush that what remains of partisan rancor must now be put aside, and may God bless his stewardship of this country.

Neither he nor I anticipated this long and difficult road. Certainly neither of us wanted it to happen. Yet it came, and now it has ended, resolved, as it must be resolved, through the honored institutions of our democracy.

Over the library of one of our great law schools is inscribed the motto, "Not under man but under God and law." That's the ruling principle of American freedom, the source of our democratic liberties. I've tried to make it my guide throughout this contest as it has guided America's deliberations of all the complex issues of the past five weeks.

Now the U.S. Supreme Court has spoken. Let there be no doubt, while I strongly disagree with the court's decision, I accept it. I accept the finality of this outcome which will be ratified next Monday in the Electoral College. And tonight, for the sake of our unity of the people and the strength of our democracy, I offer my concession.

I also accept my responsibility, which I will discharge unconditionally, to honor the new president elect and do everything possible to help him bring Americans together in fulfillment of the great vision that our Declaration of Independence defines and that our Constitution affirms and defends.

Let me say how grateful I am to all those who supported me and supported the cause for which we have fought. Tipper and I feel a deep gratitude to Joe and Hadassah Lieberman who brought passion and high purpose to our partnership and opened new doors, not just for our campaign but for our country.

This has been an extraordinary election. But in one of God's unforeseen paths, this belatedly broken impasse can point us all to a new common ground, for its very closeness can serve to remind us that we are one people with a shared history and a shared destiny.

Indeed, that history gives us many examples of contests as hotly debated, as fiercely fought, with their own challenges to the popular will.

Other disputes have dragged on for weeks before reaching resolution. And each time, both the victor and the vanquished have accepted the result peacefully and in the spirit of reconciliation.

So let it be with us.

I know that many of my supporters are disappointed. I am too. But our disappointment must be overcome by our love of country.

ENDURING DEMOCRACY

And I say to our fellow members of the world community, let no one see this contest as a sign of American weakness. The strength of American democracy is shown most clearly through the difficulties it can overcome.

Some have expressed concern that the unusual nature of this election might hamper the next president in the conduct of his office. I do not believe it need be so.

President-elect Bush inherits a nation whose citizens will be ready to assist him in the conduct of his large responsibilities.

I personally will be at his disposal, and I call on all Americans—I particularly urge all who stood with us to unite behind our next president. This is America. Just as we fight hard when the stakes are high, we close ranks and come together when the contest is done.

And while there will be time enough to debate our continuing differences, now is the time to recognize that that which unites us is greater than that which divides us.

While we yet hold and do not yield our opposing beliefs, there is a higher duty than the one we owe to political party. This is America and we put country before party. We will stand together behind our new president.

As for what I'll do next, I don't know the answer to that one yet. Like many of you, I'm looking forward to spending the holidays with family and old friends. I know I'll spend time in Tennessee and mend some fences, literally and figuratively.

Some have asked whether I have any regrets and I do have one regret: that I didn't get the chance to stay and fight for the American people over the next four years, especially for those who need burdens lifted and barriers removed, especially for those who feel their voices have not been heard. I heard you and I will not forget.

I've seen America in this campaign and I like what I see. It's worth fighting for and that's a fight I'll never stop.

As for the battle that ends tonight, I do believe as my father once said, that no matter how hard the loss, defeat might serve as well as victory to shape the soul and let the glory out.

So for me this campaign ends as it began: with the love of Tipper and our family; with faith in God and in the country I have been so proud to serve, from Vietnam to the vice presidency; and with gratitude to our truly tireless campaign staff and volunteers, including all those who worked so hard in Florida for the last 36 days.

Now the political struggle is over and we turn again to the unending struggle for the common good of all Americans and for those multitudes around the world who look to us for leadership in the cause of freedom.

In the words of our great hymn, "America, America": "Let us crown thy good with brotherhood, from sea to shining sea."

And now, my friends, in a phrase I once addressed to others, it's time for me to go.

Thank you and good night, and God bless America.

From Dot-Com to Dot-Gone: The Rise and Fall of E-Commerce

John Schwartz

Entrepreneurs in the mid-1990s came to see the Internet as a re-markable new medium for selling services and products to the millions of people who regularly surfed the World Wide Web. Instead of driving to "brick and mortar" stores in crowded shopping malls, the Internet customer could simply point and click their way through a "virtual store." New companies, known as "dot-coms," began forming at an incredible rate to tap the Internet's selling potential, concentrating in trendy urban neighborhoods from San Francisco to New York. The hype surrounding these ventures was phenomenal, and many Internet entrepreneurs became overnight millionaires, at least on paper, through the initial public offerings, or IPOs, of their companies' stock. Thousands of talented young people dropped out of elite business schools to join the dot-com gold rush.

By late 2000, however, it had become painfully clear that too many dot-coms were based on shoddy business models and were losing investors' money at an alarming rate. Dot-com after dot-com collapsed and along with them the sense of heady optimism that had characterized the booming economy of the 1990s. John Schwartz in the following article contends that the country abruptly shifted away from the greed and self-absorption that characterized the fleeting dot-com era. According to Schwartz, the dream of easy dot-com riches and promise of the "New Economy" were exposed as belonging to a "revolution" rife with hyperbole and mislaid priorities.

M ark Leibovich recalled the day in 1999 when he showed up early for an appointment at a Washington dot-com. Mr. Leibovich, a reporter for *The Washington Post,* was there to interview the company's executives. "I got there just in time to see the C.E.O. himself wheeling a foosball table into the lobby" to give the impression that the high-tech firm possessed the desired quantum of wackiness that its Silicon Valley counterparts are famous for.

FROM REVOLUTION TO CULTURAL BONEYARD

That is so over, and so much more over, even, than before. The popular obsession with the dot-com revolution, fading for more than a year, seems to have simply winked out since mid-September [2001], as firemen and warriors have become the new heroes, and e-commerce's whiz kids are consigned to the cultural boneyard.

Not much more than a year ago, boosters of the New Economy and their true believers in the press were claiming to have changed all the rules. Not just in tech-fetish magazines like *Wired,* but in self-styled cultural arbiters like *New York* magazine, which declared the 1990's the "e-Decade." In a 1999 cover story, the essayist Michael Wolff—himself a failed dot-com executive—announced a brave new world. "There is, at the elusive center of the e-experience, the fantasy that we might become free of economic laws," he wrote. "All it takes to make otherworldly riches is the will and desire." It wasn't enough to make money. They had to make history.

Now they themselves are history. Each day, the old idols seem to fade further into the dim past, barely recollected in a country where the languages of "revolution" and "warfare" are no longer just business metaphors. This is the next step after the bursting of the dot-com economic bubble—the bursting of the cultural bubble, the end of the nerd as a crossover hit, of the I.P.O. (initial public offering) zillionaire as role model to college students.

The changing of the guard can be seen in little things. Like Henry Blodget, the industry analyst who became famous for predicting early that Amazon.com would reach $400 a share, announcing that he is taking a buyout and leaving Merrill Lynch at the grand old age of 35.

Like the growing wave of books that focus not on the dot-com path to riches but on the wild plunge into the abyss. Having failed to sell their dreams, they are now attempting to sell their failure. A documentary of the rise and fall of a Silicon Alley company was chronicled in "Startup.Com" by Sebastian Nokes, released in the winter of 2000. Books by former dot-com executives are arriving in stores. Two of the first are *A Very Public Offering: A Rebel's Story of Business Excess, Success, and Reckoning* by Stephan Paternot, founder of Theglobe.com, and *Dot.bomb: My Days and Nights at an Internet Goliath,* by J. David Kuo. Another is coming soon: *Boo Hoo,* the chronicle of the spectacular failure of Boo.com, the luxury fashion site that burned through $185 million of its investors' cash and had an online life of just six months, told by its profligate founders.

Did we mention that Mr. Blodget is writing a book?

SHIFTING VALUES

For the most part, however, the flood of dot-com failure stories is being met with a national yawn. The tell-all books have bounced around the Amazon.com rankings without making inroads into best-seller territory. And why not? Because former idols have feet of clay. In *A Very Public Offering,* a book written as amateurishly as the company was run, did we need the image of Mr. Paternot dancing the night away in plastic pants?

Ellen DeGeneres's new sitcom, "The Ellen Show," is built around the notion of an executive returning to her hometown after the collapse of her dot-com, but the show sits at the miserable ranking of 93rd for the season—behind "Emeril," the celebrity chef comedy—despite Ms. DeGeneres's own considerable appeal.

To Amitai Etzioni, a sociologist at George Washington University, the country is experiencing an abrupt cultural shift away from the libertarian, individualistic values that were expressed in the celebration of the New Economy and toward more old-fashioned values in the wake of the terrorist attacks, when government is not The Problem and people are not The Market. "There's been a sea change," he said. The surge in charitable giving and blood donations after Sept. 11, he said, underscores "the sense that you're willing to give priority to the common good, to public safety and public health."

Paulina Borsook, the author of *Cyberselfish,* a critical look at dot-com values published [in 2000], said: "People really crave a reminder of human bonds that have to do with sacrifice and fellowship and getting to know each other over time. It's not about changing jobs every six months and getting stock options."

In the 90's, college students hoping to emulate Marc Andreessen of Netscape and other geek stars migrated to Silicon Valley or New York's Silicon Alley with thin résumés and visions of Testarossas dancing in their heads. That's all changing, said Thomas T. Field, director of the Center for the Humanities at the University of Maryland, Baltimore County. "Many of the young adults that I see coming to campus now say they want fulfilling jobs, not just ways of earning money," he said. "Sounds awfully familiar, when you come from the 60's generation."

Professor Field suggested that protests over globalism, and the sense of security that flourished during the boom, made young people more willing to question the status quo and to take chances. During the I.P.O. frenzy, he said, students could not wait to get out of school and begin earning. This year, many of his students have chosen to study abroad in China, Nepal, India and Egypt.

The country is in dot-com denial, Ms. Borsook said, adding, "No one wants to admit that they were caught up in it," an attitude she calls "I don't want to think that I drank the Kool-Aid."

Good riddance, said Thomas Frank, the author of *One Market Under God: Extreme Capitalism, Market Populism and the End of Economic Democracy.* The book is a withering attack on the ideas underlying the selling of the New Economy, which he says co-opted hipness and the language of populism to serve greed and gain. The book has come out in paperback with a new afterword. "It's going to take some time for it to sink in," Mr. Frank said. "The Dow isn't going to go to 36,000, and the dot-coms aren't going to come back—and a lot of people lost a lot of money."

OPTIMISTS PERSIST WHILE STOCKS PLUMMET

Though dot-com executives might seem irrelevant these days, the technologies they sold, by and large, are not, pointed out Paul Saffo, an analyst at the Institute for the Future in Menlo Park, Calif. "People haven't stopped using the Internet," he said. "The fact is that it is changing the world, and it has changed the world." People now expect to be able to buy a book or make an airline reservation in the middle of the night, "and it's washed into the rest of their lives."

Kevin Kelly, who as a longtime editor of *Wired* magazine helped create the heroic ethos surrounding dot-com entrepreneurs, acknowledged "it came tumbling down with the towers." But Mr. Kelly insisted that these people would rise again. The generation of tyro executives who crashed and burned "got better business education than they could if they had gotten a Harvard M.B.A.," he said. "They didn't set out to learn, but, boy, they are much smarter now." He predicts that the last decade has been the "layup" for a true cultural revolution to come—he could not be specific, and his words may strike many as more dot-com hyperbole.

It takes a special kind of gall for the same people who argued that the "long boom" suspended the laws of economics, and even unraveled the cycles of history, to fall back now on analysis of historical cycles to support their arguments.

But to believe any less goes against the American grain, argued Jason McCabe Calacanis, the editor of the now-defunct *Silicon Alley Reporter*. The dot-commer, seen today as a scam artist, will be reborn, he said, smarter and tougher, because he represents optimism itself. "It's the belief that the future—the individual's future and the future of the economy—are going to be better in five years than they are today."

But still. Take a look at the book *Radical E* by Glenn Rifkin and Joel Kurtzman, which offers "Lessons on How to Rule the Web" after the bust. It extols companies that truly understand how to marry the World Wide Web to business. "After five tumultuous years of hype and hysteria," the authors promise, "the real advent of the Web and e-business is now."

One of the book's chief examples of a company that does it right, Enron, has been in the news a lot lately, though not because of astute exploitation of e-commerce. No, Enron—which trades energy via the Web—has seen its stock collapse 90 percent. [Enron filed for bankruptcy protection in December 2001. Enron executives were accused of looting the company's assets prior to its unexpected collapse.]

THE COLLAPSE OF THE ENRON CORPORATION

THOMAS FRANK

The booming American economy in the latter half of the 1990s rewarded Americans with ample job opportunities and fostered public faith in large corporations as a source of secure and upwardly mobile employment. In the fall of 2001, however, the image of the American corporation as a beacon of prosperity based around fundamentally ethical business practices was shattered by the collapse of the Enron corporation, a Houston, Texas–based energy giant. Enron's corporate leaders misrepresented the true state of its assets to both shareholders and employees, painting a picture of glowing prosperity as the company teetered on the brink of bankruptcy. Many executives and top managers sold their stock in the company shortly before its collapse, making off with millions of dollars while lower-level employees were left jobless, and in many cases, holding pension funds heavily invested in near-worthless Enron stock. The public outcry over such repugnant behavior led to congressional hearings into Enron's accounting practices and stock trades, but most executives called to testify exercised their right to remain silent.

In the following essay on the Enron debacle, Thomas Frank maintains that the unregulated boomtimes of the 1990s caused the public to turn a blind eye to the shady salesmanship, political wheeling and dealing, and deceptive bookkeeping of corporate America. According to Frank, without the necessary regulatory oversight, business leaders have no incentive to abide by standards of ethical decency, and they will attempt to get away with whatever shenanigans the free market allows. To prevent future Enron meltdowns and achieve true economic democracy, the author contends that free markets must be better regulated. Frank is the author of *One Market Under God*.

I n happier times the Enron corporation used to run a TV commercial in which a clever young executive punctured the pretensions of a panel of windbag politicians with a single sharp word: "Why?" It was supposed to be a thirty-second demonstration of the populist wisdom of electricity deregulation: Anyone could see that our legislators were arrogant fogies who kept us from having economic "choices" simply because they thought they knew better than the people.

TAKING THE FIFTH

These days, the clever young executives of Enron are taking the Fifth, not cracking wise at the Man. And the notion of Enron acting in the public interest—of Enron acting in anyone's interest other than that of those same clever young executives—can only register as a sort of sick joke. Consider just the stories that have made the front pages over the past few months. Thanks to the failure of a series of shady accounting tricks, Enron had to amend its profits for the past few years by hundreds of millions of dollars. Naturally, this destroyed investors' faith in Enron management, causing a catastrophic drop in the company's share price and a downgrading of its debt rating, leading immediately to bankruptcy. Enron employees, who had been encouraged to buy shares right up to the end, found they were not allowed to sell and watched helplessly as their 401(k)s were wiped out. While encouraging their workers to stand pat, top Enron managers were unloading the soon-to-be-worthless stuff as fast as they could.

Then it was the turn of Arthur Andersen, the accounting firm that had OK'd the fatal transactions, and whose managers were discovered feverishly shredding Enron-related documents. Before long Andersen found itself indicted and hemorrhaging clients. The chain reaction soon spread over the rest of the corporate landscape, where Enron had long been regarded as a leader in the field of clever accounting tricks. Copycat bankruptcies broke out. Markets drooped sorrowfully.

This would be enough to seal the eternal disgrace of most companies. But the Enron story only got worse. We are accustomed to associating corporate interests with conservatism, but Enron seems to have had its own ideology, a swaggering free-market evangelism that it promoted not so much by argument as by financial might. Enron not only bankrolled pundits and endowed university chairs in economics and political science, but it ingratiated itself with those very politicians it gloried in mocking in its ads. Forever pushing for the deregulation of the various fields in which it operated, the company gave campaign contributions to nearly half the members of Congress. Its influence in state legislatures was sufficiently great that journalists now speak of Enron as the main force behind the movement for electricity deregulation that swept the nation in the late 1990s. National politicians received seats on the Enron board after doing their good deeds for the company, while others were rotated from Enron into the upper echelons of the Administration. And, as everyone now knows, [President] George W. Bush was Enron's special pet, nurtured on Enron money, Enron jets and Enron connections. He had been in office for only a few weeks before the favors that Enron paid for began to flow: friendly appointments, special consideration in energy policy-making.

ANGER AND DISBELIEF

Right up to the end, Enron was described in the exalted realms of management theory and business journalism with virtually unmodulated adoration. Fortune compared Enron to Elvis. Superguru Gary Hamel, who devoted a section of Leading the Revolution to the company, waxed enthusiastic about Enron's "genius for innovation" and its "capacity for revolution."

The effect of this has been to promote what could have been a simple tale of corporate crime into the staggering revelation that everyone you listened to in the New Economy years was either a liar or an ignoramus. Despite all the recent lamentations about public "cynicism," Americans seem generally to have believed that they lived in a world where the depictions of the business press were fairly accurate, where pundits argued for things because they believed in them, where accountants and stock analysts spoke truthfully, where politicians represented their constituents and not just those with money, where the stock market had been cleansed of crooks and was now safe enough for little old ladies from Beardstown. The Enron story has flattened each of these faiths simultaneously. It's a perfect ideological reversal, a narrative that was supposed to prove the goodness of the New Economic Order and that has instead discredited it in every respect.

Thanks to the vast chasm between the populist promise of the New Economy and what it has actually delivered, a corporation is today the target of a species of outrage usually reserved for enemy dictators or mass murderers. The other day an artist friend—a man who has never talked about big business issues with me before—volunteered without any prompting his ferocious feelings toward Enron CEO Ken Lay. All the way from the South Side of Chicago to O'Hare a Nigerian taxi driver shared with me his anger and disbelief at the reach of Enron's malign influence. According to a poll taken in February by the Pew Center for the People and the Press, more people were following the Enron scandal than the Olympics.

The epicenter of this earthquake is the Enron headquarters in Houston, familiar by now to television viewers around the world with its crooked-E logo out front. I read in a management book about the building's state-of-the-art trading floor where the Enron hotshots conducted the energy business of the nation, and in the *National Enquirer* about the plush upper-story "bachelor pads" where the Enron brass conducted their trysts with secretaries, but what I saw was a bland fifty-story glass tower, built in the smooth and ornament-free corporate style of the 1980s, and connected by many enclosed walkways to similar-looking office buildings in the neighborhood. From one of these climate-controlled tubes I could look down on the Antioch Baptist Church, one of the oldest African-American institutions in the city, its lot now little more than an island between the busy downtown streets, and its gothic tower with its somehow defiant sign, Jesus Saves, dwarfed by the encircling skyscrapers.

A LOT OF BULL

The ATMs here were still displaying jaunty Enron propaganda and a stock ticker was still telling passers-by where Enron stood in the market's all-knowing estimation (at a humble 29 cents on the day I visited), while an incongruous slogan touting Enron's "endless possibilities" zipped by underneath. In the tower next door, where laid-off Enron employees used computers to look for new jobs, the walls were still covered with framed motivational posters illustrating the company's four "values": "Respect," "Integrity," "Communication," "Excellence." Few of the ironies are lost on the skyscraper's inhabitants, one imagines.

In fact, in the lobby someone had actually assembled a collection of embarrassing Enroniana, placed each slogan-bearing coffee cup or boasting paperweight under a museum-quality vitrine, and given the resulting works of "art" some sarcastic title: "A Lot of Bull." "Not a Shred of Evidence."

Bitterness of this sort isn't hard to come by in Houston. Mentioning Enron to the proprietors of a shop in the tony River Oaks neighborhood earned me an earful of righteous disgust toward Mrs. Ken Lay, who had tearfully announced on TV a few nights before that the company's demise might force her to sell off two of her many homes. Rachel Hernandez, who worked in Enron's relocation department until that operation was outsourced some years ago, told me she thought her former bosses deserved jail time for what they had done. And a former systems administrator for Enron Broadband named Barry La Valla recalled how Enron persuaded him to give up a house in Portland and take a significant pay cut to move to Houston, just six months before the company declared bankruptcy. Everywhere I heard angry stories of ruined 401(k)s, of personal losses in the range of $60,000, $100,000, a million.

AMBIVALENCE AMIDST THE CRITICISM

But what surprised me was the number of former Enronites I came across who had more ambivalent feelings about the disgraced corporation, who were willing to accept the damage the company has inflicted on the nation and on their savings, and to defend what Enron did, or at least what Enron set out to do. This is partly because the company chose its employees well: They are, after all, traders and MBAs, true believers in free-market theory even though they themselves have now become international symbols of its resounding failure. For several of the people I talked to, Enron had been their first job out of college or even out of high school, and they knew no other world than the New Economy 1990s, with its saintly CEOs and its many shrines to Our Lady of Perpetual Privatization. How are you supposed to criticize the laissez-faire order when you've never heard a competing theory in your life?

Such weird ambivalence was also clearly a response to the fact that the international press corps has descended on Houston as though a whole flock of toddlers had been caught in wells, and has proceeded to make an instant mini-celebrity of every laid-off Enron employee who wants to play ball. Nearly everyone I met had been on TV, or had their picture in the paper, or told me about some other media moment. And with the entire world screaming for Ken Lay's head, many of the ex-Enronians have decided to cast themselves as voices of moderation. After all, they worked there, too: They contributed money to the infamous PAC, they cheered when electricity deregulation swept the nation, and when I talked to them they still referred almost universally to former CEO Jeffrey Skilling as "Jeff."

"It's a spectacle," says Bilal Bajwa, who came from Pakistan to work for Enron and whom I found searching for a new job from a computer in a downtown office building. "I might feel bitter a year down the road," but for now such emotions are lost in the glare. Instead of the usual disgruntled-former-employee mentality, what he notices among his ex-colleagues is a variation on the Stockholm syndrome, in which "the only one who defends the kidnapper is the kidnapped."

This curious contradiction came up again when I talked to John Allario, a smart and articulate energy business development professional who clearly understands the complex business dealings that brought Enron down. As such, he is in high demand among radio, TV and print reporters from around the world, fielding phone calls, in just the few hours that I spent with him, from ABC News and TV crews from France and Japan. He spends his time these days running an ex-Enron website called Laydoff.com, which burns with the outrage of the wrongfully terminated, magnified by the spectacular self-aggrandizement of Enron upper management. Allario's Enron career ended when he was simply told to clear out one day on his cell phone. And now, as he puts it on the website, "your 401k is depleted, your after-tax severance packages are reduced to one month's mortgage payment, and those who sent you packing are buying Hill Country or ski slope vacation properties with their exorbitant retention bonuses." He reads aloud from a typical e-mail to the Laydoff.com chat room: "I cannot express how incensed I am by the plight of you all." Allario also sells a line of T-shirts printed with anti-Enron jokes. (I bought one that reads: "Loss of job—$100,000. Watching 401K disappear—$225,000. Losses on company stock options—$505,000. Ten years hard time for guilty executives—Priceless.") He shows me a lucite computer mouse, a bit of Enroniana issued in 2000 to commemorate the first year of EnronOnline and marked with the staggering sum ("gross notional value") of $274,602,202,016. It's a perfect example of what was wrong with the company. "It is total obfuscation!" Allario says. "These figures are more than the GNP of Poland. Even if you knew what gross national value meant, the calculations of these numbers were internal secrets, which were not open to verification by employees."

Drinking Enron "Kool-Aid"

On the other hand, Allario is moved not to anger but to a sort of empathy at the sight of Jeff Skilling testifying before the House Energy and Commerce subcommittee on CNN. "I still respect some of those guys for their mental acuity," he says. They have "a creative, special brainpower." What's more, Congress will find it difficult to prove actual fraud, he suspects. "Enron knew the laws as well, and sometimes better, than our own accountants," he tells me. "The job of Enron's finance and accounting groups was to find a way to structure around unfavorable accounting rules. It was a game to them."

Allario's TV goes on the blink and we head over to a local brew pub to watch Skilling's testimony on their set. Nobody in the place objects when we ask them to turn off the classic rock and crank the volume on CNBC. The details of the deals Skilling is being asked to explain are almost nightmarishly complicated. Allario, though, is riveted to the screen. "This is such compelling TV," he says. "As good as the World Series." Back in Washington, the notoriously quick-tempered Skilling is doing his best to impersonate a sensitive, concerned person. He gets out of one question by relating how the power went out during a crucial meeting. In the corner of the screen, both the Dow and the Nasdaq go from green to red.

"One of the legacies of the Enron debacle," Allario tells me later, "will be how so many smart MBAs drank the Enron Kool-Aid. Listening to Jeff, I'm falling for it again. I want to take another sip." He thinks for a while about the better times at Enron, about the Promethean free-market ambitions of all those young executives. "We set ourselves apart," he says. "We were for free thinking. For doing something good." Enron lived to open new markets in previously unimagined areas. "We could commoditize anything," Allario continues. "Water, paper, air freight capacity, weather, computer chips, ad space on TV."

Again and again during my stay in Houston I am told—by TV commentators, by business magazines, by former Enronians in whatever state of outrage—that what did the company in was greed. That Enron's true mission was a glorious one, that deregulation is a noble goal, but that greed in the upper echelons got in the way. Obviously, there is considerable truth to this. After all, Andrew Fastow, Michael Kopper and the rest of the clever Enron financiers received many millions of dollars as compensation for running the partnerships that inflated Enron's numbers and ultimately destroyed the company. And other top Enron executives were promised royal bonuses when the company's shares hit a certain price target—a clear incentive to do whatever was necessary to make Enron look attractive to Wall Street.

EXPOSING NEW ECONOMY MYTHS

In previous years, though, greed was regarded as the fuel that drove Enron's spectacular intervention in so many different markets. Way back in 2000, Gary Hamel identified the opportunity that Enron executives had to indulge in what he quaintly called "personal wealth accumulation" as a critical element of the company's success. And for Hamel—for nearly everyone in the New Economy amen corner—that was perfectly OK, if not downright virtuous. The great myth of the 1990s was the fundamental decency of capitalist motivations. Free markets were democracy at its finest. CEOs were men of the people, lovable friends of rich and poor alike. The disappearance of job security and labor unions was "free agency." Even the endless cycles of obsolescence and destruction and ruin were something creative, something cool. Only when such destruction threatens to derail the stock market and discredit the entire New Economy does the moral turpitude of top management become an issue. Only then do the Aquinases of business journalism discover the fine distinctions between sensitivity to incentives and base greed.

However spectacular its effects, the wreck of Enron is a far more ordinary matter than such moralizing makes it appear. This is not the result of sin; this is the way markets work. It is simply what happens when regulatory oversight is systematically shut down, bought off and defunded; when business journalism becomes salesmanship; when investment banking becomes salesmanship; and when political power is a prize that goes to the highest bidder. There can be little doubt that the kind of microscopic scrutiny that Enron is now undergoing would uncover similar accounting and compensation scandals at many other companies in America. And it is well-known that industry lobbyists routinely craft the legislation that is supposed to regulate their industries. Credit-card lobbyists write the bankruptcy laws; broadcasting lobbyists write the telecommunications laws. It's not because they're greedy, it's because they can.

REPEAT SHENANIGANS

These are mistakes that the country seems determined to repeat every few decades or so. In the early 1930s the Senate Banking Committee performed a long investigation of Wall Street's practices during the just-ended bull market, and many of the shenanigans they unearthed seem straight out of the Enron playbook: lucrative options deals for insiders, dummy corporations set up to disguise liabilities, friendly politicians, financial institutions using their own endlessly rising stock to secure questionable deals and, of course, the rampant transformation of investment bankers into salesmen. (One critical difference: That time, the mighty men of Wall Street, concerned about their industry's reputation, actually testified.)

Years after those revelations, Ferdinand Pecora, the committee's counsel, wrote about the small investor who was surprised to find all of this going on, who had somehow believed that everything on Wall Street was regulated, overseen, safe: "He has reckoned without the ingenuity of the legal technicians and the complaisance of governmental authorities toward powerful financial and business groups during the lamented pre-New Deal era." Nor was this malign ingenuity—what the Enron brass called "creativity"—finally extirpated by the 1930s reforms. "Under the surface of the governmental regulation of the securities market," Pecora warned, "the same forces that produced the riotous speculative excesses of the 'wild bull market' of 1929 still give evidences of their existence and influence." Such corruption wasn't merely the product of individual greed; it was a force of free-market nature, and it would reassert itself by default if we didn't remain vigilant.

And, of course, we didn't. (And we won't, either, if Dubya has his way.) Amid a frenzy of New Economy exuberance we came to believe that the rules had been somehow suspended. That only if we left markets free to do their special thing would we ever achieve real economic democracy. In life Enron was hailed as the great exemplar of this bankrupt idea; so it should be in death as well.

THE UNITED STATES ABANDONS THE GLOBAL WARMING TREATY

TIMOTHY E. WIRTH

In March 2001, newly elected president George W. Bush announced that his administration was rejecting the 1997 Kyoto
Protocol—the international treaty to reduce emissions of carbon
dioxide and other pollutants believed to cause global warming.
The United States had signed the treaty with over one hundred
countries under President Bill Clinton's administration. President Bush's decision to withdraw from the Kyoto Protocol was
met with widespread criticism from world leaders, who viewed
the participation of the United States, responsible for a large
share of the world's atmospheric pollution, as essential to reducing the threat of global warming. Bush maintained that the
treaty would hurt the U.S. economy by requiring that the nation
reduce its carbon dioxide emissions to below 1990 levels by
2012. In the following viewpoint, Timothy E. Wirth describes
the events leading up to Bush's abandonment of the treaty and
what it bodes for future international efforts to combat global
warming. The author is president of the United Nations Foundation and is a former Democratic U.S. senator from Colorado.

From "Hot Air over Kyoto: The United States and the Politics of Global Warming," by
Timothy E. Wirth, *Harvard International Review*, Winter 2002. Copyright © 2002 by Harvard International Relations Council. Reprinted with permission.

The year 2001 has been the most turbulent year in international global-warming policy since the tumultuous final round of negotiations on the UN Framework Convention on Climate Change (UNFCCC) in 1992. US President George W. Bush's decision in March [2001] to withdraw from further talks on the 1997 Kyoto Protocol may seem to be a potentially fatal blow to current international efforts to control greenhouse gas emissions. However, as the year draws to a close, the outlook for real progress is actually more mixed. The outlook is in many ways even more positive than it was in the final years of President [Bill] Clinton's administration, which never mounted a serious campaign internationally or domestically after retreating from its public commitment to aggressive action on global warming within 24 hours of the successful conclusion of the Kyoto talks in December 1997.

SLOW PROGRESS ON GLOBAL WARMING

The morning after the Kyoto agreement, Republican congressional leaders held a news conference declaring the Protocol "dead on arrival" in the US Senate, arguing that the document's failure to set binding emissions-reduction targets for China, India, and other major developing countries would economically disadvantage the United States. In response, the Clinton administration chose not to defend the Protocol's basic premise: industrialized nations, whose fossil fuel-based economic growth in the 20th century is largely responsible for today's increased level of greenhouse gas concentrations, should act first to curb their emissions growth. Instead, the White House announced that it would not send the agreement to the Senate for ratification without obtaining emissions-reduction commitments from key developing countries—a posture that directly contradicted the international negotiating position it had maintained for more than two years.

As it emerged from Kyoto, the Protocol was only a barebones framework of reduction targets and a hazy statement of the principles for meeting them. It would require several years of additional negotiations to build an international agreement on actual reduction mechanisms. But having trapped itself in a conflict between its international and domestic positions, the Clinton administration put the Kyoto process on a political back burner.

Progress at home also was slow in the wake of the Kyoto negotiations. While it was readily apparent that the debate over carbon dioxide emissions-reduction measures must begin quickly if the United States was to have any chance of meeting the targets it accepted at Kyoto, the Clinton administration never advanced a serious legislative proposal to begin the process. In August 1998, then-Vice President Al Gore summarily rejected a request from environmental organizations that the Clinton administration mount a fight in the US Congress to reduce emissions from electric utilities, which account for nearly 40 percent of US greenhouse gas emissions. Similarly, Clinton repeatedly signed into law Republican-sponsored riders to appropriations bills that barred the promulgation of new automobile fuel-efficiency standards.

To be fair, the Clinton White House faced a difficult domestic political situation. Control of both the House and Senate by Republicans closely allied with the oil, coal, utility, and automobile industries made domestic action to reduce carbon dioxide emissions difficult. This difficulty was compounded by alliances between a significant number of congressional Democrats and mining and autoworkers' unions. Achieving rapid ratification of an international global-warming agreement requiring a two-thirds Senate majority was clearly impossible under the circumstances. Breaking this complex knot of opposition over several years would have required a sustained commitment from the highest levels of the administration to spend a substantial amount of political capital on the issue.

A CHANGING POLITICAL SITUATION

That level of commitment, of course, was not forthcoming. Throughout 1998, scandal and impeachment absorbed much of the White House's energy. By the time the US Senate acquitted Clinton in January 1999, the 2000 presidential campaign was in its initial stages, intensifying a number of imperatives for the Clinton administration. As a domestic political issue, global warming had been strongly associated with Gore since the publication of his 1992 book, *Earth in the Balance.* Any new administration initiative on climate change, domestic or international, could be expected to be exploited by Gore's electoral opponents; his advisers were already concerned that the initial Kyoto Protocol itself would be a political liability. For three years, the oil, coal, utility, and automobile industries had been generating studies predicting economic disaster for the United States if the Protocol were implemented. Taking on the United Mine Workers and the United Auto Workers in a battle to reduce carbon emissions was similarly unattractive at a time when Gore was courting labor's support in both primary and general election contests. Global warming was an issue best kept off the political stage in the view of many, if not most, in the White House.

The political dynamics changed only after the 2000 election, when the sixth Conference of the Parties to the UNFCCC convened in The Hague at the height of the Florida recount controversy in the United States. With the possibility of a Bush presidency becoming more likely, the Clinton administration launched a last-minute push to resolve in two weeks a host of issues that had been left unsettled for three years. Unfortunately, European nations (with the exception of the United Kingdom) failed to recognize the implications of an incoming US administration headed by a president and vice president with oil-industry backgrounds who had opposed the Protocol during their electoral campaigns. In the end, the European Union allowed the talks to collapse over proposals that would have shrunk the US emission reduction commitment by 150 million tons out of 500 million tons total, a difference of 25 percent. Clinton worked aggressively to convince foreign leaders during the negotiations, but to no avail.

Thus, 2001 had opened with a very dark outlook for real progress on global warming. Three years had passed since the agreement on targets in Kyoto, with very little serious negotiating progress; the most recent round of talks had failed completely. No public challenge had been mounted to US congressional opponents of the Kyoto Protocol, and most congressional supporters of the agreement remained silent. Finally, a new administration opposed to the Protocol was preparing to take office.

THE EARLY BUSH MONTHS

Bush came to office with contradictory international and domestic positions on climate change. While he had vocally opposed the Kyoto Protocol as a threat to the US economy during his campaign, as president he embraced aggressive domestic emissions-reduction measures that the Clinton administration had never seriously considered. In trying to resolve this contradiction, the Bush administration inadvertently rearranged the entire US political landscape on global warming. Between March and July 2001, the Bush White House laid the foundation of a bipartisan coalition in the US Congress for mandatory carbon dioxide emissions reductions, effectively put an end to the industry-promoted debate over the adequacy of climate-change science, and generated the political will among other industrialized nations to complete the Kyoto Protocol.

On September 29, 2000, in an energy policy speech in Lansing, Michigan, then-Governor Bush proposed a major departure from the voluntary emissions-reductions policies first embraced by his father's administration almost a decade earlier. He proposed amending the Clean Air Act to require mandatory carbon dioxide emissions reductions from the nation's utilities as part of a comprehensive program that would reduce emissions of other principal air pollutants as well. While the initiative may have been largely intended to protect him in the televised presidential debates from criticism of his poor record on cleaning up air pollution by Texas utilities, the inclusion of carbon emissions set the stage for a high-profile controversy over global warming that persisted through the first nine months of his administration.

Bush had been in office only a matter of weeks when Environmental Protection Agency (EPA) Administrator Christine Todd Whitman's restatement of Bush's commitment to reduce carbon dioxide emissions touched off a storm of criticism from conservative Republicans. By mid-March, the White House could only calm the storm by releasing a letter from the president to a prominent congressional foe of carbon emissions reductions renouncing his campaign pledge. Soon afterwards, word leaked to the *Washington Post* of a private lunch held by European ambassadors in Washington at which the guest of honor, US National Security Adviser Condoleezza Rice, remarked that the Kyoto Protocol was "dead, as far as the President is concerned." The Post also reported that the Bush White House had sought US State Department advice on procedures for reversing Clinton's 1996 decision to sign the Protocol. At a subsequent press appearance, Bush reaffirmed the position taken by his national security adviser, ill-advisedly using the word "dead" himself to describe the Kyoto Protocol.

QUESTIONING THE PRESIDENT'S ENVIRONMENTAL POLICIES

In a breathtakingly short time, these clumsily executed moves reversed years of assiduous and successful Clinton administration work to keep climate change out of the political spotlight.

Instead, global warming was forced to the front of the president's international and domestic agenda by the heavy criticism generated by the administration's actions. For the European Union, US rejection of the Kyoto agreement was the first symptom of a new and highly objectionable "unilateralist" approach to foreign policy. This feeling was followed by similar Bush administration decisions to reject international agreements on biological weapons and trade in small arms, and by threats to exercise the six-month notice provision of the Anti-Ballistic Missile Treaty to abrogate the agreement.

On the domestic front, the about-face on power plant carbon dioxide emissions and the controversy over the Protocol became prominent symbols of the administration's highly unpopular environmental policies. They were likened in the media to decisions to re-examine Clinton administration standards on arsenic in drinking water, changes to policies limiting logging in national forests, and a host of other such actions. Throughout the spring and summer, global warming was the subject of literally hundreds of newspaper articles, editorials, columns, and radio and television news stories—far more attention than the issue had received since 1997. More than 40 major newspapers editorialized in favor of action to reduce US greenhouse gas emissions, many taking such a position for the first time.

Equally importantly, the Bush administration's mishandling of the issue energized congressional Democrats. For four years, few had been willing to actively support the Kyoto Protocol or to advocate aggressive domestic action to reduce emissions, largely due to opposition from labor. But the highly critical media coverage of the administration's rejection of the agreement and the reversal of the president's campaign pledge emboldened many to take far more outspoken positions. For example, House Democratic Leader Richard Gephardt, whose home state, Missouri, is second only to Michigan in automobile union membership, publicly called for ratification of the Protocol. Other Democrats lined up behind legislation to reduce power plant carbon dioxide emissions.

The administration's posture also galvanized support for international and domestic action on climate change among Republicans. Moderates from northeastern states, where the environment is a top-tier political issue, distanced themselves from the president. Then-Senate Environment and Public Works Committee Chairman Bob Smith (R-NH) made it clear that he supported a carbon dioxide emissions-reduction program for power plants and designated the legislation as a top priority for his panel. US Senator John McCain (R-AZ), Bush's 2000 primary opponent, joined with Senator Joe Lieberman (D-CT), the 2000 Democratic vice-presidential nominee, in calling for an economy-wide greenhouse gas emissions-reduction program.

AN ABANDONED PLEDGE BACKFIRES

On June 7, 2001, one of the Bush White House's principal efforts to justify reversal of the president's campaign pledge on power plants and rejection of the Kyoto Protocol backfired spectacularly. For the past decade, public-relations campaigns sponsored by the oil, coal, utility, and automobile industries have attempted to portray the scientific evidence of climate change as uncertain, touting the opinions of a handful of industry-funded scientists who dissent from a very broad international scientific consensus.

In 2001, the newly released assessment reports by the UN-sponsored Intergovernmental Panel on Climate Change (IPCC), involving over 2,000 scientists in the United States and abroad, demonstrated with further scientific certainty that human contributions to atmospheric greenhouse gas concentrations are accelerating global warming. Having little personal background in the field, senior White House staff members accepted arguments by industry and conservative groups that the IPCC reports did not reflect the views of mainstream US scientists. In May 2001, John M. Bridgeland, deputy assistant to the president for domestic policy, and Gary Edson, deputy assistant for international economic affairs, requested a "fast-track" review of climate change science from the National Academy of Sciences, questioning the IPCC studies. Only days before Bush's first meeting with European heads of government in Goteborg, Sweden, where the Kyoto Protocol would rise as a principal issue, an 11-member Academy panel released its report. It was an authoritative rebuff to earlier administration statements questioning the IPCC's assessments: the panel reaffirmed the mainstream scientific conclusion that "greenhouse gases are accumulating in earth's atmosphere as a result of human activities, causing surface air temperatures and subsurface ocean temperatures to rise." The scientists also warned that "national policy decisions made now and in the longer-term future will influence the extent of any damage suffered by vulnerable human populations and ecosystems later in the century." Ironically, Academy panels had taken this position in earlier reports, of which both the Bush White House and many reporters were unaware. The White House-initiated review, so clearly an embarrassment to the administration, generated headlines and editorials all over the country. Even the most prominent congressional skeptics were forced to admit that science had reached a stage where action was required. US Senator Chuck Hagel (R-NB), the leading Senate opponent of the Protocol, told the *New York Times*, "This report does provide us with enough evidence to move forward in a responsible, reasonable way to reduce greenhouse gas emissions.

The administration's declaration that the Kyoto Protocol was "dead" also produced unexpected results at the negotiating table. European governments that had rejected even minor modifications to the Kyoto emissions-reduction targets during The Hague talks were suddenly forced to confront the reality that the entire agreement might collapse if the Protocol were not completed in July 2001 at the next negotiating session in Bonn, Germany. And while Bush pledged not to obstruct the Bonn meeting, US administration officials identified Japan as the weakest link among industrialized nations and worked to convince the new government of Prime Minister Junichiro Koizumi to await a US proposal before agreeing to anything in Bonn. In the end, this effort failed: in order to save the treaty, European governments made substantial concessions to the Japanese— concessions that would have been unthinkable six months earlier in the Hague—and an agreement was announced on July 23 that substantially completed the Protocol.

DYNAMICS OF 2002

While there are no public indications today that the Bush administration is considering softening its position on the Kyoto Protocol or domestic emissions reductions, political pressures for it to do so are likely to intensify over the coming year. For one, 2002 is a critical congressional election year for both parties: Republicans control the House by a razor-thin margin and Democrats control the Senate only by courtesy of Vermont's James Jeffords, now an Independent. While many of the Democrats' most popular domestic issues were temporarily swept off the table by the September 11 terrorist attacks, it is unlikely that the 90-percent presidential approval ratings from which Republicans are benefiting will survive through next November. (Bush senior enjoyed similar ratings following the Gulf War in 1991, but went on to be defeated in his re-election bid the following year.) As the ship of state rights itself and elections loom, national security may remain by far the most prominent national issue, but it is unlikely to remain the only one of concern to voters.

The Bush administration certainly recognizes that a significant amount of repair work must be done to its environmental image. Bush's flurry of press conferences in national parks during the spring and summer of 2001 did not move his poll numbers on environmental issues at all; those in the White House arguing that the problem is not policy but presentation have now seen their message-only approach fail. One important early sign of preparation for the 2002 congressional elections was Whitman's about-face on standards for arsenic in drinking water: in a *Washington Post* interview on September 10, 2001, she said she would not announce a new standard any less stringent than the one she inherited from the Clinton administration. With an EPA decision on the issue scheduled for February, neither Whitman nor the White House likely relished the prospect of kicking off an election year with another controversy about arsenic in the nation's drinking water.

On both domestic and international fronts, the Bush administration faces the prospect that global warming will continue to be a prominent environmental issue. Jeffords' departure from the Republican Party in May not only switched Senate control to the Democrats but also gained him the chairmanship of the Senate Environment and Public Works Committee. As one of five often-isolated moderate Republicans, Jeffords was the principal author of legislation to establish the first mandatory carbon dioxide emissions-reduction program, which the White House was able to ignore. Now, as chairman, he is aggressively moving that legislation through his committee; by January or February [on February 14, 2002, Bush announced a voluntary carbon dioxide emission-reduction plan], it is likely that the White House will face a committee-approved bill that will be debated on the US Senate floor sometime during 2002, placing carbon dioxide emissions reductions squarely in the middle of the domestic environment debate as US congressional elections approach.

INTERNATIONAL PRESURE

At the same time, the international dynamic around the Kyoto Protocol has intensified. British Prime Minister Tony Blair, who has assumed the role of the administration's strongest international supporter in antiterrorism efforts, has made clear both publicly and in private meetings with US administration officials since September 11, 2001, that a cooperative US policy on global warming is a high priority to him. His views will be very difficult for the president to ignore. Germany and France, both of whom have been strong supporters in the aftermath of the attacks, offering participation by their troops, are also among the strongest backers of Kyoto.

Equally important, following legal text negotiations in Marrakech, Morocco, in October and November, 2002, the European Union and many other nations will proceed to formal ratification. Japan recently informed US State Department officials that Japanese ratification will swiftly follow the Marrakech talks. This creates a difficult international situation with potential domestic political consequences: in September 2002, less than two months before the US congressional elections, world leaders will meet at the second "Earth Summit" in Johannesburg, South Africa, to celebrate the 10th anniversary of the Rio summit. Global warming will be a high-profile issue at the meeting, and Bush faces the prospect of appearing at home to be isolated and out-of-step on the environment once again. Ironically, this is exactly the situation his father faced at Rio before the 1992 elections, when he rejected provisions of the draft UNFCCC that required binding emissions-reduction targets.

GETTING BUSH ON BOARD

If international pressure is to be successful in softening the Bush administration's position on agreeing to a binding international agreement on carbon dioxide emissions reductions, the United States must be given a face-saving means of rejoining the international community on this issue. There is a way to accomplish the above goal that, at the same time, acknowledges a fundamental reality. The United States cannot now meet the reductions targets agreed to in Kyoto four years ago. A reduction from business-as-usual emissions of more than 30 percent by approximately 2010 was ambitious, even if the Clinton administration had begun to press Congress immediately for action on domestic emissions reductions. Now, following the September 11 attacks, there is simply no indication that the United States can reach that goal. If Congress completed legislation mandating such reductions by the end of 2002—not in itself likely—completing regulations implementing the law would take at least two years. Industries facing reductions would then be only three years away from the Protocol's first budget period (2008–2012) and meeting the targets would be physically impossible.

It is critical at this point that the European Union, Japan, and other nations recognize this reality—something that will be politically difficult for them at home. But such a recognition would allow the Bush administration to come back to the table: Bush has consistently argued that the Kyoto targets would have a serious economic impact on the United States, but his administration has equally consistently supported the flexible international trading mechanisms that have been negotiated to implement the Protocol. In addition, utilities facing the prospect of mandated emissions reductions have begun to make the case that access to the international mechanisms is critical to their ability to make cost-effective carbon dioxide emissions reductions. Making it clear to the Bush White House that US proposals to join the Protocol in the second budget period would be looked upon favorably and would provide a politically palatable resolution to the situation. This would allow the Bush administration to join the agreement while renegotiating the targets agreed to by its predecessor.

The turbulence of 2001 has almost completely altered the political landscape around global-warming issues, and 2002 offers critical opportunities to capitalize on these changes. They must not be lost. The next year may produce a unique political dynamic and the best foreseeable opportunity to shift US policy onto a constructive path. The European Union, in particular, must participate in creating an atmosphere that both presses for change and shapes a constructive US response.

The United States must partner with others around the world on a program to develop alternative energy systems. The technological revolution needed for the urgent move to a hydrogen economy, for example, coupled with increased national investment in research for environmentally safe transportation, would yield huge results for the global environment. Such a far-reaching program would have a major stimulative effect for the world economy and would place the United States again in a position of genuine global vision and leadership.

2001 and Beyond: A Tragic Introduction to a New Era

CHAPTER 4

September 11, 2001: A Day of Infamy

Scott Anderson

On September 11, 2001, commercial airliners hijacked by terrorists carrying small knives and box cutters became guided missiles that killed thousands of Americans. Two planes originating from Boston's Logan Airport were steered into the upper floors of the 110-story Twin Towers of the World Trade Center complex in downtown New York City. The first plane crashed into Tower One at 8:30 A.M. Thousands of office workers on the floors below the crash began a desperate evacuation of the tower. Twenty minutes later, a second plane hit Tower Two. At 9:59 A.M., Tower Two collapsed, sending scores of evacuees, rescue workers, and onlookers scrambling for their lives. Thirty minutes later, Tower One also collapsed. In the meantime, a third hijacked plane had slammed into the Pentagon outside Washington, D.C., after takeoff from Dulles International Airport. A fourth hijacked plane, originating from Newark International Airport in New Jersey and presumed to have been diverted toward the White House, crashed in rural Pennsylvania after desperate passengers attempted to foil the hijackers.

The attacks, carried out by Islamic extremists willing to die for their cause, left Americans struggling to comprehend what had provoked the most catastrophic assaults ever committed on domestic soil. Close to three thousand people were killed at the World Trade Center, including hundreds of firemen and police officers. At the Pentagon, 125 workers lost their lives. All 246 passengers and crew members on board the four airplanes were killed. Many people felt immobilized by fears of further attacks, but in New York City, thousands of residents showed immense courage and volunteered to help with the rescue and recovery efforts at what became known as "Ground Zero," the site of the devastated World Trade Center. In the following essay, Scott Anderson delivers a first-person account of the events of September 11 as they unfolded in New York City. Anderson describes how the city was transformed into a war-zone that tested the strengths of ordinary New Yorkers, who suddenly found themselves in the midst of a nightmarish landscape of death and destruction. Anderson is a contributing editor at *Harper's* magazine and has reported on conflicts in Chechnya, El Salvador, and Uganda for numerous publications.

I t is an odd thing, probably not what one would predict or remember afterward, but when a person encounters true horror, the body's first response almost always occurs in the hands. With women, the hands tend to immediately come up to cover the mouth or press the cheeks. Among men, they tend to form a steeple over the nose and mouth or to clutch tightly onto the sides of the head. It is as if, in this moment of utter incomprehension and helplessness, the hands are trying to give comfort.

SHOCKING SCENES OF DESTRUCTION

I'm not sure where I first noticed this. It might have been in Belfast in 1989, when a large car bomb went off downtown and the people around me didn't know which way to run as glass rained down around us. Or it might have been before that, in Beirut in 1983 or in Sri Lanka in 1987, but it does seem to be a universal reflex, this thing with the hands. I saw it again at 9:59 on the morning of September 11 in New York City.

At that moment, I was standing on the roof of an apartment building in the East Village, watching the billows of white smoke pouring off the upper floors of the World Trade Center towers, perhaps two miles away. On the surrounding rooftops were scores, maybe hundreds, of other onlookers. At 9:59, there appeared to be a sudden bulging outward around the midpoint of Tower Two, a quick glittering of either fire or the morning sun reflecting off dislodged windows, and then Tower Two started straight down with a speed that seemed to defy gravity. On the rooftops all around me, men gripped their heads, women their faces. Just down from me, a man in his late thirties with a long ponytail and tattooed forearms began screaming, "No, no!" then dropped to his knees and wrapped his arms tightly over his chest. I remember looking at him with a mix of pity and envy—pity for his pain but envy because he was the first among us to find his voice, the first to move from shock to despair, and this seemed the healthiest reaction to have. I was still just standing there, mute, numb, clutching my head.

Over the past eighteen years, I've been to a dozen-odd war zones around the world. Usually, I went as a journalist, with all the detachment and comparative immunity that implies. Of course, there were times when both detachment and immunity fell away, when I witnessed things that affected me deeply, or I found myself in harm's way, but in all these places, I was, first and foremost, an outsider; what was happening fundamentally did not involve me, it was not my war. Nor could I ever reasonably claim to be shocked by what I saw; after all, I had gone there for the very purpose of seeing it. All that ended, as it did for millions of other New Yorkers, on the morning of September 11. For the first time, I had not gone to war, but war had come to me—and with as little warning as it comes to most—and if a lot of it felt very familiar, a lot of it didn't at all.

After Tower One collapsed at 10:28, I left the apartment

The Twin Towers of the World Trade Center no longer grace New York's skyline. Their collapse buried almost three thousand people.

rooftop. Like everyone else in the city, I didn't know what to do, I just knew that I needed to do something, and maybe if I began to walk I would discover it. I started south, toward the plume of white smoke and dust in the sky.

The four lanes of First Avenue were virtually empty save for an occasional racing ambulance or police car, but along the side-walks came a flood of people heading north. There was a hush to them, hardly anyone speaking, and here and there in the crowd was someone caked in fine beige powder. I don't think any of them knew where they were going, either, just away from the ugly cloud, further into the warmth and sunlight of this beautiful late-summer morning.

Walking against the current, I spotted a middle-aged busi-nessman approaching at a brisk pace, weaving and overtaking "traffic" the way New Yorkers do on sidewalks. He was dressed in an expensive suit and clutched a fine leather briefcase, but it was as if he'd been dipped in buckwheat flour from head to toe, and the briskness of his walk was causing little spumes of dust to fly off him with each step. As we passed, he gave me a quick, slightly annoyed glance, as if to say, "What the hell are you looking at?" He obviously had been close when the towers came down, had undoubtedly sprinted for his life, and had done so in such blind terror that it never occurred to him to drop the briefcase. Now, a half hour and two miles away, he was still pumped up, still moving on the adrenaline that might give out on the next block or might carry him all the way to wherever he imagined he was headed.

SEARCHING FOR WAYS TO HELP

In war, the fabric of society—the rules and laws and customs that are lived by—frays in direct proportion to one's nearness to the battlefield. In most wars, this fraying occurs over a dis-tance of provinces or valleys or mountain ranges, but in New York on September 11 it was happening over the space of a few city blocks. By 11:00, the authorities were trying to establish a security perimeter at Canal Street, a demarcation line between civilization and madness that civilians would not be allowed past. The problem was, the police detailed to this task were just as lost and stunned as the rest of us; their authority had de-serted them. A policeman stopped me, ordered me back. I nod-ded at him and continued on, and he simply turned to try his luck with someone else. Once past this line, authority had little to do with rank or uniforms; in the peculiar kind of meritocracy that takes over in a place of chaos, leadership now fell to anyone with the surety or charisma to seize it.

I first saw this at a forward triage unit being set up in the lobby of the Department of Health building near City Hall, where a black woman in her mid-thirties in a white coat was in command of people twice her age. Perhaps she was a doctor, perhaps a nurse, but her authority stemmed from her calm, her ability to focus on each person who came before her and to give them orders. It didn't matter if the commands she gave were impossible to fulfill, it was the certainty with which she gave them that made the rest of us trust her; in our collective impotence, we were all just looking for someone to tell us what to do.

I helped unload boxes of medical supplies coming off trucks, stacked them along the walls of the lobby. It felt good to do this, like I was being useful, and I was spurred on by a man somewhere in the crowd who repeatedly shouted, "Come on, people, we have to get organized. They're going to be coming in any minute now." Except they didn't come in. No one came in. No one was coming out anymore from the awful cloud a few blocks away, and we were all just there—doctors, nurses, grunts like me—stacking boxes, erecting eyewash kits, making neat little arrays of gauze bandages and syringes and antiseptic wash, because it was only by staying busy that our minds could detach from the enormity of what had happened, could let us believe we were doing something to help.

After a time, I wandered outside. Another set of wooden barricades had been set out on the far side of the street, and as I walked toward them, a policewoman called out to me: "Sir, you're not allowed past there."

"Okay," I called back, and continued on. She was not a cop anymore; she knew it and I knew it, and if I'd had the presence of the woman in the Health Department lobby, I could have told the cop to go across the street and start counting paper cups and she would have done it.

I walked a little ways down a deserted side street, and, finally, out of the gloom came two women caked in dust. One was middle-aged and white, the other elderly and black with tightly braided hair, limping. I couldn't tell if they were friends or coworkers or simply found each other on the way out, but they were very protective of each other, the white woman hovering close as the other settled into a chair on the sidewalk. I asked if there was anything I could do for them; they thanked me and said they were fine.

"I was at my desk on the ninety-first floor," the white woman said. "I think the plane must have hit right above us, maybe on ninety-three or ninety-four. They told us to leave."

A Terrifying Escape

She told of her long descent down the stairwell of Tower One, how after a few flights she felt a second shudder, softer than the first, and figured this must have been from the other plane hitting Tower Two. She related all this in a flat, matter-of-fact voice, but her face was trembling, her knees unsteady.

"When I got outside, I saw people jumping. I didn't know they were people at first. I thought maybe it was just different things falling, you know? Maybe bits of the building or chairs or lamps. I really didn't know. Even now, I'm not sure that's what I saw, that maybe it wasn't people. Have you heard anything about people jumping?"

Her eyes were desperate and terribly sad, and they searched my face for a clue. I'd seen that look many times before—after car bombings or artillery attacks, on the faces of mothers looking for lost sons—and it seemed that her mind was trying to erase what her eyes had seen, that with the right words at this fragile moment, the memory might be erased altogether.

"No," I told her. "I haven't heard anything about that. There's a lot of wild rumors flying around, but I haven't heard that one."

This seemed to calm her, and I asked if she'd like me to find her a chair.

"No, thank you," she said, wiping at her cheek with shaking fingers. "I just want to stand for a while, wait for the others."

I stayed with them, and we all gazed down the side street from which they had emerged, from which any other survivors coming this way would probably emerge. After a time, a lone figure appeared. She was a very pretty Hispanic woman in her mid-twenties, and she seemed oblivious to the fact that she had lost her shoes and was leaving behind drops of blood with each step. Just about the only way to reach someone in severe shock is to look directly into their eyes and talk softly, but this woman only stared straight ahead, so as she passed, I leaned close and whispered that she was bleeding, that there was a medical unit just ahead. She continued on without any indication she'd heard me.

We waited awhile longer, the two ladies and I, but no one else came down the street, and, finally, the white woman turned to her friend. "Well," she said, with that exaggerated exhalation that usually suggests impatience or that it's time to get motivated, "are you ready?"

The black woman nodded and got to her feet, and the two went off together down the sidewalk. I was sorry to see them go, because even just standing beside them in their vigil, I felt I was doing something. With them gone, I had no purpose again.

ORGANIZING SEARCH-AND-RESCUE TEAMS

I came upon a large crowd gathered in Foley Square, in front of the New York Supreme Court building. Groups were being organized and corralled into little pens delineated with yellow police tape. It appeared most people were there to donate blood, their blood type marked in big black letters on their arms or T-shirts, and one young man moved about shouting in a hoarse voice, "O-negatives, we urgently need O-negatives." Except there was no one around to actually take blood, no vehicles to take anyone to a place where it might be done. It was organization for organization's sake, a plan of action being devised in the absence of either plan or action. But if it was absurd, it was also inspiring; what I was seeing was the very first steps toward rebuilding an ordered society in a corner of Manhattan where it had suddenly vanished, and it was being done with black Magic Markers and yellow police tape by the natural leaders among us.

At one corner of the park, search-and-rescue volunteers were being divided into various groups, and I joined the one consisting of current and former members of the military. I chose the group both because I figured it would be among the first to go in and because I was drawn to its self-appointed leader: an athletic, bespectacled man in his late thirties with a crew cut and a bullhorn. Through the hot afternoon, he put us through our paces, ordering us to "form up" in columns or "fall out," to "rehydrate" ourselves, to "listen up, and listen good" to whatever new bits of information he had gleaned from somewhere. "Stay loose, men, and stay focused," our "commander" exhorted us. "There's a lot of desperate people in there, and they're counting on us."

"We kept running over body parts," the fireman whispered. He was staring into my eyes with a pleading look, as if seeking forgiveness. "I mean, the ash was so thick, you'd see things in the street, but you couldn't tell what they were until you ran over them. I mean, what the fuck were we supposed to do?"

I nodded, patted him on the shoulder, and when I did, he let out a single sharp sob, almost like a hiccup. I looked past him at the 150 or so other firemen resting in a tunnel nearby.

At about four o'clock, I and the rest of the "military team" had been bused over to the West Side of Manhattan, just above the ruins. We had assumed we were about to go in, but instead we'd been told that another high-rise building was about to collapse and were ordered back toward the West Side Highway. In our retreat, we'd come upon the firemen in the tunnel.

I'd heard many rumors over the course of that day—that the Capitol had been hit, that another hijacked plane was shot down over the Hudson River—but a recurrent one held that a huge number of New York City firefighters were dead or missing; as I passed the firemen, I studied their faces for some clue as to its validity. I couldn't detect a pattern. At some tables they were talking, even laughing at some shared story, while at the next table over they were sleeping or simply staring into space.

One day in Chechnya, I'd come upon a group of Russian soldiers stranded on a remote firebase. The night before, they'd been attacked by the rebels, had taken a number of casualties, but now, in the false calm of day, they were scattered over the ground, some sound asleep, others crying, others contentedly playing cards or listening to music. It occurred to me then how in moments of emotional collapse, we simply mimic those around us—if you sit next to a laugher, you laugh, next to a crier, you cry, that if you get enough shell-shocked people together in one place, you won't discern any pattern at all.

On the West Side Highway, we linked up with some of the other search-and-rescue teams waiting to go in and huddled around to wait some more. The sun set over the river and for a while, maybe a half hour, there was a stunning gold tinge to the sky and the buildings around us. Up the highway stretched a line of emergency vehicles and knots of waiting firemen and medics and police as far as the eye could see, and, as hard as it was for us to accept—and it was very, very hard—I think it began to dawn on all of us volunteers that if they were not going into the ruins and flames, neither were we.

At about midnight, I finally gave up hope and began the long walk north toward the perimeter line and the "normal" city that lay beyond. I remember that I passed a man walking his dog. For a fleeting instant, I felt an absolute rage at the sight, but the very next instant, I felt my eyes well up for reasons I wouldn't have been able to explain. I decided to keep to the quieter, less-peopled streets as I made my way home.

RETURNING TO THE DISASTER SITE

The following evening, I reached the edge of the disaster site, not as a "deputized" search-and-rescue volunteer but as a mere onlooker. A measure of official authority had been established by then, but only a measure; by cutting through the backstreets below the Brooklyn Bridge, I charted a path past the police barricades and emerged onto Broadway at the corner of Ann Street. Across the street, the graves of St. Paul's were covered in ash and scattered papers, and along the wall next to me was an enormous pile of crudely made wood stretchers. Yesterday, one of the construction teams had gone off to make stretchers, and here they sat, unused, never to be used, gathering ash from the fires that still burned.

Walking south on Broadway, I came to the corner of Liberty Street, just a block from where the World Trade towers had once stood. It was, of course, a bizarre scene, made more so by the ghostly glow of stage lights that illuminated the workers scrambling over the ruins. Enormous sections of the Tower Two facade jutted up at odd angles, and as shovels dug at the pile, little bursts of flame appeared beneath. I stood on the corner and watched for a time, but what I eventually began to notice were all the shoes scattered in the street before me. There were ladies' pumps, men's dress shoes, high heels, but they all looked much the same, twisted and mangled by either their owner's flight or the wheels of emergency vehicles, all half sunken in the ash-mud that coated everything here.

I can recall only one other time that I've ever written about shoes. It was in a book I wrote with my brother, an oral history of five wars taking place around the world. In the epilogue I had tried to sum up what war now meant to me, and the image that came to me was of a young man, a lotus-blossom seller I had met in Sri Lanka, sitting in his hut and holding up a pair of small green shoes. Two years earlier, guerrillas had suddenly appeared at the Buddhist shrine where he sold his flowers and started shooting anyone not quick enough to get out of their way—and that included the man's five-year-old son. The boy had lost four inches of his left leg, and that was now compensated for by a four-inch heel on his left shoe.

"And I suppose for me that is war," were the last words I'd written in the book, "that for a variety of reasons, all of which sound good, men shoot the children of lotus-blossom sellers and leave behind them little green shoes."

And now here I was again, not in Sri Lanka or Chechnya, but on the corner of Broadway and Liberty Street in downtown Manhattan, looking at the shoes that war leaves behind, and all at once, in this place I had tried so hard to reach, I didn't want to stay any longer, I didn't ever want to see it again.

EMERGING FROM THE SHOCK

On the night of Thursday, September 13, a dramatic thunderstorm approached New York from the northwest. It had been sixty hours since the attacks, and the people of the city were slowly emerging from their shock, their emotions settling down into anger and sadness. Throughout the city that day, impromptu memorials had been erected, little altars of flowers and cards and candles wherever enough people decided to place them. What had also blossomed were a million small posters, photographs of those still missing, appeals from their families for any information on their whereabouts; they reminded me of so many other posters and families that I'd seen around the world—in Bosnia, in Guatemala—holding on to the memory of those who had vanished, refusing to relinquish hope that they might miraculously return. On that day, no one had been found alive at the World Trade Center.

At about one o'clock on Friday morning, the storm finally reached Manhattan. There had been times in the past when, coming back from a war zone, it had taken me time to get used to such storms, when I couldn't get out of my head how much the roar of thunder can sound like artillery or a collapsing building, how much the flash of lightning can look like something exploding in the distance. If it is possible to be simultaneously comforted and saddened by a thought—and, believe me, any crazy combination of emotions is possible in New York after September 11—then I was comforted and saddened right then, knowing that across my city were hundreds of thousands of other people just like me, unable to sleep, unable to fully believe that what was passing over us was nothing more than a late-summer storm.

In the Wake of September 11: Declaring War on Terrorism

George W. Bush

In the following speech delivered on September 20, 2001, nine days after thousands of Americans were killed in terrorist attacks on the Pentagon and the World Trade Center, President George W. Bush outlined his plans for a war against terrorism. According to Bush, this war would involve military action, diplomacy, intelligence gathering, law enforcement, and freezing the financial assets of terrorists. Most important, nations that acted as safe havens for terrorists were to be considered hostile to the security of the United States.

One nation that had clearly tolerated terrorist activity was Afghanistan. In the speech, the president mentioned evidence linking the al-Qaeda terrorist organization and its leader, Osama bin Laden, to the catastrophic attacks of September 11, 2001. Afghanistan's Taliban government, a regime of Islamic extremists, had allowed bin Laden and al-Qaeda to train terrorists in camps around the country. The president demanded that the Taliban hand over bin Laden and the leaders of al-Qaeda in Afghanistan or face the consequences of war. The war against terrorism entered its first military action on October 7, 2001, after the Taliban refused to cooperate. President George W. Bush, the former governor of Texas, entered office in January 2001.

Excerpted from George W. Bush's address delivered to a Joint Session of Congress and the American People, Washington, D.C., September 20, 2001.

M r. Speaker, Mr. President pro tempore, Members of Congress, and fellow Americans: In the normal course of events, presidents come to this chamber to report on the state of the Union. Tonight, no such report is needed. It has already been delivered by the American people.

We have seen it in the courage of [airline] passengers, who rushed terrorists to save others on the ground—passengers like an exceptional man named Todd Beamer. Please help me to welcome his wife, Lisa Beamer, here tonight.

We have seen the state of our Union in the endurance of rescuers, working past exhaustion. We have seen the unfurling of flags, the lighting of candles, the giving of blood, the saying of prayers—in English, Hebrew, and Arabic. We have seen the decency of a loving and giving people, who have made the grief of strangers their own.

My fellow citizens, for the last nine days, the entire world has seen for itself the state of our Union—and it is strong.

FREEDOM UNDER ATTACK

Tonight we are a country awakened to danger and called to defend freedom. Our grief has turned to anger, and anger to resolution. Whether we bring our enemies to justice, or bring justice to our enemies, justice will be done.

I thank the Congress for its leadership at such an important time. All of America was touched on the evening of the tragedy [September 11, 2001] to see Republicans and Democrats, joined together on the steps of this Capitol, singing "God Bless America." And you did more than sing, you acted, by delivering forty billion dollars to rebuild our communities and meet the needs of our military.

Speaker Hastert and Minority Leader Gephardt—Majority Leader Daschle and Senator Lott—I thank you for your friendship and your leadership and your service to our country.

And on behalf of the American people, I thank the world for its outpouring of support. America will never forget the sounds of our National Anthem playing at Buckingham Palace, and on the streets of Paris, and at Berlin's Brandenburg Gate. We will not forget South Korean children gathering to pray outside our embassy in Seoul, or the prayers of sympathy offered at a mosque in Cairo. We will not forget moments of silence and days of mourning in Australia and Africa and Latin America.

Nor will we forget the citizens of eighty other nations who

died with our own. Dozens of Pakistanis. More than 130 Israelis. More than 250 citizens of India. Men and women from El Salvador, Iran, Mexico, and Japan. And hundreds of British citizens. America has no truer friend than Great Britain. Once again, we are joined together in a great cause. The British Prime Minister has crossed an ocean to show his unity of purpose with America, and tonight we welcome Tony Blair.

On September the eleventh, enemies of freedom committed an act of war against our country. Americans have known wars—but for the past 136 years, they have been wars on foreign soil, except for one Sunday in 1941 [when Japanese forces attacked Pearl Harbor, Hawaii]. Americans have known the casualties of war—but not at the center of a great city [New York] on a peaceful morning. Americans have known surprise attacks—but never before on thousands of civilians. All of this was brought upon us in a single day—and night fell on a different world, a world where freedom itself is under attack.

EVIDENCE POINTS TO ISLAMIC TERRORIST ORGANIZATIONS

Americans have many questions tonight. Americans are asking:

Who attacked our country?

The evidence we have gathered all points to a collection of loosely affiliated terrorist organizations known as al-Qaida. They are the same murderers indicted for bombing American embassies in Tanzania and Kenya [1998], and responsible for the bombing of the U.S.S. Cole [2000].

Al-Qaida is to terror what the mafia is to crime. But its goal is not making money; its goal is remaking the world—and imposing its radical beliefs on people everywhere.

The terrorists practice a fringe form of Islamic extremism that has been rejected by Muslim scholars and the vast majority of Muslim clerics—a fringe movement that perverts the peaceful teachings of Islam. The terrorists' directive commands them to kill Christians and Jews, to kill all Americans, and make no distinctions among military and civilians, including women and children.

This group and its leader—a person named Usama bin Ladin—are linked to many other organizations in different countries, including the Egyptian Islamic Jihad and the Islamic Movement of Uzbekistan.

There are thousands of these terrorists in more than sixty

countries. They are recruited from their own nations and neighborhoods, and brought to camps in places like Afghanistan where they are trained in the tactics of terror. They are sent back to their homes or sent to hide in countries around the world to plot evil and destruction.

The leadership of al-Qaida has great influence in Afghanistan, and supports the Taliban regime in controlling most of that country.

In Afghanistan, we see al-Qaida's vision for the world. Afghanistan's people have been brutalized—many are starving and many have fled. Women are not allowed to attend school. You can be jailed for owning a television. Religion can be practiced only as their leaders dictate. A man can be jailed in Afghanistan if his beard is not long enough.

The United States respects the people of Afghanistan—after all, we are currently its largest source of humanitarian aid—but we condemn the Taliban regime. It is not only repressing its own people, it is threatening people everywhere by sponsoring and sheltering and supplying terrorists. By aiding and abetting murder, the Taliban regime is committing murder. And tonight, the United States of America makes the following demands on the Taliban:

Deliver to United States authorities all the leaders of al-Qaida who hide in your land.

Release all foreign nationals—including American citizens—you have unjustly imprisoned, and protect foreign journalists, diplomats, and aid workers in your country.

Close immediately and permanently every terrorist training camp in Afghanistan and hand over every terrorist, and every person in their support structure, to appropriate authorities.

Give the United States full access to terrorist training camps, so we can make sure they are no longer operating.

These demands are not open to negotiation or discussion. The Taliban must act and act immediately. They will hand over the terrorists, or they will share in their fate.

I also want to speak tonight directly to Muslims throughout the world: We respect your faith. It is practiced freely by many millions of Americans, and by millions more in countries that America counts as friends. Its teachings are good and peaceful, and those who commit evil in the name of Allah blaspheme the name of Allah. The terrorists are traitors to their own faith, trying, in effect, to hijack Islam itself. The enemy of America is not our many Muslim friends; it is not our many Arab friends. Our enemy is a radical network of terrorists, and every government that supports them.

DECLARING WAR ON TERRORISM

Our war on terror begins with al-Qaida, but it does not end there. It will not end until every terrorist group of global reach has been found, stopped, and defeated.

Americans are asking: Why do they hate us?

They hate what we see right here in this chamber—a democratically elected government. Their leaders are self-appointed. They hate our freedoms—our freedom of religion, our freedom of speech, our freedom to vote and assemble and disagree with each other.

They want to overthrow existing governments in many Muslim countries, such as Egypt, Saudi Arabia, and Jordan. They want to drive Israel out of the Middle East. They want to drive Christians and Jews out of vast regions of Asia and Africa.

These terrorists kill not merely to end lives, but to disrupt and end a way of life. With every atrocity, they hope that America grows fearful, retreating from the world and forsaking our friends. They stand against us, because we stand in their way.

We are not deceived by their pretenses to piety. We have seen their kind before. They are the heirs of all the murderous ideologies of the twentieth century. By sacrificing human life to serve their radical visions—by abandoning every value except the will to power—they follow in the path of fascism, and Nazism, and totalitarianism. And they will follow that path all the way, to where it ends: in history's unmarked grave of discarded lies.

Americans are asking: How will we fight and win this war?

We will direct every resource at our command—every means of diplomacy, every tool of intelligence, every instrument of law enforcement, every financial influence, and every necessary weapon of war—to the disruption and defeat of the global terror network.

This war will not be like the war against Iraq a decade ago [1991], with its decisive liberation of territory and its swift conclusion. It will not look like the air war above Kosovo two years ago [1999], where no ground troops were used and not a single American was lost in combat.

Our response involves far more than instant retaliation and

isolated strikes. Americans should not expect one battle, but a lengthy campaign, unlike any other we have seen. It may include dramatic strikes, visible on television, and covert operations, secret even in success. We will starve terrorists of funding, turn them one against another, drive them from place to place, until there is no refuge or rest. And we will pursue nations that provide aid or safe haven to terrorism. Every nation, in every region, now has a decision to make. Either you are with us, or you are with the terrorists. From this day forward, any nation that continues to harbor or support terrorism will be regarded by the United States as a hostile regime.

PROTECTING AMERICANS AT HOME

Our nation has been put on notice: We are not immune from attack. We will take defensive measures against terrorism to protect Americans.

Today, dozens of federal departments and agencies, as well as state and local governments, have responsibilities affecting homeland security. These efforts must be coordinated at the highest level. So tonight I announce the creation of a Cabinet-level position reporting directly to me—the Office of Homeland Security.

These measures are essential. But the only way to defeat terrorism as a threat to our way of life is to stop it, eliminate it, and destroy it where it grows.

Many will be involved in this effort, from FBI agents to intelligence operatives to the reservists we have called to active duty. All deserve our thanks, and all have our prayers. And tonight, a few miles from the damaged Pentagon, I have a message for our military: Be ready. I have called the armed forces to alert, and there is a reason. The hour is coming when America will act, and you will make us proud.

This is not, however, just America's fight. And what is at stake is not just America's freedom. This is the world's fight. This is civilization's fight. This is the fight of all who believe in progress and pluralism, tolerance and freedom.

We ask every nation to join us. We will ask, and we will need, the help of police forces, intelligence services, and banking systems around the world. The United States is grateful that many nations and many international organizations have already responded—with sympathy and with support. Nations from Latin America, to Asia, to Africa, to Europe, to the Islamic world. Perhaps the NATO Charter reflects best the attitude of the world: an attack on one is an attack on all.

The civilized world is rallying to America's side. They understand that if this terror goes unpunished, their own cities, their own citizens may be next. Terror, unanswered, can not only bring down buildings, it can threaten the stability of legitimate governments. And we will not allow it.

Americans are asking: What is expected of us?

I ask you to live your lives and hug your children. I know many citizens have fears tonight, and I ask you to be calm and resolute, even in the face of a continuing threat.

I ask you to uphold the values of America, and remember why so many have come here. We are in a fight for our principles, and our first responsibility is to live by them. No one should be singled out for unfair treatment or unkind words because of their ethnic background or religious faith.

I ask you to continue to support the victims of this tragedy with your contributions. Those who want to give can go to a central source of information, libertyunites.org, to find the names of groups providing direct help in New York, Pennsylvania, and Virginia.

The thousands of FBI agents who are now at work in this investigation may need your cooperation, and I ask you to give it.

I ask for your patience, with the delays and inconveniences that may accompany tighter security—and for your patience in what will be a long struggle.

I ask your continued participation and confidence in the American economy. Terrorists attacked a symbol of American prosperity. They did not touch its source. America is successful because of the hard work, and creativity, and enterprise of our people. These were the true strengths of our economy before September eleventh, and they are our strengths today.

Finally, please continue praying for the victims of terror and their families, for those in uniform, and for our great country. Prayer has comforted us in sorrow, and will help strengthen us for the journey ahead.

Tonight I thank my fellow Americans for what you have already done and for what you will do. And ladies and gentlemen of the Congress, I thank you, their representatives, for what you have already done, and for what we will do together.

Tonight, we face new and sudden national challenges. We will come together to improve air safety, to dramatically expand the number of air marshals on domestic flights, and take new measures to prevent hijacking. We will come together to promote stability and keep our airlines flying with direct assistance during this emergency.

We will come together to give law enforcement the additional tools it needs to track down terror here at home. We will come together to strengthen our intelligence capabilities to know the plans of terrorists before they act, and find them before they strike.

We will come together to take active steps that strengthen America's economy, and put our people back to work.

Tonight we welcome here two leaders who embody the extraordinary spirit of all New Yorkers: Governor George Pataki, and [then–New York City] Mayor Rudy Giuliani. As a symbol of America's resolve, my administration will work with the Congress, and these two leaders, to show the world that we will rebuild New York City.

STANDING STRONG AND DETERMINED

After all that has just passed—all the lives taken, and all the possibilities and hopes that died with them—it is natural to wonder if America's future is one of fear. Some speak of an age of terror. I know there are struggles ahead, and dangers to face. But this country will define our times, not be defined by them. As long as the United States of America is determined and strong, this will not be an age of terror; this will be an age of liberty, here and across the world.

Great harm has been done to us. We have suffered great loss. And in our grief and anger we have found our mission and our moment. Freedom and fear are at war. The advance of human freedom—the great achievement of our time, and the great hope of every time—now depends on us. Our nation—this generation—will lift a dark threat of violence from our people and our future. We will rally the world to this cause, by our efforts and by our courage. We will not tire, we will not falter, and we will not fail.

It is my hope that in the months and years ahead, life will return almost to normal. We'll go back to our lives and routines, and that is good. Even grief recedes with time and grace. But our resolve must not pass. Each of us will remember what happened that day, and to whom it happened. We will remember the moment the news came—where we were and what we were doing.

Some will remember an image of fire, or a story of rescue. Some will carry memories of a face and a voice gone forever.

And I will carry this. It is the police shield of a man named George Howard, who died at the World Trade Center trying to save others. It was given to me by his mom, Arlene, as a proud memorial to her son. This is my reminder of lives that ended, and a task that does not end.

I will not forget this wound to our country, or those who inflicted it. I will not yield—I will not rest—I will not relent in waging this struggle for the freedom and security of the American people.

The course of this conflict is not known, yet its outcome is certain. Freedom and fear, justice and cruelty, have always been at war, and we know that God is not neutral between them.

Fellow citizens, we will meet violence with patient justice—assured of the rightness of our cause, and confident of the victories to come. In all that lies before us, may God grant us wisdom, and may He watch over the United States of America. Thank you.

Responding to Terror: Waging War in Afghanistan

Charles Krauthammer

On October 7, 2001, the United States entered a military campaign against the Taliban government in Afghanistan and the network of terrorists who were using the country as a safe haven. The war was being fought in response to the devastating terrorist attacks of September 11, 2001, on the Pentagon outside Washington, D.C., and the World Trade Center in New York City, which resulted in the deaths of over three thousand Americans. The nineteen terrorists responsible for the September 11 attacks had been linked to Osama bin Laden, a Saudi Arabian exile whose al-Qaeda terrorist network was operating openly within Afghanistan's borders.

The Taliban government had come to power in Afghanistan in 1994 and imposed a rigid strain of Islamic fundamentalism on the nation. All affairs of the nation were conducted under a strict interpretation of Islamic law. Radio and television were banned. Women were required to wear the *burqa*, an outfit which covered them from head to toe, and were denied work and education. Following the September 11 attacks, the United States government requested that the Taliban's leader, Mullah Muhammad Omar, hand over Osama bin Laden and the leaders of al-Qaeda and provide the United States full access to terrorist training camps. Omar refused, and the United States began a bombing campaign against military and terrorist targets. At the same time, the Northern Alliance, an Afghan resistance group opposed to

From "Only in Their Dreams: Why Is the 'Arab Street' Silent? Because a Radical Muslim Fantasy Has Met Reality," by Charles Krauthammer, *Time*, December 24, 2001. Copyright © 2001 by Time, Inc. Reprinted with permission.

the Taliban, engaged in a ground war, soon capturing key Taliban strongholds. By mid-December 2001, the Taliban had been removed from power and many al-Qaeda terrorists were presumed dead. The whereabouts of Osama bin Laden and Mullah Muhammad Omar, however, remained unknown.

In the following essay, Charles Krauthammer describes how the swift defeat of the Taliban delivered a significant blow to the cause of Islamic fundamentalism. According to Krauthammer, the recruitment of young men to radical Islamic sects and terrorist activity will be much more difficult in the wake of the Taliban's shameful fall from power. Krauthammer is a journalist who writes frequently for *Time* magazine.

T he West has not fought a serious religious war in 350 years. America is too young to have fought any. Our first reaction, therefore, to the declaration of holy war made upon us on September 11 was to be appalled, impressed and intimidated. Appalled by the primitivism, impressed by the implacability, intimidated by the fanaticism.

Intimidation was pervasive during the initial hand-wringing period. What have we done to inspire such rage? What can we do? Sure, we can strike back, but will that not just make the enemy even more angry and determined and fanatical? How can you defeat an enemy who thinks he's on a mission from God?

How? A hundred days and one war later, we know the answer: B-52s, for starters.

We were from the beginning a little too impressed. There were endless warnings that making war on a Muslim nation would succeed only in recruiting more enraged volunteers for [Osama] bin Laden, with a flood of fierce mujahedin going to Afghanistan to confront the infidel. Western experts warned that the seething "Arab street" would rise up against us.

Look around. The Arab street is deathly quiet. The mobs, exultant on September 11 and braying for American blood, have gone home. There are no recruits headed to Afghanistan to fight the infidel. The old recruits, battered and beaten and terrified, are desperately trying to sneak their way out of Afghanistan.

The reason is simple. We won. Crushingly. Astonishingly. Destroying a regime 7,000 miles away, landlocked and almost inaccessible, in nine weeks.

The logic of victory often eludes the secular West. We have a hard time figuring out an enemy who speaks in religious terms. He seems indestructible. Cut him down, and 10 more will rise in his place. How can you destroy an idea?

This gave rise to the initial soul searching, the magazine covers plaintively asking WHY DO THEY HATE US? The feeling that we might be responsible for the hatred directed against us suggested that we should perhaps seek to assuage and placate. But there is no assuaging those who see your very existence as a denial of the faith and an affront to God. There is no placating those who offer you the choice of conversion or death.

There is only war and victory.

Mullah Omar and bin Laden are animated by a vision. They really do believe—or perhaps did believe—that their destiny was to unite all the Muslim lands from the Pyrenees to the Philippines and re-establish the original caliphate of a millennium ago. Omar took the sacred robe, attributed to Muhammad and locked away for more than 60 years, and triumphantly donned it in public as if to declare his succession to the Prophet's earthly rule. (Osama harbored similar fantasies about himself, although he fed Omar's, as a form of flattery and enticement.)

Such visions are not new. Omar's and Osama's are just as expansive, just as eschatological, and yet no more crazy than Hitler's dream of the Thousand-Year Reich or Napoleon's of dominion over all Europe. The Taliban and al-Qaeda, like Nazi Germany and revolutionary France, represent not just political parties or power seekers; they also represent movements. And a movement carries with it an idea, an ideology, a vision for the future.

That is where the mad dreamers are vulnerable: the dream can be defeated by reality. What was left of Nazi ideology with Hitler buried in the rubble of Berlin? What was left of Bonapartism with Napoleon rotting in St. Helena? What was left of Fascism, an idea that swept Europe and entranced a generation, with Mussolini's body hanging upside down, strung up by partisans in 1945?

What is left of the great caliphate today? It is a ruin. Caliph Omar is in hiding; Caliph Osama, on the run.

This is not to say that Islamic fundamentalism is dead. But it has suffered a grievous blow. Its great appeal was not just its revival of a glorious past but also the promise that it was the wave of the future, the inexorable tide that would sweep through not just Arabia but all Islam—and one day the world.

That is why Afghanistan is such a turning point. It marks the first great reversal of fortune for radical Islam. For two decades it tasted one victory after another: the Beirut bombings of 1983 that chased America out of Lebanon; "Black Hawk Down" that chased America out of Somalia; the first Afghan war that chased the Soviet Union out of Afghanistan—and led to the collapse of a superpower, no less. These were heady victories, as were the wounds inflicted with impunity on the other superpower: the 1993 attack on the World Trade Center, the 1998 destruction of two U.S. embassies in Africa, the 2000 attack on the U.S.S. Cole. The limp and feckless American reaction to these acts of war— a token cruise missile here, a showy indictment there, empty threats everywhere—only reinforced the radical Islamic conviction that America was a paper tiger, fat and decadent, leader of a civilization grown weak and cowardly and ripe for defeat.

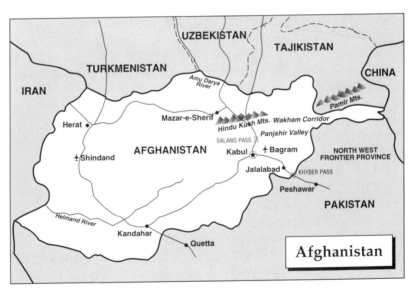

For the fundamentalist, success has deep religious significance. The logic of the holy warrior is this:

My God is great and omnipotent. I am a warrior for God. Therefore victory is mine.

What then happens to the syllogism if he is defeated? To understand, we must enter the mind of primitive fundamentalism. Or, shall we say, re-enter. Our Western biblical texts speak of a time 3,000 years ago when victory in battle was seen as the victory not only of one people over another but also of one god over another. Triumph over the "hosts of Egypt" was of theological importance: it was living proof of the living God—and the powerlessness and thus the falsity of the defeated god.

The secular West no longer thinks in those terms. But radical Islam does. Which is why the Osama tape, reveling in the success of September 11, is such an orgy of religious triumphalism: so many dead, so much fame, so much joy, so many new recruits—God is great.

By the same token, with the total collapse of the Taliban, everything has changed. Omar has lost his robe. The Arab street is silent. The joy is gone. And recruitment? The Pakistani mullahs who after September 11 had urged hapless young men to join the Taliban in fighting America and now have to answer to bereaved parents are facing ostracism and disgrace. Al-Qaeda agents roaming the madrasahs of Pakistan and the poorer neighborhoods of the Arab world will have a much harder sell. The syllogism of invincibility that sustained Islamic fanaticism is shattered.

We have just witnessed something new in the modern world: the rollback of Islamic fundamentalism. We have just witnessed the first overthrow of a radical Islamic regime, indeed, the destruction of radical Islam's home base. Yesterday the base was Afghanistan. Today it is a few caves and a few hidden cells throughout the world. Al-Qaeda controls no state, no sovereign territory. It is an outlaw on the run.

Rollback is, of course, a cold war term. For decades our approach to Islamic terrorism was like our approach to communism: containment. Do not invade its territory, but keep it, as Clinton liked to say of Saddam, "in a box." We tried containing al-Qaeda with a few pinprick bombings and an attack on a pharmaceutical factory in Sudan. These were nothing but an evasion, a looking the other way. September 11 proved the folly of that approach. President Bush therefore announced a radically new doctrine. We would no longer contain. We would attack, advance and destroy any government harboring terrorists. Afghanistan is now the signal example. Just as the Reagan doctrine reversed containment and marked the beginning of the end of the Soviet empire, the Bush doctrine marks the beginning of the rollback of the Islamic terror empire.

Of course, the turning of the tide is not the end of the war. This is the invasion of Normandy; we must still enter Berlin. The terrorists still have part of their infrastructure. They still have their sleeper cells. They can still, if they acquire weapons of mass destruction, inflict unimaginable damage and death. Which is why eradicating the other centers of terrorism is so urgent.

We can now, however, carry on with a confidence we did not have before Afghanistan. Confidence that even religious fanaticism can be defeated, that despite its bravado, it carries no mandate from heaven. The psychological effect of our stunning victory in Afghanistan is already evident. We see the beginning of self-reflection in the Arab press, asking what Arab jihadists are doing exporting their problems to places like Afghanistan and the West; wondering why the Arab world uniquely has not developed a single real democracy; and asking, most fundamentally, how a great religion like Islam could have harbored a malignant strain that would rejoice in the death of 3,000 innocents. It is the kind of questioning that Europeans engaged in after World War II (asking how Fascism and Nazism could have been bred in the bosom of European Christianity) but that was sadly lacking in the Islamic world. Until now.

It is beginning now not because our propaganda is good. Not because al-Jazeera changed its anti-American tune. Not because a wave of remorse spontaneously erupted in places like Saudi Arabia. But because, with our B-52s, our special forces, our smart bombs, our daisy cutters—our power and our will—we scattered the enemy.

What the secular West fails to understand is that in fighting religious fanaticism the issue—for the fanatic—is not grievance but ascendancy. What must be decided is not who is right and wrong—one can never appease the grievances of the religious fanatic—but whose God is greater. After Afghanistan there can be no doubt. In the land of jihad, the fall of the Taliban and the flight of al-Qaeda are testimony to the god that failed.

CIVIL LIBERTIES AND THE WAR AGAINST TERRORISM

SALIM MUWAKKIL

Following the devastating terrorist attacks on the Pentagon and the World Trade Center on September 11, 2001, many observers blamed the country's federal intelligence gathering agencies—the FBI and the CIA—for failing to prevent the attacks. Critics of the FBI contended that the agency could not properly engage in the electronic surveillance of suspected terrorists due to the inadequate authority it was granted for this type of activity. The CIA was blamed for failing to gather human intelligence on terrorist activity.

Faced with a ruthless enemy willing to die for its cause, Attorney General John Ashcroft made the case to the public and to political leaders that law enforcement officials needed greater flexibility if the war on terrorism was to be a success. In response, Congress passed the USA Patriot Act of 2001, which grants law enforcement agencies sweeping new powers in the course of investigations related to terrorism. In the following commentary, Salim Muwakkil expresses alarm at the threat the Patriot Act poses to civil liberties in the United States. According to Muwakkil, legislators have moved too far toward severely limiting personal freedom in their zeal to protect Americans from terrorism. The author is the senior editor of *In These Times* magazine and a columnist with the *Chicago Tribune*.

C itizens of the United States, be advised that the federal government can now examine your medical, educational and financial history, all without your knowledge and without even presenting evidence of a crime.

Police now can obtain court orders to conduct so-called sneak-and-peak searches of your homes and offices and remove or alter your possessions without your knowledge. Internet service providers and telephone companies can be compelled to turn over your customer information, including the phone numbers you've called and Internet sites you've surfed—all, again, without a court order, if the FBI claims the records are relevant to a "terrorism investigation." A secret court can permit roving wiretaps of any telephone or computer you might possibly use; reading your e-mail is allowed, even before you open it.

CIVIL LIBERTIES IN JEOPARDY

These are just some of the provisions of the USA PATRIOT Act of 2001—the bill's title is an acronym for "Uniting and Strengthening America by Providing Appropriate Tools Required to Intercept and Obstruct Terrorism"—which President George W. Bush signed into law on October 26, 2001. In passing the legislation, Senate Majority Leader Thomas Daschle said Congress was "able to find what I think is the appropriate balance between protecting civil liberties, privacy, and ensuring that law enforcement has the tools to do what it must."

The fears provoked by the kamikaze hijackings and the anthrax incidents that followed explain why many legislators have been less protective of civil liberties. Those progressive legislators who supported the legislation said the unique and deadly circumstances of the 9/11 attacks already had predisposed them to support strong action, and many noted that a sunset provision would allow the bill's most controversial surveillance sections to expire in 2005. But the Bill of Rights was designed to offer a judicial sanctuary from political passions. If progressive legislators don't make that clear, who will?

The events of 9/11 make it plain that the United States has enemies willing to die for their cause, and it would be impractical, even foolish, to deny the need for increased national vigilance. Ratcheting up our security is necessary, if only to enhance citizens' sense of well-being. And, according to a *Newsweek* poll reported in the publication's December 10, 2001, edition, "86 percent think the administration has not gone too far in restricting civil liberties in its response to terrorism."

The import of the USA PATRIOT Act was presaged by the Clinton administration's anti-terrorism bill of 1996, which broadened the government's investigative and prosecutorial powers. And even before that, the Foreign Intelligence Surveillance Act of 1978 allowed the wiretapping of non-citizens by approval of a secret court with secret evidence. But this new legislation ups the ante considerably. "This new legislation goes far beyond any powers conceivably necessary to fight terrorism in the United States," says Laura Murphy of the American Civil Liberties Union. "The long-term impact on basic freedoms in this legislation cannot be justified."

BYPASSING THE CONSTITUTION

Leading the charge in the wake of 9/11 is Attorney General John Ashcroft, who, for starters, launched a nationwide dragnet that rounded up more than 1,000 foreign nationals and detained most of them on minor immigration charges. Many have since been released after officials found they had no connection to terrorism. As of December 6, 603 foreign nationals remain in custody. On Halloween, Ashcroft issued an order allowing federal authorities to monitor communications between federal prisoners and their lawyers without first obtaining a judicial warrant. He argued that this new power is necessary to prevent terrorist attacks planned under cover of lawyer-client privilege.

The administration's power grab is so audacious that it has prompted a new alliance between the civil-liberties left and the libertarian right. *New York Times* columnist William Safire characterized Bush's strategy as "a sudden seizure of power by the executive branch, bypassing all constitutional checks and balances." The American Civil Liberties Union (ACLU), joined by 16 other civil rights and human rights groups, filed suit on December 5, 2001, charging the Justice Department with violating the Constitution and federal law through its detention policies.

Mining public fears for all the right-wing treasures he can get, Ashcroft also has proposed relaxing restrictions on the FBI's spying on religious and political organizations. The guidelines Ashcroft has targeted were imposed on the FBI in the '70s after the death of J. Edgar Hoover and revelations about the COINTELPRO program—which included disclosures of the agency's surveillance and harassment of Martin Luther King Jr. In Chicago, activists recently commemorated another poignant signpost of COINTELPRO infamy: the police assassination of Black Panther leaders Fred Hampton and Mark Clark on December 4, 1969. COINTELPRO ultimately was condemned as "little more than a sophisticated vigilante action" by the Congress and shut down.

But under Section 802 of the USA PATRIOT Act, a person commits the crime of "domestic terrorism" if he engages in activity "that involves acts dangerous to human life that violate the laws of the U.S. or any state and appear to be intended: to intimidate or coerce a civilian population; to influence the policy of a government by intimidation or coercion; or to affect the conduct of a government by mass destruction, assassination or kidnapping." This definition of terrorism could allow the feds to go after environmental, civil rights or anti-globalization groups, among others, for their dissenting views or direct-action protests.

ECHOING PAST EXCESSES

Right-wing extremism is always fertilized by external threats. At its most notorious extreme, Adolph Hitler's Nazi Party rose like a rocket after the 1933 Reichstag fire convinced the German people that the Bolsheviks were out to get them. At the Nuremberg Trials, Hitler's second-in-command, Hermann Goering, aptly explained the process: "The people can always be brought to do the bidding of the leaders. That is easy. All you have to do is tell them they are being attacked, and denounce the pacifists for lack of patriotism and exposing the country to danger."

This eerily familiar formula is so effective that it has become enshrined in U.S. traditions, even if it violates strictures of the Constitution. During times of war, the chief executive has implemented many extra-constitutional edicts: Abraham Lincoln unilaterally suspended *habeas corpus* during the Civil War; the infamous, anti-Communist Palmer Raids of 1920 arrested thousands of people without warrants or due process; Franklin D. Roosevelt ordered the internment of more than 100,000 Japanese-Americans in squalid camps. In retrospect, these excessive actions invariably have been condemned as historical blemishes.

But today's policy-makers seem oblivious to the lessons of history as they implement actions that echo—and amplify—those past excesses. Roosevelt also ordered a special military tribunal for eight accused Nazi spies, six of whom were later executed. The Supreme Court upheld Roosevelt's tribunal as it has most other questionable actions of wartime presidents. And the Bush administration has used the top court's 8–0 decision in 1942 as a precedent to bolster the president's own proposed military tribunals. Bush has assumed unchecked power as commander-in-chief to detain and try any non-citizen he suspects of committing terrorist acts or helping international terrorists. These suspects can be secretly arrested, tried, convicted and executed even if prosecutors failed to prove their case beyond a reasonable doubt.

Like the Bush administration's war, the future of our civil liberties is fuzzy and indeterminate. Since this is a war on the tactic of "terrorism" rather than on a tangible enemy, there is no entity to offer a formal surrender. The "war"—and the concomitant wartime powers and prerogatives—can be extended indefinitely; only the Bush administration has the power to declare the war's end.

Soon after 9/11, Bush said the people who perpetuated the terrorist murders hate America because of "our freedoms." After a few more executive orders and congressional capitulations, they won't have much left to hate.

THE RISE OF ANTI-AMERICANISM IN THE POST–COLD WAR ERA

STANLEY HOFFMANN

Following the September 11, 2001, terrorist attacks on the Pentagon and the World Trade Center in New York City, Americans were forced to examine how the world had come to view the United States in the post–Cold War era. Many Americans were startled to discover that the country's image as a benign protector and champion of human rights was being called into question abroad. In many corners of the world, including parts of Western Europe, people were unsympathetic toward America following the September 11 attacks. In Great Britain, Philip Lader, the former U.S. ambassador to Britain, was shouted down on the BBC television program *Question Time* by audience members who claimed that America itself was to blame for the terrorist attacks. In France, protesters refused to observe three minutes of silence on September 14 in memory of the terrorist victims.

In the following analysis, Stanley Hoffmann asserts that the rise of America as the sole superpower in the post–Cold War era has generated resentment and distrust throughout the world. Many people base their criticism on U.S. foreign policies, which have often supported authoritarian and oppressive regimes, in Hoffmann's opinion. Other criticisms surround U.S. support for Israel and a lack of concern for the growing poverty in developing countries. According to Hoffmann, the international response to the September 11 attacks reveals that Americans must pay more attention to the outside world and listen carefully to criticisms of U.S. policy. The author is the Paul and Catherine Buttenwieser University Professor at Harvard University.

I t wasn't its innocence that the United States lost on September 11, 2001. It was its naivete. Americans have tended to believe that in the eyes of others the United States has lived up to the boastful cliches propagated during the Cold War (especially under President Ronald Reagan) and during the Clinton administration. We were seen, we thought, as the champions of freedom against fascism and communism, as the advocates of decolonization, economic development, and social progress, as the technical innovators whose mastery of technology, science, and advanced education was going to unify the world.

Some officials and academics explained that U.S. hegemony was the best thing for a troubled world and unlike past hegemonies would last—not only because there were no challengers strong enough to steal the crown but, above all, because we were benign rulers who threatened no one.

But we have avoided looking at the hegemon's clay feet, at what might neutralize our vaunted soft power and undermine our hard power. Like swarming insects exposed when a fallen tree is lifted, millions who dislike or distrust the hegemon have suddenly appeared after September 11, much to our horror and disbelief. America became a great power after World War II, when we faced a rival that seemed to stand for everything we had been fighting against—tyranny, terror, brainwashing—and we thought that our international reputation would benefit from our standing for liberty and stability (as it still does in much of Eastern Europe). We were not sufficiently marinated in history to know that, through the ages, nobody—or almost nobody—has ever loved a hegemon.

Past hegemons, from Rome to Great Britain, tended to be quite realistic about this. They wanted to be obeyed or, as in the case of France, admired. They rarely wanted to be loved. But as a combination of high-noon sheriff and proselytizing missionary, the United States expects gratitude and affection. It was bound to be disappointed; gratitude is not an emotion that one associates with the behavior of states.

This is an old story. Two sets of factors make the current twist a new one. First, the so-called Westphalian world has collapsed.[1] The world of sovereign states, the universe of Hans Morgenthau's and Henry Kissinger's Realism, is no longer.[2] The unpopularity of the hegemonic power has been heightened to incandescence by two aspects of this collapse. One is the irruption of the public, the masses, in international affairs. Foreign policy is no longer, as Raymond Aron had written in *Peace and War*, the closed domain of the soldier and the diplomat. Domestic publics—along with their interest groups, religious organizations, and ideological chapels—either dictate or constrain the imperatives and preferences that the governments fight for. This puts the hegemon in a difficult position: It often must work with governments that represent but a small percentage of a country's people—but if it fishes for public support abroad, it risks alienating leaders whose cooperation it needs. The United States paid heavily for not having had enough contacts with the opposition to the shah of Iran in the 1970s. It discovers today that there is an abyss in Pakistan, Saudi Arabia, Egypt, and Indonesia between our official allies and the populace in these countries. Diplomacy in a world where the masses, so to speak, stayed indoors, was a much easier game.

The collapse of the barrier between domestic and foreign affairs in the state system is now accompanied by a disease that attacks the state system itself. Many of the "states" that are members of the United Nations are pseudo-states with shaky or shabby institutions, no basic consensus on values or on procedures among their heterogeneous components, and no sense of national identity. Thus the hegemon—in addition to suffering the hostility of the government in certain countries (like Cuba, Iraq, and North Korea) and of the public in others (like, in varying degrees, Pakistan, Egypt, and even France)—can now easily become both the target of factions fighting one another in disintegrating countries and the pawn in their quarrels (which range over such increasingly borderless issues as drug trafficking, arms trading, money laundering, and other criminal enterprises). In addition, today's hegemon suffers from the

1. The Peace of Westphalia, negotiated in 1648, ended the Thirty Year's War in Europe. It is widely recognized as having introduced the era of modern international relations among sovereign states.   2. Hans Morgenthau is a political theorist and author of the book *Politics Among Nations: The Struggle for Power and Peace*. Henry Kissinger served as secretary of state under President Nixon. Both men were adherents of political Realism—a theory that maintains that politics is governed by objective laws that are rooted in human nature.

volatility and turbulence of a global system in which ethnic, religious, and ideological sympathies have become transnational and in which groups and individuals uncontrolled by states can act on their own. The world of the nineteenth century, when hegemons could impose their order, their institutions, has been supplanted by the world of the twenty-first century: Where once there was order, there is now often a vacuum.

What makes the American Empire especially vulnerable is its historically unique combination of assets and liabilities. One has to go back to the Roman Empire to find a comparable set of resources. Britain, France, and Spain had to operate in multipolar systems; the United States is the only superpower.

But if America's means are vast, the limits of its power are also considerable. The United States, unlike Rome, cannot simply impose its will by force or through satellite states. Small "rogue" states can defy the hegemon (remember Vietnam?). And chaos can easily result from the large new role of nonstate actors. Meanwhile, the reluctance of Americans to take on the Herculean tasks of policing, "nation building," democratizing autocracies, and providing environmental protection and economic growth for billions of human beings stokes both resentment and hostility, especially among those who discover that one can count on American presence and leadership only when America's material interests are gravely threatened. (It is not surprising that the "defense of the national interest" approach of Realism was developed for a multipolar world. In an empire, as well as in a bipolar system, almost anything can be described as a vital interest, since even peripheral disorder can unravel the superpower's eminence.) Moreover, the complexities of America's process for making foreign-policy decisions can produce disappointments abroad when policies that the international community counted on—such as the Kyoto Protocol [global warming treaty] and the International Criminal Court—are thwarted. Also, the fickleness of U.S. foreign-policy making in arenas like the Balkans has convinced many American enemies that this country is basically incapable of pursuing long-term policies consistently.

None of this means, of course, that the United States has no friends in the world. Europeans have not forgotten the liberating role played by Americans in the war against Hitler and in the Cold War. Israel remembers how President Harry Truman sided with the founders of the Zionist state; nor has it forgotten all the help the United States has given it since then. The democratizations of postwar Germany and Japan were huge successes. The Marshall Plan [Secretary of State George C. Marshall's program for the reconstruction of Europe following World War II] and the Point Four Program [President Harry Truman's program of technical assistance to developing countries] were revolutionary initiatives. The decisions to resist aggression in Korea and in Kuwait demonstrated a commendable farsightedness.

But Americans have a tendency to overlook the dark sides of their course (except on the protesting left, which is thus constantly accused of being un-American), perhaps because they perceive international affairs in terms of crusades between good and evil, endeavors that entail formidable pressures for unanimity. It is not surprising that the decade following the [1991] Gulf War was marked both by nostalgia for the clear days of the Cold War and by a lot of floundering and hesitating in a world without an overwhelming foe.

STRAINS OF ANTI-AMERICANISM

The main criticisms of American behavior have mostly been around for a long time. When we look at anti-Americanism today, we must first distinguish between those who attack the United States for what it does, or fails to do, and those who attack it for what it is. (Some, like the Islamic fundamentalists and terrorists, attack it for both reasons.) Perhaps the principal criticism is of the contrast between our ideology of universal liberalism and policies that have all too often consisted of supporting and sometimes installing singularly authoritarian and repressive regimes. (One reason why these policies often elicited more reproaches than Soviet control over satellites was that, as time went by, Stalinism became more and more cynical and thus the gap between words and deeds became far less wide than in the United States. One no longer expected much from Moscow.) The list of places where America failed at times to live up to its proclaimed ideals is long: Guatemala, Panama, El Salvador, Chile, Santo Domingo in 1965, the Greece of the colonels, Pakistan, the Philippines of Ferdinand Marcos, Indonesia after 1965, the shah's Iran, Saudi Arabia, Zaire, and, of course, South Vietnam. Enemies of these regimes were shocked by U.S. support for them—and even those whom we supported were disappointed, or worse, when America's cost-benefit analysis changed and we dropped our erstwhile allies. This Machiavellian scheming behind a Wilsonian facade has alienated many clients, as well as potential friends, and bred strains of anti-Americanism around the world.[3]

A second grievance concerns America's frequent unilateralism and the difficult relationship between the United States and the United Nations. For many countries, the United Nations is, for all its flaws, the essential agency of cooperation and the protector of its members' sovereignty. The way U.S. diplomacy has "insulted" the UN system—sometimes by ignoring it and sometimes by rudely imposing its views and policies on it—has been costly in terms of foreign support.

Third, the United States' sorry record in international development has recently become a source of dissatisfaction abroad. Not only have America's financial contributions for narrowing the gap between the rich and the poor declined since the end of the Cold War, but American-dominated institutions such as the International Monetary Fund and the World Bank have often dictated financial policies that turned out to be disastrous for developing countries—most notably, before and during the Asian economic crisis of the mid-1990s.

Finally, there is the issue of American support of Israel. Much of the world—and not only the Arab world—considers America's Israel policy to be biased. Despite occasional American attempts at evenhandedness, the world sees that the Palestinians remain under occupation, Israeli settlements continue to expand, and individual acts of Arab terrorism—acts that Yasir Arafat can't completely control—are condemned more harshly than the killings of Palestinians by the Israeli army or by Israeli-sanctioned assassination squads. It is interesting to note that Israel, the smaller and dependent power, has been more successful in circumscribing the United States' freedom to maneuver diplomatically in the region than the United States has been at getting Israel to enforce the UN resolutions adopted after the 1967 war (which called for the withdrawal of Israeli forces from then-occupied territories, solving the refugee crisis, and establishing inviolate territorial zones for all states in the region). Many in the Arab world, and some outside, use this state of affairs to stoke paranoia of the "Jewish lobby" in the United States.

3. Niccolo Machiavelli was a 16th century Italian philosopher who advised using any means necessary to achieve political power. Woodrow Wilson, the 28th President of the United States, propounded the view that it was America's role to ensure peace and democracy around the world.

ANTIGLOBALISM AND ANTI-AMERICANISM

Those who attack specific American policies are often more ambivalent than hostile. They often envy the qualities and institutions that have helped the United States grow rich, powerful, and influential.

The real United States haters are those whose anti-Americanism is provoked by dislike of America's values, institutions, and society—and their enormous impact abroad. Many who despise America see us as representing the vanguard of globalization—even as they themselves use globalization to promote their hatred. The Islamic fundamentalists of al-Qaeda—like Iran's Ayatollah Khomeini 20 years ago—make excellent use of the communication technologies that are so essential to the spread of global trade and economic influence.

We must be careful here, for there are distinctions among the antiglobalist strains that fuel anti-Americanism. To some of our detractors, the most eloquent spokesman is bin Laden, for whom America and the globalization it promotes relentlessly through free trade and institutions under its control represent evil. To them, American-fueled globalism symbolizes the domination of the Christian-Jewish infidels or the triumph of pure secularism: They look at the United States and see a society of materialism, moral laxity, corruption in all its forms, fierce selfishness, and so on. (The charges are familiar to us because we know them as an exacerbated form of right-wing anti-Americanism in nineteenth- and twentieth-century Europe.) But there are also those who, while accepting the inevitability of globalization and seem eager to benefit from it, are incensed by the contrast between America's promises and the realities of American life. Looking at the United States and the countries we support, they see insufficient social protection, vast pockets of poverty amidst plenty, racial discrimination, the large role of money in politics, the domination of the elites—and they call us hypocrites. (And these charges, too, are familiar, because they are an exacerbated version of the left-wing anti-Americanism still powerful in Western Europe.)

On the one hand, those who see themselves as underdogs of the world condemn the United States for being an evil force because its dynamism makes it naturally and endlessly imperialistic—a behemoth that imposes its culture (often seen as debased), its democracy (often seen as flawed), and its conception of individual human rights (often seen as a threat to more communitarian and more socially concerned approaches) on other societies. The United States is perceived as a bully ready to use all means, including overwhelming force, against those who resist it: Hence, Hiroshima, the horrors of Vietnam, the rage against Iraq, the war on Afghanistan.

On the other hand, the underdogs draw hope from their conviction that the giant has a heel like Achilles'. They view America as a society that cannot tolerate high casualties and prolonged sacrifices and discomforts, one whose impatience with protracted and undecisive conflicts should encourage its victims to be patient and relentless in their challenges and assaults. They look at American foreign policy as one that is often incapable of overcoming obstacles and of sticking to a course that is fraught with high risks—as with the conflict with Iraq's Saddam Hussein at the end of the Gulf War; as in the flight from Lebanon after the terrorist attacks of 1982; as in Somalia in 1993; as in the attempts to strike back at bin Laden in the Clinton years.

Thus America stands condemned not because our enemies necessarily hate our freedoms but because they resent what they fear are our Darwinian aspects, and often because they deplore what they see as the softness at our core. Those who, on our side, note and celebrate America's power of attraction, its openness to immigrants and refugees, the uniqueness of a society based on common principles rather than on ethnicity or on an old culture, are not wrong. But many of the foreign students, for instance, who fall in love with the gifts of American education return home, where the attraction often fades. Those who stay sometimes feel that the price they have to pay in order to assimilate and be accepted is too high.

WHAT BRED BIN LADEN

This long catalog of grievances obviously needs to be picked apart. The complaints vary in intensity; different cultures, countries, and parties emphasize different flaws, and the criticism is often wildly excessive and unfair. But we are not dealing here with purely rational arguments; we are dealing with emotional responses to the omnipresence of a hegemon, to the sense that many people outside this country have that the United States dominates their lives.

Complaints are often contradictory: Consider "America has neglected us, or dropped us" versus "America's attentions corrupt our culture." The result can be a gestalt of resentment that strikes Americans as absurd: We are damned, for instance, both for failing to intervene to protect Muslims in the Balkans and for using force to do so.

But the extraordinary array of roles that America plays in the world—along with its boastful attitude and, especially recently, its cavalier unilateralism—ensures that many wrongs caused by local regimes and societies will be blamed on the United States. We even end up being seen as responsible not only for anything bad that our "protectorates" do—it is no coincidence that many of the September 11 terrorists came from America's proteges, Saudi Arabia and Egypt—but for what our allies do, as when Arabs incensed by racism and joblessness in France take up bin Laden's cause, or when Muslims talk about American violence against the Palestinians. Bin Laden's extraordinary appeal and prestige in the Muslim world do not mean that his apocalyptic nihilism is fully endorsed by all those who chant his name. Yet to many, he plays the role of a bloody Robin Hood, inflicting pain and humiliation on the superpower that they believe torments them.

Bin Laden fills the need for people who, rightly or not, feel collectively humiliated and individually in despair to attach themselves to a savior. They may in fact avert their eyes from the most unsavory of his deeds. This need on the part of the poor and dispossessed to connect their own feeble lot to a charismatic and single-minded leader was at the core of fascism and of communism. After the failure of pan-Arabism, the fiasco of nationalism, the dashed hopes of democratization, and the fall of Soviet communism, many young people in the Muslim world who might have once turned to these visions for succor turned instead to Islamic fundamentalism and terrorism.

One almost always finds the same psychological dynamics at work in such behavior: the search for simple explanations— and what is simpler and more inflammatory than the machinations of the Jews and the evils of America—and a highly selective approach to history. Islamic fundamentalists remember the promises made by the British to the Arabs in World War I and the imposition of British and French imperialism after 1918 rather than the support the United States gave to anticolonialists in French North Africa in the late 1940s and in the 1950s. They remember British opposition to and American reluctance toward intervention in Bosnia before Srebrenica, but they forget about NATO's actions to save Bosnian Muslims in 1995, to help Albanians in Kosovo in 1999, and to preserve and improve Albanians' rights in Macedonia in 2001. Such distortions are manufactured and maintained by the controlled media and schools of totalitarian regimes, and through the religious schools, conspiracy mills, and propaganda of fundamentalism.

WHAT CAN BE DONE?

Americans can do very little about the most extreme and violent forms of anti-American hatred—but they can try to limit its spread by addressing grievances that are justified. There are a number of ways to do this:

• First—and most difficult—drastically reorient U.S. policy in the Palestinian-Israeli conflict.

• Second, replace the ideologically market-based trickledown economics that permeate American-led development institutions today with a kind of social safety net. (Even *New York Times* columnist Thomas Friedman, that ur-celebrator of the global market, believes that such a safety net is indispensable.)

• Third, prod our allies and proteges to democratize their regimes, and stop condoning violations of essential rights (an approach that can only, in the long run, breed more terrorists and anti-Americans).

• Fourth, return to internationalist policies, pay greater attention to the representatives of the developing world, and make fairness prevail over arrogance.

• Finally, focus more sharply on the needs and frustrations of the people suffering in undemocratic societies than on the authoritarian regimes that govern them.

America's self-image today is derived more from . . . pride than from reality, and this exacerbates the clash between how we see ourselves and foreign perceptions and misperceptions of the United States. If we want to affect those external perceptions (and that will be very difficult to do in extreme cases), we need to readjust our self-image. This means reinvigorating our curiosity about the outside world, even though our media have tended to downgrade foreign coverage since the Cold War. And it means listening carefully to views that we may find outrageous, both for the kernel of truth that may be present in them and for the stark realities (of fear, poverty, hunger, and social hopelessness) that may account for the excesses of these views.

Terrorism aimed at the innocent is, of course, intolerable.

Safety precautions and the difficult task of eradicating the threat are not enough. If we want to limit terrorism's appeal, we must keep our eyes and ears open to conditions abroad, revise our perceptions of ourselves, and alter our world image through our actions. There is nothing un-American about this. We should not meet the Manichaeanism of our foes with a Manichaeanism of self-righteousness. Indeed, self-examination and self-criticism have been the not-so-secret weapons of America's historical success. Those who demand that we close ranks not only against murderers but also against shocking opinions and emotions, against dissenters at home and critics abroad, do a disservice to America.

1992

March 26: Professional boxer Mike Tyson is sentenced to ten years in prison for raping eighteen-year-old Miss Black America contestant Desiree Washington.

April 7: President George Bush signs a decree recognizing the independence of Bosnia-Herzegovina, Croatia, and Slovenia, which were republics of the former Yugoslavia.

April 29: Rioting breaks out on the streets of Los Angeles in reaction to the acquittal of white police officers accused of beating black motorist Rodney King.

May: Representatives of 153 nations convene in Rio de Janeiro, Brazil, at the Rio Earth Summit to address the problem of global warming.

May 22: After thirty years as host of the *Tonight Show,* comedian Johnny Carson makes his final appearance.

June: Librarian Jean Armour Polly coins the phrase "surfing the Internet" in an article published in the *Wilson Library Bulletin.*

August 24: Hurricane Andrew roars through south Florida, leaving thousands homeless and causing billions of dollars in damages.

September 12: Mae C. Jemison becomes the first African American woman to go into space, traveling aboard the space shuttle *Endeavor.*

November 3: William Jefferson Clinton is elected the forty-second president of the United States.

December 9: U.S. troops land in Somalia to deliver famine relief and humanitarian aid.

December 17: The presidents of the United States, Canada, and Mexico sign the North American Free Trade Agreement.

1993

February 26: The World Trade Center in New York City is bombed by men connected with Islamic terrorist groups; six people are killed and over a thousand are injured.

March 10: A fanatical antiabortion protester assassinates Dr. David Gunn as he enters an abortion clinic in Pensacola, Florida.

April 19: On the outskirts of Waco, Texas, the compound of the Branch Davidian religious group is engulfed in flames during a raid conducted by federal agents, ending a fifty-one-day standoff; seventy-five Davidians are killed.

May 20: The final episode of the television comedy *Cheers* airs, receiving the second largest audience ever for an episodic television program.

July/August: Heavy spring rains cause severe flooding in the upper Mississippi River valley, affecting Missouri, Illinois, Kansas, and other Midwestern states.

October: New software allows easier navigation of the Internet, drawing in millions to "surf" the World Wide Web; President Clinton orders six U.S. destroyers to Haiti to enforce the UN trade embargo against the military-led regime.

October 3–4: Eighteen U.S. Army Rangers are killed during a gun battle with local militiamen in Mogadishu, Somalia.

October 7: Toni Morrison, an African American author, is awarded the Nobel Prize for literature.

December 7: Deranged gunman Colin Ferguson opens fire on passengers leaving New York City on a crowded Long Island Railroad commuter train, killing six.

1994

January: The Justice Department begins investigations into President Clinton's dealings with Whitewater Development, a real estate venture, while governor of Arkansas.

January 17: The Northridge earthquake, centered twenty miles northwest of Los Angeles, California, kills fifty-seven people and causes significant damage to buildings and homes.

February: President Clinton's policy of "don't ask, don't tell" for gays in the U.S. military takes effect; the military will no longer ask recruits about their sexual orientation.

April 8: Kurt Cobain, the twenty-seven-year-old singer of the popular rock band Nirvana, is found dead in his Seattle home; the cause is suicide.

May 19: Former first lady Jacqueline Kennedy Onassis dies of cancer and is later buried beside her first husband, President John F. Kennedy, in Arlington Cemetery outside Washington, D.C.

June 17: Former professional football star O.J. Simpson is arrested for the murders of his ex-wife Nicole Brown Simpson and her acquaintance Ronald Goldman.

August 4: Kenneth W. Starr is appointed independent counsel to head the ongoing Whitewater investigation.

December 11: Russian forces invade the republic of Chechnya to prevent its secession.

1995

January: President Clinton authorizes a $42-billion loan to Mexico following the collapse of its currency.

February: Bernard A. Harris Jr. becomes the first African American astronaut to walk in space during the first flight of the joint Russian-American space program.

April 19: A total of 168 people are killed after a van filled with explosives is detonated outside the Alfred P. Murrah federal building in Oklahoma City, Oklahoma; Timothy McVeigh is later executed for his role in the bombing, and accomplice Terry Nichols receives a life sentence.

June/July: A U.S. Supreme Court ruling sets a stringent new standard for justifying federal affirmative action programs for blacks and other minorities; the regents of the University of California vote to end all affirmative action programs at University of California campuses.

September 19: The *Washington Post* and the *New York Times* jointly publish "Industrial Society and Its Future," a treatise written by "the Unabomber"; a terrorist long sought by FBI, the Unabomber had claimed that he would not kill again if the papers published his treatise.

October 3: A jury finds O.J. Simpson not guilty of murdering Ronald Goldman and Nicole Brown Simpson.

October 16: Nation of Islam leader Louis Farrakhan leads the "Million Man March" in Washington, D.C.; the march, affirming family values and personal responsibility, attracts black men from all over the country.

December 14: All parties in the war in Bosnia sign the Dayton Agreement.

1996

January: Sheik Omar Abdel-Rahman is sentenced to life in prison for his role in the 1993 World Trade Center bombing; nine coconspirators also receive severe sentences.

April 3: The Unabomber, Theodore Kaczynski, is arrested by federal agents; Kaczynski targeted university professors and business leaders with mail bombs, killing three people and injuring more than two dozen over a seventeen-year period.

June 15–16: Over one hundred thousand people attend the Tibetan Freedom Concert in San Francisco, held to raise awareness of the Chinese occupation of Tibet; the concert features popular rock bands and speakers condemning the Chinese government.

July 17: Trans World Airlines flight 800 explodes in midair shortly after takeoff from John F. Kennedy International airport in Queens, New York; terrorism is initially suspected, but a lengthy investigation finds no evidence of foul play.

July 27: A pipe bomb explosion in Centennial Olympic Park kills one person and injures over one hundred during the Olympic games in Atlanta, Georgia.

August: Twenty-year-old Tiger Woods announces that he is joining the professional golf tour and signs an endorsement deal with Nike worth nearly $40 million.

September 13: "Gangsta" rapper Tupac Shakur is killed in a drive-by shooting in Las Vegas, Nevada.

November 5: Bill Clinton becomes the first Democrat since Franklin Roosevelt to win a second presidential election.

December: The Oakland, California, school board recognizes Ebonics, or black English, as a distinct language and proposes to incorporate it into the classroom; the proposal draws a storm of protest from educational and political leaders.

1997

February: Scientists at the Roslin Institute in Scotland announce that they have cloned an adult sheep, marking the first-ever cloning of an adult mammal. The clone is named Dolly.

February 4: A jury in a civil trial finds O.J. Simpson responsible for the deaths of his ex-wife Nicole Brown Simpson and Ronald Goldman. Goldman's parents are awarded $8.5 million in compensatory damages.

March/April: The Hale-Bopp comet, the brightest comet to pass through the solar system in more than twenty years, becomes visible to stargazers. Thirty-nine members of the Heaven's Gate cult are found dead in a home outside San Diego, California. Followers believed that the approach of the Hale-Bopp comet marked the arrival of spacecraft that would carry them to a new world.

March 9: New York rap artist Notorious B.I.G. is murdered in Los Angeles.

April 5: Poet Allen Ginsberg, who sprung from the Beat literary movement of the late 1950s, dies of liver cancer.

July 1: After a century and a half of colonial rule, Great Britain returns Hong Kong to Communist China.

July 4: The Mars *Pathfinder,* an unmanned space probe, lands on Mars; it releases the *Sojourner* rover to analyze soil samples and record pictures that are transmitted back to Earth; the mission ends in November after NASA scientists lose contact with the probe.

August: Four New York City police officers are arrested on charges that they sodomized Abner Louima, a Haitian immigrant, with the handle of a toilet plunger at a Brooklyn stationhouse.

August 14: Timothy McVeigh is sentenced to death for the 1995 bombing of the Alfred P. Murrah federal building in Oklahoma City, Oklahoma.

1998

January 12: Linda Tripp contacts Whitewater investigator Kenneth W. Starr, informing him of secretly recorded tapes she has made of conversations with former White House intern Monica Lewinsky; the tapes detail Lewinsky's affair with President Clinton.

January 16: Kenneth W. Starr expands his investigation of President Clinton to include allegations that the president had an affair with Lewinsky and then pressured her to deny it.

February 3: A U.S. Marine jet on a routine training mission severs a ski-tram cable in the Italian Alps, killing twenty tram passengers.

March 24: Two boys ages thirteen and eleven kill four students and a teacher at Westside Middle School in Jonesboro, Arkansas.

May: Both India and Pakistan announce that they have successfully developed nuclear weapons.

May 14: Millions watch the final episode of the television comedy *Seinfeld.*

August 7: U.S. embassies in Kenya and Tanzania are bombed by terrorists, killing more than two hundred and injuring thousands; Saudi Arabian exile Osama bin Laden, living in Afghanistan, is considered a prime suspect; the United

States retaliates by bombing terrorist targets in Afghanistan and Sudan.

September 21: President Clinton's August 17 four-hour appearance before Kenneth W. Starr's grand jury airs on television; Starr alleges that the president has lied about his affair with Lewinsky and has obstructed justice to cover it up; the president denies the allegations and criticizes Starr's four-year, $40-million investigation as politically motivated.

October 18: The U.S. Department of Justice begins its trial against the Microsoft corporation for allegedly attempting to bully, bribe, and collude with competitors.

November: At age seventy-seven, John Glenn, the first American to be launched into orbit in 1962, becomes the oldest astronaut, following a nine-day mission aboard the space shuttle *Discovery.*

December 19: The U.S. House of Representatives votes to impeach President Clinton for committing perjury and obstructing justice.

1999

February 12: The U.S. Senate acquits President Clinton of charges that he committed perjury and obstructed justice, ending the impeachment process.

March 24: U.S. war planes under NATO command begin a bombing campaign to force Serbian president Slobodan Milosevic to negotiate the political fate of Kosovo; Serbian forces respond by forcing Kosovars from their homes and killing thousands, driving more than eight hundred thousand refugees out of the country.

April 20: Two students go on a shooting rampage at Columbine High School in Littleton, Colorado, killing twelve students, one teacher, and themselves.

July: John F. Kennedy Jr. is killed after the small plane he is piloting crashes off the Massachusetts coast; his wife, Carolyn, and her sister Lauren are also killed.

July 23–25: The Woodstock '99 rock festival is marred by violence and looting; it is later disclosed that several women were raped in front of a central stage during musical performances.

August 10: White supremacist Buford Furrow Jr. wounds five people at the North Valley Jewish Community Center in Los Angeles, California; he then kills a Filipino American postal worker.

November: Five-year-old Elian Gonzales is found by fishermen clinging to an inner tube two miles off the coast of Fort Lauderdale, Florida; Elian becomes the center of an international custody battle between his Florida relatives and Cuban father and is later returned to Cuba.

December: Hundreds of demonstrators are arrested in Seattle after protests against a meeting of the World Trade Organization turn violent.

December 29: Former Beatle George Harrison is stabbed in the chest by an intruder who breaks into Harrison's mansion outside London, England; Harrison suffers a collapsed lung but survives the attack.

December 31: Fears that the Y2K computer bug will crash millions of computers around the world and cause widespread calamity reach a fever pitch, as clocks near the stroke of midnight.

2000

January 1: The world enters the year 2000 with few reports of Y2K-related computer problems.

March: "Dot-com" businesses in San Francisco, New York, and other cities begin to collapse under the weight of too much hype and too few profits; once-hot real estate districts like the Mission in San Francisco are faced with an exodus of dot-com tenants.

June 26: International scientists with the government-funded Human Genome Project announce that they have completed a map of the human genome; the chemical mapping for more than 90 percent of human DNA is regarded as a major scientific breakthrough.

October 12: The USS *Cole*, a navy destroyer, is attacked by suicide bombers while refueling in Yemen; the explosion kills seventeen sailors; once again, Osama bin Laden is connected to the bombing.

November 7: The U.S. presidential election between Al Gore and George W. Bush is left undecided after election results in Florida are too close to call; legal battles over hand recounts in several Florida counties ensue.

December 12: The U.S. Supreme Court overrules a Florida Supreme Court decision allowing a statewide manual recount of votes requested by presidential candidate Gore; the following day, Gore concedes the election to Bush.

2001

January 20: George W. Bush is sworn in as the forty-third president of the United States.

March: The U.S. economy officially enters a recession. President Bush announces the United States is abandoning the 1997 Kyoto Protocol.

September 11: Nineteen terrorists hijack four commercial airliners, crashing two into the Twin Towers of the World Trade Center in New York City and one into the Pentagon outside Washington, D.C.; a fourth plane, thought to have been headed for the White House, crashes in Pennsylvania after passengers stage a last-ditch effort to stop the hijackers; the hijackers are Islamic extremists with ties to Osama bin Laden and the al-Qaeda terrorist network in Afghanistan; over three thousand Americans are killed.

September 20: In a speech to Congress and the American people, President Bush declares war on terrorism; countries harboring terrorists are to be considered a threat to U.S. security; in particular, Afghanistan's Taliban government must deliver Osama bin Laden and al-Qaeda terrorists to U.S. authorities or prepare for military action.

October 7: The United States launches a war against the Taliban government in Afghanistan after it fails to comply with U.S. demands to hand over Osama bin Laden and leaders of the al-Qaeda terrorist group.

November: Air travel is down more than 25 percent over the previous year in the United States due to fears of further terrorist attacks.

Fall: Enron, a Houston, Texas–based energy giant, files for bankruptcy. It is revealed that top-level executives misrepresented the state of the company's finances.

December: Afghanistan's Taliban government collapses under bombings from U.S. aircraft and a ground war led by the Northern Alliance, an Afghan resistance group; the hunt for Osama bin Laden and Taliban leader Mullah Muhammad Omar continues.

2002

January: New Year's Eve celebrations in New York City proceed without incident; New York City mayor Rudy Giuliani steps aside after eight years as mayor.

FOR FURTHER RESEARCH

CULTURE AND THE ARTS

Jim Berkenstadt and Charles R. Cross, *Nevermind: Nirvana*. New York: Schirmer Books, 1998.

Louis Chunovic, *One Foot on the Floor: The Curious Evolution of Sex on Television from* I Love Lucy *to* South Park. New York: TV Books, 2000.

Charles R. Cross, *Heavier than Heaven: A Biography of Kurt Cobain*. New York: Hyperion, 2001.

Chuck D., *Fight the Power: Rap, Race, and Reality*. New York: Dell, 1998.

Jimi Fritz, *Rave Culture: An Insider's Overview*. Victoria, BC: Smallfry, 1999.

Nelson George, *Hip Hop America*. New York: Viking, 1998.

Bonnie Hinman, *John F. Kennedy Jr. (They Died Too Young)*. New York: Chelsea House, 2001.

Geoffrey T. Holtz, *Welcome to the Jungle: The Why Behind "Generation X."* New York: St. Martin's Press, 1995.

William Irwin, Mark T. Conrad, and Aeon J. Skoble, eds., *The Simpsons and Philosophy: The D'oh! of Homer*. Chicago: Open Court, 2001.

Adam Krims, *Rap Music and the Poetics of Identity*. New York: Cambridge University Press, 2000.

Mark I. Pinsky, *The Gospel According to the Simpsons: The Spiritual Life of the World's Most Animated Family*. Louisville, KY: Westminster John Knox Press, 2001.

Ronin Ro, *Gangsta: Merchandising the Rhymes of Violence*. New York: St. Martin's Press, 1996.

Tim Rosaforte, *Raising the Bar: The Championship Years of Tiger Woods*. New York: St. Martin's Press, 2000.

Jerry Seinfeld and Larry David, *Seinfeld Script Collection*. New York: HarperPerennial, 1998.

FOREIGN POLICY

David L. Boren and Edward J. Perkins, *Preparing America's Foreign Policy for the 21st Century*. Norman: University of Oklahoma Press, 1999.

Mark Bowden, *Black Hawk Down: A Story of Modern War*. New York: Penguin Books, 2000.

Lester H. Brune, *The United States and Post–Cold War Interventions: Bush and Clinton in Somalia, Haiti, and Bosnia, 1992–1998*. Claremont, CA: Regina Books, 1998.

Stephen J. Cimbala, ed., *Clinton and Post–Cold War Defense*. Westport, CT: Praeger, 1996.

Cecil V. Crabb Jr., Leila E. Sarieddine, and Glenn J. Antizzo, *Charting a New Diplomatic Course: Alternative Approaches to America's Post–Cold War Foreign Policy*. Baton Rouge: Lousiana State University Press, 2001.

Ivan Eland, *Putting "Defense" Back into U.S. Defense Policy: Rethinking U.S. Security in the Post–Cold War World*. Westport, CT: Praeger, 2001.

Thomas H. Henriksen, *Clinton's Foreign Policy in Somalia, Bosnia, Haiti, and North Korea*. Stanford, CA: Hoover Institution Press, 1996.

Thomas H. Henriksen, ed., *Foreign Policy for America in the Twenty-First Century: Alternative Perspectives*. Stanford, CA: Hoover Institution Press, 2001.

Karin von Hippel, *Democracy by Force: U.S. Intervention in the Post–Cold War World*. New York: Cambridge University Press, 2000.

Robert D. Kaplan, *The Coming Anarchy: Shattering the Dreams of the Post Cold War*. New York: Random House, 2000.

Jonathan Stevenson, *Losing Mogadishu: Testing U.S. Policy in Somalia*. Annapolis, MD: Naval Institute Press, 1995.

POLITICS

James Bovard, *"Feeling Your Pain": The Explosion and Abuse of Government Power in the Clinton-Gore Years.* New York: St. Martin's Press, 2000.

Robert Busby, *Defending the American Presidency: Clinton and the Lewinsky Scandal.* New York: Palgrave, 2001.

James W. Ceaser and Andrew E. Busch, *The Perfect Tie: The True Story of the 2000 Presidential Election.* Lanham, MD: Rowman & Littlefield, 2001.

William Crotty, ed., *America's Choice 2000.* Boulder, CO: Westview Press, 2001.

Philip John Davies and Fredric A. Waldstein, eds., *Political Issues in America Today: The 1990s Revisited.* New York: St. Martin's Press, 1996.

Elizabeth Drew, *The Corruption in American Politics: What Went Wrong and Why.* Woodstock, NY: Overlook Press, 1999.

Abner Greene, *Understanding the 2000 Election: A Guide to the Legal Battles That Decided the Presidency.* New York: New York University Press, 2001.

Martin L. Gross, *The Great Whitewater Fiasco: An American Tale of Money, Power, and Politics.* New York: Ballantine Books, 1994.

Paul S. Herrnson and Dilys M. Hill, *The Clinton Presidency: The First Term, 1992–1996.* New York: St. Martin's Press, 1999.

John Hoenberg, *Reelecting Bill Clinton: Why America Chose a "New" Democrat.* Syracuse, NY: Syracuse University Press, 1997.

David A. Kaplan, *The Accidental President: How 413 Lawyers, 9 Supreme Court Justices, 5,963,110 (Give or Take a Few) Floridians Landed George W. Bush in the White House.* New York: William Morrow, 2001.

Douglas Kellner, *Grand Theft 2000: Media Spectacle and a Stolen Election.* Lanham, MD: Rowman & Littlefield, 2001.

Fedwa Malti-Douglas, *The Starr Report Disrobed.* New York: Columbia University Press, 2000.

Jim McDougal and Curtis Wilkie, *Arkansas Mischief: The Birth of a National Scandal*. New York: Henry Holt, 1998.

Dick J. Reavis, *The Ashes of Waco: An Investigation*. New York: Simon and Schuster, 1995.

Craig A. Rimmerman, *Gay Rights, Military Wrongs: Political Perspectives on Lesbians and Gays in the Military*. New York: Garland, 1996.

Larry J. Sabato, Mark Stencel, and S. Robert Lichter, *Peepshow: Media and Politics in an Age of Scandal*. Lanham, MD: Rowman & Littlefield, 2000.

Steven E. Schier, ed., *The Postmodern Presidency: Bill Clinton's Legacy in U.S. Politics*. Pittsburgh: University of Pittsburgh Press, 2000.

Susan Schmidt and Michael Weisskopf, *Truth at Any Cost: Ken Starr and the Unmaking of Bill Clinton*. New York: HarperCollins, 2000.

Kenneth Starr, *The Starr Report: The Findings of Independent Counsel Kenneth W. Starr on President Clinton and the Lewinsky Affair*. New York: Public Affairs, 1998.

George Stephanopoulos, *All Too Human: A Political Education*. Boston: Little, Brown, 1999.

Jack Tapper, *Down and Dirty: The Plot to Steal the Presidency*. Boston: Little, Brown, 2001.

Evan Thomas et al., *Back from the Dead: How Clinton Survived the Republican Revolution*. New York: Atlantic Monthly Press, 1997.

Jeffrey Toobin, *A Vast Conspiracy: The Real Story of the Sex Scandal That Nearly Brought Down a President*. New York: Random House, 1999.

Washington Post Company, *Deadlock: The Inside Story of America's Closest Election*. New York: PublicAffairs, 2001.

Stuart A. Wright, ed., *Armageddon in Waco*. Chicago: University of Chicago Press, 1995.

Science and Technology

Charles R. Cantor and Cassandra L. Smith, *Genomics: The Science and Technology Behind the Human Genome Project*. New York: Wiley, 1999.

John Cassidy, *Dot.Con: The Greatest Con Story Ever Told*. New York: HarperCollins, 2002.

John Heilemann, *Pride Before the Fall: The Trials of Bill Gates and the End of the Microsoft Era*. New York: HarperCollins, 2001.

Philip J. Kaplan, *F'd Companies: Spectacular Dot Com Flameouts*. New York: Simon and Schuster, 2002.

Leon R. Kass and James Q. Wilson, *The Ethics of Human Cloning*. Washington, DC: AEI Press, 1998.

J. David Kuo, *dot.bomb: My Days and Nights at an Internet Goliath*. Boston: Little, Brown, 2001.

Robert E. Litan and Alice M. Rivlin, eds., *The Economic Payoff from the Internet Revolution*. Washington, DC: Brookings Institution Press, 2001.

Glenn McGee, ed., *The Human Cloning Debate*. Berkeley, CA: Berkeley Hills Books, 2000.

Christos J.P. Moschovitis et al., *History of the Internet: A Chronology, 1843 to the Present*. Santa Barbara, CA: ABC-CLIO, 1999.

Andrew L. Shapiro, *The Control Revolution: How the Internet Is Putting Individuals in Charge and Changing the World We Know*. New York: PublicAffairs, 2000.

James Slevin, *The Internet and Society*. Malden, MA: Blackwell, 2000.

Anthony G. Wilhelm, *Democracy in the Digital Age: Challenges to Political Life in Cyberspace*. New York: Routledge, 2000.

James Wilsdon, *Digital Futures: Living in a Dot-Com World*. Sterling, VA: Earthscan, 2001.

Gray Young, *The Internet*. New York: H.W. Wilson, 1998.

SOCIAL ISSUES

Elliot Aronson, *Nobody Left to Hate: Teaching Compassion After Columbine*. New York: Worth, 2000.

Lou Cannon, *Official Negligence: How Rodney King and the Riots Changed Los Angeles and the LAPD*. New York: Time Books, 1997.

Chuck Collins and Felice Yeskel, *Economic Apartheid in America: A Primer on Economic Inequality and Insecurity*. New York: The New Press, 2000.

C.P. Ewing, *Youth Violence*. Chichester, NY: Wiley, 2001.

John George and Laird Wilcox, *American Extremists: Militias, Supremacists, Klansmen, Communists, and Others*. Amherst, NY: Prometheus Books, 1996.

Jewelle Taylor Gibbs, *Race and Justice: Rodney King and O.J. Simpson in a House Divided*. San Francisco: Josey-Bass, 1996.

Juan Gonzalez, *Roll Down Your Window: Stories of a Forgotten America*. New York: Verso, 1995.

Kathleen M. Heide, *Young Killers: The Challenge of Juvenile Homicide*. Thousand Oaks, CA: Sage, 1999.

Robert A. Ibarra, *Beyond Affirmative Action: Reframing the Context of Higher Education*. Madison: University of Wisconsin Press, 2001.

Susan Mitchell, *American Attitudes: Who Thinks What About the Issues That Shape Our Lives*. Ithaca, NY: New Strategist, 1998.

Geoff Payne, *Social Divisions*. New York: St. Martin's Press, 2000.

Jerry Reiter, *Live from the Gates of Hell: An Insider's Look at the Antiabortion Underground*. Amherst, NY: Prometheus Books, 2000.

Joseph F. Sheley and James D. Wright, *In the Line of Fire: Youth, Guns, and Violence in Urban America*. New York: A. de Gruyter, 1995.

John David Skrentny, *Color Lines: Affirmative Action, Immigration, and Civil Rights Options for America*. Chicago: University of Chicago Press, 2001.

Stephen Steinberg, *Turning Back: The Retreat from Racial Justice in American Thought and Policy.* Boston: Beacon Press, 2001.

Curtis Stokes, Theresa Melendez, Genice Rhodes-Reed, eds., *Race in 21st Century America.* East Lansing: Michigan State University Press, 2001.

James D. Tabor and Eugene V. Gallagher, *Why Waco? Cults and the Battle for Religious Freedom in America.* Berkeley: University of California Press, 1995.

Franklin E. Zimring and Gordon Hawkins, *Crime Is Not the Problem: Lethal Violence in America.* New York: Oxford University Press, 1999.

Wendy Murray Zoba, *Columbine and the Search for America's Soul.* Grand Rapids, MI: Brazos Press, 2000.

TERRORISM

Yonah Alexander and Milton Hoenig, *Super Terrorism: Biological, Chemical, and Nuclear.* Ardsley, NY: Transnational, 2001.

Yonah Alexander and Michael S. Swetnam, *Usama Bin Laden's al-Qaida: Profile of a Terrorist Network.* Ardsley, NY: Transnational, 2001.

Yossef Bodansky, *Bin Laden: The Man Who Declared War on America.* Rocklin, CA: Forum, 2001.

Peter L. Bergen, *Holy War, Inc.: Inside the Secret World of Osama Bin Laden.* New York: Free Press, 2001.

Danny O. Coulson and Elaine Shannon, *No Heroes: Inside the FBI's Secret Counter-Terror Force.* New York: Pocket Books, 1999.

Mark S. Hamm, *Apocalypse in Oklahoma: Waco and Ruby Ridge Revenged.* Boston: Northeastern University Press, 1997.

Mark Huband, *Warriors of the Prophet: The Struggle for Islam.* Boulder, CO: Westview Press, 1998.

Marsha Kight, ed., *Forever Changed: Remembering Oklahoma City, April 19, 1995.* Amherst, NY: Prometheus Books, 1998.

Lou Michel and Dan Herbeck, *American Terrorist: Timothy McVeigh & the Oklahoma City Bombing.* New York: Regan Books, 2001.

Louis R. Mizell, *Target U.S.A.: The Inside Story of the New Terror-ist War*. New York: John Wiley & Sons, 1998.

Laurie Mylroie, *Study of Revenge: The First World Trade Center At-tack and Saddam Hussein's War Against America*. Washington, DC: AEI Press, 2001.

Simon Reeve, *The New Jackals: Ramzi Yousef, Osama Bin Laden, and the Future of Terrorism*. Boston: Northeastern University Press, 1999.

Stephen Singular, *The Uncivil War: The Rise of Hate, Violence, and Terrorism in America*. Beverly Hills, CA: New Millennium Press, 2001.

Robert L. Snow, *The Militia Threat: Terrorists Among Us*. New York: Plenum Trade, 1999.

INDEX